SHAPE IT! 4

COMBO

STUDENT'S BOOK
WITH DIGITAL PACK

Samantha Lewis
with Daniel Vincent

CAMBRIDGE
UNIVERSITY PRESS

CONTENTS

STARTER

WELCOME!

VOCABULARY

Travel

S.01 **1 Match the words in the box with the photos. Then listen, check, and repeat.**

accommodation	☐	sightseeing	1
backpacking	☐	tourist attractions	☐
resort	☐	trip	☐

1 
2 
3 
4 
5 
6 

S.02 **2 Complete the comments with the words from Exercise 1. Then, listen and check.**

Where did you go on vacation this summer?

London. It's a great city for [1] ________ because there are so many [2] ________, like Big Ben.

To a [3] ________ in Greece. The [4] ________ was amazing – a beautiful hotel right next to the beach.

I went [5] ________ in Mexico this summer – just me, my bag, and a paper map. It was the best [6] ________ of my life.

LEARN TO LEARN

Personalizing Vocabulary

Writing sentences helps you remember words.

Use It!

3 Write true sentences about your vacations with the words in Exercise 1.

____

____

____

Music and Theater

S.03 **4 Match the nouns in the box with the definitions. Then listen, check, and repeat.**

audience lines part rehearsal scene show

1 when people practice a play ________
2 live performance in a theater ________
3 the words actors say ________
4 a character in a play ________
5 the people who watch ________
6 a part of a play ________

Use It!

5 Complete the questions with words from Exercise 4. Discuss the questions.

1 Have you ever been in a ________ at school? What ________ did you play? How did you learn your ________? Did you have any ________ before the show?
2 How is the ________ at the theater and movies different from at a concert?
3 If you were in a movie, would you want to appear all the way through the movie or be in one big, important ________?

Explore It!

Guess the correct answer.

What movies do these lines come from?

a "To infinity and beyond!"

b "Just keep swimming."

Write other famous lines from movies in English. Can your partner guess the movie?

READING

An Interview in a School Magazine

S.04 **1** Look at the photo. What do you think the boy is doing? Read the interview and check your answer.

Now that we're back in school, everybody's talking about what they did during the summer. Some of you probably went to a resort or went sightseeing with your family, and most of you probably spent time at the pool with friends. But not Joshua Wills. His summer was very different. Let's find out why.

Joshua, you didn't have a normal summer vacation this year, did you? What did you do?

No, I didn't. I went to a theater camp for teenagers. Our teachers were real actors from the theater and TV. They taught us all about acting – you know, how to develop a character, how to project your voice and use your body. It was a lot of fun.

Did you put on a show?

We put on a musical about a detective. I played the part of the detective's assistant. We had one rehearsal every day for a week and then three performances. A lot of my friends and family came.

How did it go?

It was great, but on the first night, in the final scene, I forgot my lines. Everything was going really well and then suddenly I couldn't remember anything! Everyone in the audience was looking at me, thinking, "What's wrong? He's not speaking. He's not even moving!"

Were you panicking?

I wasn't panicking. I was just frozen! But in the end, I remembered the lines and it was all OK.

Do you want to do more theater?

Definitely! I don't want to stop. In fact, I'm writing a play. It's more difficult than I expected, but I'm really enjoying it. I want to put it on at school.

Are you looking for any actors?

Of course! Why? Do you want to join us?

Maybe! It sounds like fun!

2 Read the interview again and answer the questions.

1. Why was Joshua's summer vacation unusual?
2. What did the theater camp participants learn?
3. How often did the group practice their play?
4. What problem did Joshua have?
5. How did the audience react to the problem?
6. Why is Joshua looking for actors now?

3 Find words in the interview that mean …

1. speak loudly and clearly (phrase). ______
2. somebody who helps someone do their job (n). ______
3. unable to move (adj). ______
4. 100 percent yes! (adv). ______

Voice It!

4 Discuss the questions.

1. Joshua's teachers were real actors. What is good about this?
2. Have you ever acted or spoken in front of a big group of people? How was it?

GRAMMAR IN ACTION

Past and Present, Simple and Continuous

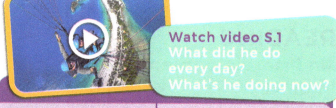

Watch video S.1
What did he do every day?
What's he doing now?

	Simple Present	Present Continuous	Simple Past	Past Continuous
+	It **sounds** like fun.	I 3 ______ **writing** a play.	We **had** one rehearsal every day.	Everyone in the audience 7 ______ **looking** at me.
–	I 1 don't **want** to stop.	He **isn't speaking**.	You 5 ______ **have** a normal summer vacation this year.	I 8 ______ **panicking**.
?	2 ______ you **want** to join us?	4 ______ you **looking** for any actors?	What 6 ______ you **do**?	**Were** you **panicking**?

1 **Complete the examples in the chart above with the correct form of *to be* or *to do*. Use the interview on page 5 to help you.**

S.05 2 **Complete the sentences with the correct form of the verbs in parentheses. Then listen and check.**

1 Mike goes (go) sightseeing every year.
2 Amalia ______ (not learn) her lines until the night before the first show.
3 A Where's Harry? B He ______ (read) in his room.
4 You didn't like the play, did you, Eddie? You ______ (sleep) during it!
5 I'm so happy we ______ (not stay) in that resort last week when the terrible storm came.
6 Ana's not at the rehearsal because she ______ (not feel) well right now.

3 **Complete Esme's blog with the correct form of the verbs in the box.**

begin do get up go ~~have~~ not finish
not forget practice start think

Hi, everyone. Yesterday we 1 had our last rehearsal for the musical. I 2 ______ practicing until 11 p.m., and when I 3 ______ to bed, some of the others 4 ______ still ______. The first show 5 ______ at 7:30 tonight. I didn't feel nervous when I 6 ______ this morning, but I 7 ______ to feel nervous now – I hope I 8 ______ my lines. But I'm also really excited. I 9 ______ it's going to be a great night. Anyway, 10 ______ you ______ anything this weekend? Why don't you come and see me?

Use It!

4 **Write the questions.**

1 what / you / do / at nine o'clock last night
What were you doing at nine o'clock last night?
2 what time / you / get up / today
______
3 during the summer / you / prefer to go sightseeing or go to the beach
______
4 what time / you / usually / get up / when you're on vacation
______
5 speak English to anyone / last week
______
6 what / you / wear / at the moment
______

5 **Ask and answer the questions.**

What were you doing at nine o'clock last night?

I was watching some videos online.

VOCABULARY AND LISTENING

Ways of Communicating

S.06 **1 Match the verbs in the box with emoticons 1–9. Then listen, check, and repeat.**

describe	☐	shake hands	1	translate	☐
greet	☐	shout	☐	wave	☐
post	☐	smile	☐	whisper	☐

S.07 **2 Listen to the conversations and circle the correct words from Exercise 1.**

1 whisper / shake hands
2 translate / smile
3 post / shout
4 greet / translate
5 wave / describe

3 Do we express the verbs in Exercise 1 with actions or words? Complete the chart.

Actions	Words
shake hands	describe

LEARN TO LEARN

Describing Words You Don't Know with Other Words or a Gesture

When you don't know a word, use words you do know to describe it or use gestures to express what you mean.

4 Express or explain the words in the box with other words or gestures.

accommodation cry dance frozen movie sing stand up tourist attraction

It's a place where you can stay. *Accommodation?*

Use It!

5 Use gestures or tell your partner *I do this when* …. Can they guess the verb?

A Talk

S.08 **6 Listen to Mateo and mark (✓) the tips that helped him learn English.**

a Describe a word with other words. ☐
b Take a language course. ☐
c Don't worry about making mistakes. ☐
d Listen to music. ☐
e Talk as much as possible. ☐
f Translate words and make them sound English. ☐
g Watch TV. ☐

S.08 **7 Listen again and complete each sentence with one word.**

1 Mateo is studying __________ in college.
2 He didn't understand the family at first because they __________ so fast.
3 When he doesn't know a word, he describes it or __________ it and makes a word in English similar to the Spanish word.
4 A lot of things were different for him, but he liked the __________ best.

Voice It!

8 Discuss the questions.

1 Which of Mateo's tips do you use?
2 Which tips would you like to try?

GRAMMAR IN ACTION

Present Perfect and Simple Past

Watch video S.2
Where did she go last summer?
Which language has she never studied?

	Present Perfect	Simple Past
+	I'**ve been** in college now for three months.	I **started** my course in October.
–	I **haven't stopped** [1] since I was there! I'**ve** [2] ______ **been** to New York.	I **met** a lot of people in the first few weeks.
?	**Have** you [3] ______ **been** to New York?	**Did** you **go** to New York last year?

1 Complete the examples in the chart above with *ever*, *since*, or *never*.

Get It Right!

We don't use the simple present with **since**.

We've been here since Tuesday.

NOT ~~We are here since Tuesday.~~

2 Look at sentences a–d. Circle the correct options to complete the rules.

a Last year, I **spent** six months in New York.

b I **didn't understand** the kids because they **spoke** fast.

c I'**ve met** so many interesting people!

d I'**ve stayed** in contact with people I **met** in New York.

1 Use the *present perfect* / *simple past* for things that happened in a finished time period, e.g., last year.

2 Use the *present perfect* / *simple past* for things that happened in the past in an unfinished time period or when the exact time of the action is not important.

S.09 **3** Circle the correct words. Then listen and check.

BEN [1]*Have you ever been* / *Did you ever go* to a music festival?

JESSIE Yeah, [2]*I've been* / *went* to one this summer. It was great.

BEN Where [3]*has it been* / *was it*?

JESSIE Near the town where we [4]*have been* / *went* on vacation. [5]*We've stayed* / *stayed* in the town a lot of times, but this was our first time at the festival.

BEN What [6]*have you liked* / *did you like* best?

JESSIE The Night Owls [7]*have had* / *had* some amazing dancers and [8]*have sounded* / *sounded* incredible.

BEN [9]*I've never heard* / *didn't hear* of them.

JESSIE Oh, they're great! [10]*I've liked* / *liked* them for ages.

4 Complete the text with the simple past or present perfect.

I [1] have never been (be) to Mexico, but last summer I [2] ______ (get) a job in a Mexican restaurant. I [3] ______ (meet) tons of people since I [4] ______ (start) working there and I [5] ______ (make) friends. At first they [6] ______ (speak) to me in Spanish, but I [7] ______ (not understand). Since then I [8] ______ (go) to Spanish classes and I [9] ______ (learn) a lot. Our teacher [10] ______ (teach) us how to describe things when we don't know the exact word.

Use It!

5 Discuss the questions.

1 How many cities in your country have you visited?

2 How long have you known your best friend?

3 Have you ever been to a festival?

I've been to three cities. I went to the capital last month, but there are some cities I've never been to.

WRITING
An Informal Email

1 **Look at the photos. What can you see? Read Azra's email and put the photos in the correct order.**

a

b
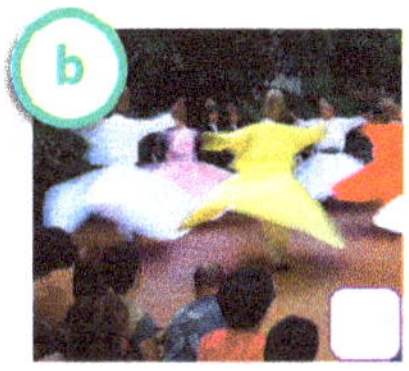
c

2 **Read the email again. Why did Azra write the email? What did she enjoy about her visit?**

[1]From: azra.kara@myemail.com

[2]To: gaby.bates@myemail.com

[3]Subject: Thank you

[4]Hi Gaby,

[5]How are things? [6]I just wanted to say thank you for a great visit to Seattle. I had an amazing time and your family is so kind!

I loved meeting your friends and visiting the city. There's so much to see! I learned so much about the U.S.A. that I didn't know before. I've listened to the playlist you made me a lot of times since I got back home, and I know all the words to the songs!

I've told my friends all about my trip and they're really looking forward to meeting you next month. I can't wait to take you sightseeing in Istanbul to show you all the tourist attractions and introduce you to my friends and family. We've bought tickets to go and watch a Turkish dance show while you're here – I hope you like it!

[7]Write back soon.

[8]Love, Azra

3 **Match a–h with the parts of the email 1–8.**

a address of the recipient ☐
b address of the sender [1]
c ending and your name ☐
d first sentence ☐
e last sentence ☐
f reason you are writing ☐
g beginning and name ☐
h topic of the email ☐

4 **Complete the *Useful Language* box with phrases from the email.**

Useful Language

Starting and ending an informal email

Start + name: Hello Gaby, / [1] ____________,

First sentence: How are you? / Thanks for your email. / [2] ____________?

The reason you are writing: I'm writing to / [3] ____________

Last sentence: See you soon. / Bye for now. / [4] ____________.

End + name: Take care, Azra / [5] ____________

PLAN

5 **Imagine you are writing an email to a penpal in an English-speaking country. You have visited their country. They are going to be visiting yours soon. Take notes.**

Where did you go? ____________

What did you do? ____________

What did you like about your visit? ____________

What are you going to do when they visit you? ____________

WRITE

6 **Write your email. Remember to include language and vocabulary from this unit, phrases from the *Useful Language* box, the parts of the email in Exercise 3, and the ideas in Exercise 5.**

CHECK

7 **Do you …**

- start and end the email correctly?
- give the reason why you are writing?
- say what you are going to do when your penpal visits?

1 What is fashion?

LEARNING OUTCOMES

I can ...

- understand texts about technology and fashion
- give my opinion politely
- comment on a blog entry
- understand how to use the present perfect simple and continuous and modifiers
- talk about and describe clothes and shoes
- categorize adjectives, record new verbs, compare British English and American English, and write different kinds of example sentences

Start It!

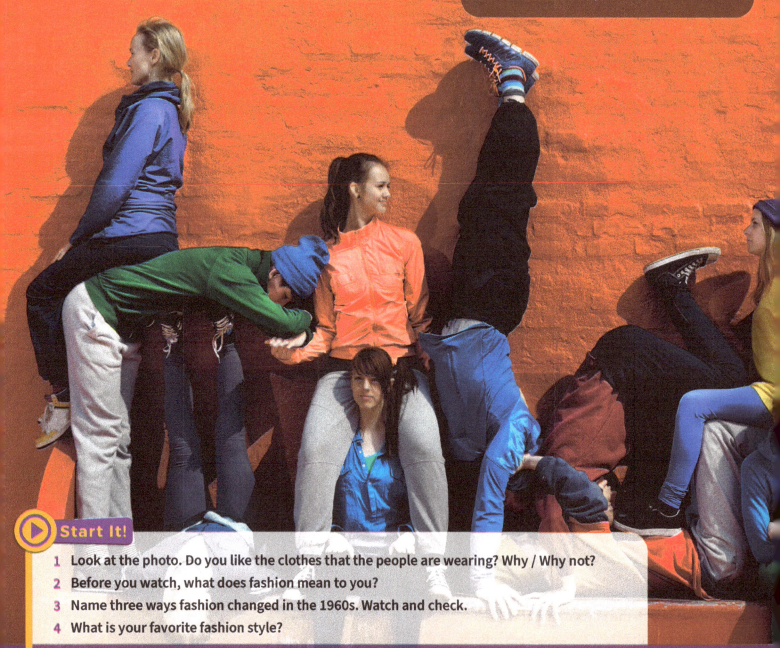

1 Look at the photo. Do you like the clothes that the people are wearing? Why / Why not?
2 Before you watch, what does fashion mean to you?
3 Name three ways fashion changed in the 1960s. Watch and check.
4 What is your favorite fashion style?

Watch video 1.1

p13

Grammar in Action 1.2

p15

Grammar in Action 1.3

p16

Everyday English 1.4

p18

Globetrotters 1.5

VOCABULARY
Describing Clothes and Shoes

1.01 **1 Match the adjectives in bold with the numbers in the photos. Then listen, check, and repeat.**

baggy jeans	☐	**long-sleeved** dress	☐
checkered skirt	☐	**plain cotton** T-shirt	☐
denim skirt	☐	**polka-dot** shoes	☐
flowery dress	☐	**striped** T-shirt	☐
high-heeled boots	☐	**tight** jeans	1
leather shoes	☐		

1.02 **2 Alex and Isabel are shopping for clothes for a school party. Listen to the conversation. Which things in Exercise 1 do they buy?**

____

____

LEARN TO LEARN

Categorizing

When we use a lot of adjectives to describe one thing, we use this order: shape, color, pattern, material.

3 Complete the chart with the adjectives from Exercise 1.

Shape	Pattern	Material
baggy		

4 Write three sentences describing the clothes in Exercise 1. Use at least two adjectives in each sentence.

1 She's wearing a blue cotton T-shirt.
2 ______________________________
3 ______________________________
4 ______________________________

5 Read your sentences in Exercise 4. Can your partner guess which person you are describing?

Use It!

6 Discuss the questions.

1 Which clothes in Exercise 1 do you have?
2 Can you describe the clothes you are wearing?
3 Which shapes, patterns, and materials do you usually wear? Which do you never wear?

Explore It!

Guess the correct answer.

Some celebrities wear special "anti-paparazzi" scarves. What do you think these scarves do?

a make their faces more beautiful
b make the photos turn black
c make the celebrities look ugly

Find out about a clothing designer. Write a question for your partner to answer.

Fashion & Technology

CONNECTED CLOTHES

Anyone who has been reading my blog for a while knows that I'm a huge fan of technology in fashion. Here are my latest discoveries.

1 ☐ We've all seen watches that measure how much we move or sleep, but what about a T-shirt? Over the last few years, scientists have been developing clothes that can record information about our heart rate or breathing and that can help us stay healthy. Most people have a denim jacket. But have you ever seen a denim jacket that can play music or send instant messages? Well, scientists have designed one that can. You just have to touch the sleeve and your music starts playing!

2 ☐ Scientists have also created clothes with sensors that take our body temperature and circulate warm or cool air through the material so that we never feel too hot or too cold. Special clothes for astronauts or emergency service workers have been using this technology for years, but now companies have created similar materials for everyday clothing and shoes. Great! No more hot, sweaty feet!

3 ☐ Now there are even smart clothes that produce energy while we're wearing them! Scientists in South Korea have created a material that turns movement into electricity. So you can charge your phone while you're doing exercise or just walking around! That's smart!

4 ☐ Finally, if you haven't been following my updates on 3-D printing, check out these trendy designs. My favorite is the high-heeled shoes. I love the fact that each design is individual and that one day we'll be able to design and print our own patterned or plain clothes and shoes at home.

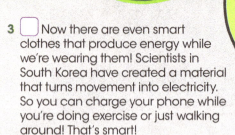

READING

A Blog Entry

1 Look at the pictures. How do they combine technology and fashion?

2 Read the blog entry. Match headings a–d with paragraphs 1–4. 1.03

a 3-D Printed Clothes
b Clothes That Change Temperature
c Connected Clothing
d Energy-Producing Clothes

3 Read the blog entry again and answer the questions.

1 How can we watch our health with connected clothing?
____

2 How does the denim jacket in the text play music?
____

3 What's good about creating electricity with clothes?
____

4 What does the blogger predict about 3-D printed clothes?
____

4 Find words in the blog that mean …

1 the part of clothing that covers your arm (1). ________
2 to move around something (2). ________
3 to put electricity into a device like a phone (3). ________
4 the latest information (4). ________
5 to produce something with a printer (4). ________

Voice It!

5 Discuss the questions.

1 Would you like to have any of the smart clothes in the blog?
2 What other things would you like clothes to do in the future?
3 Do you think smart clothes are important? Why / Why not?

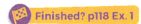

Finished? p118 Ex. 1

GRAMMAR IN ACTION

Present Perfect Simple and Present Perfect Continuous

Watch video 1.2
How long has Tara been knitting?
How many people have bought Patrick's shoes?

	Present Perfect Simple	Present Perfect Continuous
+	Scientists [1] *have* also **created** clothes with sensors.	Over the last few years, scientists [3] ______ **been developing** clothes that can record information.
–	He **hasn't bought** any 3-D printed clothing yet.	If you [4] ______ **been following** my updates on 3-D printing, check out these trendy designs.
?	[2] ______ you ever **seen** a denim jacket that can play music?	How long **have** you **been reading** my blog?

1 Complete the examples in the chart above with the correct form of *to have*.

2 Complete the rules with *simple* or *continuous*.

1 In present perfect ______ sentences, the focus is on the result of an activity.
2 In present perfect ______ sentences, the focus is on how long the activity is.

3 Put the words in the correct order to make sentences.

1 a lot of / I've / blog entries / written / .
I've written a lot of blog entries.
2 since / a fashion blog / writing / She's been / January / .
______
3 made / Have you / your own clothes / ever / ?
______
4 been / He's / two years / designing / for / clothes / .
______

1.04 **4** Complete the text with the present perfect continuous form of the verbs in the box. Then listen and check.

help make not practice ~~try~~ watch work

Recently I [1] *'ve been trying* to learn how to knit. It's really difficult! I [2] ______ a lot of videos online, but I [3] ______ very much. I [4] ______ a scarf for a few days now, but it's full of holes and looks awful. My mom [5] ______ me, too, but she [6] ______ all week and doesn't really have much free time.

1.05 **5** Complete the sentences with the present perfect simple or continuous form of the verbs in parentheses. Then listen, check, and repeat.

1 How long *has* he *been designing* clothes? (design)
2 ______ you ever ______ to knit? (learn)
3 She ______ never ______ high-heeled shoes. (wear)
4 I ______ in these shoes all morning and my feet really hurt! (walk)

Use It!

6 Imagine you are a fashion designer. Make questions with the present perfect simple or continuous. Then think of your answers.

1 What / designed?
______
2 Who / worn your designs?
______
3 How long / designing clothes?
______

7 Ask and answer the questions. Which designer makes the most interesting clothes? Why?

I've designed a coat that changes color when it gets wet!

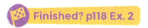

Finished? p118 Ex. 2

VOCABULARY AND LISTENING

Verbs Related to Clothes and Shoes

1.06 **1** **Read the fashion forum and match the verbs in bold with the definitions. Then listen, check, and repeat.**

ARE YOU A FOLLOWER OF FASHION?

MARIA I don't buy many clothes because they **go out of style** so quickly. I usually buy things that **go with** other clothes I already have. I like wearing green clothes because they **match** my eyes!

GISELA I'm really tall, so it's difficult to find clothes that **fit** me, especially jeans! I wear jeans so much they **wear out**! A lot of clothes don't **look good on** me because they haven't been designed for tall people.

EDU I love fashion and I work in a clothing store on Saturdays. It's great because I get to try on tons of clothes. The worst part is the dressing rooms. People leave clothes on the floor and I have to **hang up** the jackets and pants and **fold** all the T-shirts. It takes forever!

IRINA Today I had a complete fashion disaster. I was trying on a dress in a store. I managed to **zip** it **up**! But when I tried to take the dress off, I couldn't **unzip** it. How embarrassing!

1. be the right size *fit*
2. not popular any longer ______
3. wear something so much it looks old ______
4. make someone look nice ______
5. look good together ______
6. be similar or the same color/type ______
7. close zippers ______
8. open zippers ______
9. put clothes on a hanger ______
10. bend clothes so that one part lies on another part ______

Get It Right!

The word **clothes** is always plural.

Your new clothes look great!

LEARN TO LEARN

Recording New Verbs

Make sentences with new verbs so that you can remember how to use them.

2 **Complete the sentences with the correct form of the verbs in the box and the words in parentheses.**

hang up	look good on	not go with	~~wear out~~	zip up

1. You never *wear out your shoes*. They always look new. (your shoes)
2. That color ______. It matches your eyes. (you)
3. This top ______. They're different styles. (my skirt)
4. ______. It's cold. (your jacket)

3 EXAM **Discuss the questions.**

Student A:
What kinds of clothes do you like to wear?
Which clothes fit you well?

Student B:
What kinds of clothes don't you like to wear?
Which clothes look good on you?

An Interview

1.07 **4** **Listen to an interview with Carla. Where does she get her clothes from?**

1.07 **5** **Listen again and complete the text.**

Carla started looking at fashion designs online when she was [1] *12*. She enjoys upcycling – creating [2] ______ from something that exists. She also decorates [3] ______ T-shirts and tops with her own designs. She knows that people buy fast fashion because the clothes are [4] ______ and that ethical fashion is [5] ______ than fast fashion, but ethical fashion thinks about the people who [6] ______.

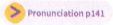

Pronunciation p141

GRAMMAR IN ACTION
Modifiers

Watch video 1.3
What are the top three fashion mistakes?
What's the problem if your bedroom is totally messy?

I've been [1] totally obsessed with fashion since I was a child.	**a** extremely / absolutely / totally / really
They look [2] ______ good.	**b** fairly / ______
These clothes are [3] ______ more expensive …	**c** ______ / a little
but they last [4] ______ longer.	**d** ______ / far

1 **Complete the examples in the chart above with *a bit*, *a lot*, *pretty*, and *totally*. Use the same words in each row.**

2 **Which words (a–d) do we use before …**

1. comparative adjectives to show a big difference? ______
2. comparative adjectives to show a small difference? ______
3. adjectives to intensify them? ______
4. adjectives to mean more than *a little* but less than *very*? ______

1.10 **3** **Circle the correct words. Then listen and check.**

Making materials like cotton or denim can be [1]*extremely* / *a lot* damaging to the environment. That's why it's [2]*absolutely* / *far* essential to create new materials from natural products that are [3]*fairly* / *a lot* better for the planet. Some materials, like bamboo, have been [4]*fairly* / *a little* successful. Others are still being developed, like a material from the rice plant, which is [5]*really* / *a bit* similar to cotton, and one made from chicken feathers, which is [6]*pretty* / *a bit* warm, like wool. Technology has also made it [7]*really* / *far* easier to recycle materials like plastic bottles into clothes such as leggings and T-shirts, which is [8]*really* / *a lot* good news for the environment!

4 **Complete the sentences with the words in parentheses.**

1. I feel pretty tired today. I need to sleep well, or I'll be extremely tired tomorrow. (extremely / pretty)
2. The shopping mall in our town is ______ good, but the one outside town is ______ better. (fairly / far)
3. He creates ______ amazing designs, which are ______ more fun than ours. (a lot / totally)
4. I'm ______ good at art, but there are people in my class who are ______ more talented than me. (far / fairly)
5. This coat is ______ beautiful and it's only ______ more expensive than the other one. (absolutely / a bit)

Use It!

5 **Complete the sentences so they are true for you.**

1. I am pretty good at ______.
2. I feel really sad when ______.
3. A subject I find a lot easier than before is ______.
4. I'm a bit more interested in ______ than before.
5. I think it's absolutely amazing that ______.

6 **Guess what your partner wrote in their sentences. Score one point for each correct guess.**

Did you say, "I am pretty good at English?"

No, I didn't. I said, "I'm pretty good at art."

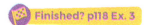

Finished? p118 Ex. 3

SPEAKING

Giving Your Opinion Politely

1.11 **1 Listen to the conversation. Does Diego like the things?**

DIEGO Hey, Dana. How's it going?
DANA Hi, Diego. I've been shopping all morning. I've bought some great stuff. Do you want to see?
DIEGO Yeah, sure.
DANA I got this striped jacket from Zaps, that new store they've just opened.
DIEGO Oh, right. Wow! [1] That's ... uh ... different!
DANA I know! It's totally out there!
DIEGO Hmm, [2] ________________ yellow and blue together, but the blue matches the color of your eyes.
DANA Thanks! And check out these pants.
DIEGO Flowery pants! Wow! Very retro!
DANA I know! They fit really well. What do you think?
DIEGO Well, [3] ________________, but I can see why you like them.
DANA Do you think they look good on me?
DIEGO Yes, I guess so.
DANA I think I might wear them to go out later, with the jacket.
DIEGO Hmm, [4] ________________ I'd wear them together. [5] ________________ the pants would go better with a plain top.
DANA No, patterns are totally in this year.
DIEGO You're such a fashion victim, Dana!

1.11 **2 Complete the conversation with the phrases from the *Useful Language* box. Then listen again and check.**

Useful Language

I don't know if ... I'm not a huge fan of ...
I think maybe ... That's ... uh ... different!
they're not exactly my style

3 Match the meanings (1–4) with the words and phrases in the *Everyday English* box.

1 someone who follows fashion
2 fashionable
3 different
4 look at

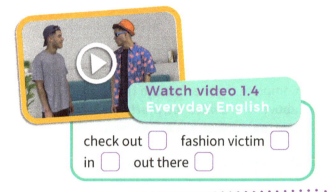

Watch video 1.4
Everyday English

check out ☐ fashion victim ☐
in ☐ out there ☐

PLAN

4 In your notebook, write about the clothes on the right.

What clothes are they?
Who bought them and why?
What do they look like?
Why do you like or not like them?

SPEAK

5 Practice the conversation with your partner. Remember to use the present perfect simple and continuous, modifiers, vocabulary from this unit, and phrases from the *Useful Language* and *Everyday English* boxes.

CHECK

6 Work with another pair. Listen to their conversation and complete the notes.

Who bought them and why? ________________
____
What do they look like? ________________
____
Does the other pair like them? Why / Why not?
____

Four Steps
to Reduce Your Fashion Footprint

Here are some ideas you can try!

- Have a clothing swap party. Swap clothes you don't want with your friends.
- Save energy. Wash clothes less often, dry clothes naturally, don't iron!
- Give old clothes to secondhand stores. Don't throw them away!
- Buy fewer, better quality new clothes.

Comments

Great post! It got me thinking about how to reduce my fashion footprint. I talked to my parents and we decided to try reduce the amount of energy we use on our clothes. Usually we wash all our clothes every time we wear them, even when they're still pretty clean; but this month we've been washing clothes less often, and we haven't ironed anything. My parents have saved money and I've been much better at hanging up my clothes! Carlos

Thanks for sharing! I had no idea that I throw so many clothes away! I had a clothing swap party last week. I got a great denim jacket that I absolutely love! I also got two long-sleeved tops and some cool high-heeled boots for free! I was absolutely amazed that we swapped everything! Since reading your post, I've decided to buy far fewer new clothes in the future. Amie

WRITING
A Blog Comment

1 **Look at the blog entry. How can people reduce their fashion footprint?**

2 **Read the blog comments. Answer the questions.**

1 Were the ideas that Carlos and Amie tried successful? How do you know?

____

2 What does Amie want to do in the future?

____

3 **Find the phrases from the *Useful Language* box in the blog comments. Which phrases can you use when you ...**

1 enjoy reading a post?

____

2 learn something new from the post?

____

3 change your behavior because of the post?

____

Useful Language

Great post! I had no idea that ...
It got me thinking about ... Since reading your post, I've ...
Thanks for sharing! We decided to ...

PLAN

4 **Write your own blog comment. Look at the ideas in the blog entry and take notes about which one to write about.**

Which idea will you try out? ______________________

____

Do you think it will go well? Why / Why not?

____

____

What other ideas would you like to try in the future? ______________________

____

WRITE

5 **Write your blog comment. Remember to include the present perfect simple and continuous, modifiers, vocabulary from this unit, and phrases from the *Useful Language* box.**

CHECK

6 **Do you ...**

- explain why an idea might or might not work well?
- explain what you would like to try in the future?

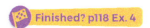

Finished? p118 Ex. 4

AROUND THE WORLD

Globetrotters
Watch video 1.5
What We Wear and Why

- Why do we wear clothes and what do they show about us?
- What is a *deel* and why do Mongolian people wear it?
- What do the colors blue, white, green, yellow, and orange represent for the Masai people?

READING
A Travel Guide

1.12 **1 Are the sentences *T* (true) or *F* (false)? Read the travel guide and check your answers.**

1. Kilts have not always been made of tartan. ___
2. Tartans today indicate where people live. ___
3. Scottish dress is different for men and women. ___
4. Tartan patterns are popular outside Scotland. ___

Voice It!

2 Discuss the questions.

1. Why do you think Scottish people wear traditional clothing for special occasions?
2. What traditional clothing do people wear in your country?
3. Why is it important to celebrate cultural traditions?

Traditional Scottish Dress

You have probably seen photos of Scotland's most famous piece of clothing, the kilt. But did you know that Scottish men have been wearing kilts for centuries? A kilt used to be an extremely long piece of heavy plain material that men from the Scottish Highlands wore every day. They wrapped the material around their waist and over one shoulder to protect them from the cold wind or rain. Nowadays, the design of the kilt is totally different. It is a knee-length **woolen** skirt, with a pattern of vertical and horizontal stripes in different colours called **tartan**. Tartan designs used to indicate the area where people lived and were far less colourful than they are today. Since the 18th century, people have been wearing designs that represent their family name or clan (group of families), and today there are over 4,500 designs! The kilt forms part of the traditional Highland **dress**, which is quite different for men and women (see box).

Highland dress is extremely popular in Scotland for special occasions such as weddings, funerals, or parties, particularly for men. Women often wear kilts to do traditional Scottish dancing at sports and cultural events. Nowadays, tartan isn't just used for traditional dress in Scotland. Fashion designers around the world use tartan to create modern designs such as tartan **trousers** or tartan shoes, and celebrities from Rihanna to Shawn Mendes have been photographed wearing tartan. Even though people have worn tartan for centuries, it is still popular today.

MEN:
- tartan kilt and a kilt pin
- leather belt
- sporran (a small leather or fur bag that hangs from the belt.)
- plain or tartan socks
- kilt knife (a small knife kept in one sock)
- ghillies (plain, flat leather shoes)

WOMEN:
- long or knee-length tartan kilt
- tartan shawl (a piece of material worn over your shoulders)
- plain or tartan socks
- ghillies

3 Use the travel guide to complete the chart.

Kilts in the 18th Century	Highland Dress for Men	Who wears traditional tartan clothes?
One long piece of cloth worn around waist and over shoulder		
Kilts in the 21st Century	**Highland Dress for Women**	**Who wears modern tartan clothes?**

LEARN TO LEARN

British English vs. American English

4 **Read the definitions and write the British English word from the text.**

1 The American English word for a pattern of vertical and horizontal stripes is *plaid*. ________________

2 A word for a set of clothes. In American English, we say *attire*. ________________

3 This clothing item covers your legs. In American English, we say *pants*. ________________

4 The American English adjective for this material is *wool*. ________________

5 **Write the American English spellings for these words.**

1 colourful ________________

2 favourite ________________

3 organise ________________

4 flavour ________________

5 centre ________________

6 neighbour ________________

7 traveller ________________

8 programme ________________

6 **Think and discuss with a partner. What other words or structures are different in British English?**

Explore It!

Guess the correct answer.

It was illegal to wear tartan in the middle of the 18th century in Scotland. True or false?

Find another fact about traditional dress. Write a question for your partner to answer.

SHAPE IT!

CULTURE PROJECT

A Fact File

A fact file presents key information about a topic. Make a fact file about traditional clothing from your culture.

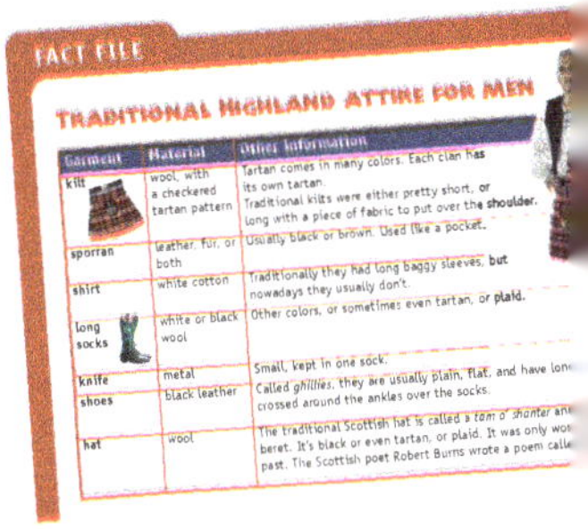

Teacher's Resource Bank

1 REVIEW

VOCABULARY

1 Circle the word that doesn't fit.

1	baggy	tight	polka-dot
2	cotton	long-sleeved	denim
3	flowery	leather	plain
4	cotton	striped	checkered
5	plain	long-sleeved	high-heeled

2 Match 1–5 with a–e.

1. **Hang up** your clothes. ☐
2. I can't **unzip** my jacket. ☐
3. These jeans are **worn out** ☐
4. This T-shirt **doesn't fit** me anymore ☐
5. Your glasses really **look good on** you. ☐

a because I've had them for ages.
b because it's too small.
c The zipper's broken.
d You look great!
e They're all over the floor.

GRAMMAR IN ACTION

3 Complete the text with the present perfect simple or continuous form of the verbs in parentheses.

Sixteen-year-old Moziah Bridges 1 ______ (design) ties since he was nine. His grandmother taught him to make bow ties and since then he 2 ______ (own) his own business. The designer 3 ______ (appear) in magazines and on TV and 4 ______ (make) a collection of ties for basketball teams in the U.S.A. Mo is still in school but 5 ______ (work) in the evenings. It 6 ______ (not be) easy, but his mom helps him and he 7 ______ (employ) more people as his business 8 ______ (grow). Mo often gives talks to other people who 9 ______ (think) about starting a business.

4 Circle the correct modifier to complete the sentences.

1. It takes *a little* / *extremely* longer to fold your clothes, but then you don't have to iron them.
2. Where did you get that jacket? I *far* / *absolutely* love it!
3. The second movie in the series was *a bit* / *pretty* better than the first one, but not much.
4. I'm *a lot* / *fairly* good at speaking Chinese, but I can't write it.
5. I'm *far* / *totally* confused by his explanation. I don't understand it at all.
6. Have you seen this video? It's *really* / *a lot* funny.
7. That T-shirt is *far* / *really* nicer than the other one, but it's *really* / *a lot* expensive.

Self-Assessment

- I can describe clothes and shoes.
- I can talk about clothes and shoes.
- I can use the present perfect simple and present perfect continuous.
- I can use modifiers.

LEARN TO ... WRITE DIFFERENT KINDS OF EXAMPLE SENTENCES

You can write different kinds of example sentences to help you understand and remember new words.

1 **Read Ela's blog. Why does she recommend using the different kinds of example sentences to remember new words?**

Ela's English Learning BLOG

Today's Tip: Example Sentences

Hi, everyone! Today we're looking at a great way to learn vocabulary: example sentences. When I learn new words, I often use them in sentences to help me learn and remember them. There are different types of example sentences you can use. They're all good for different reasons.

a Sentences about you, your family, or your friends – when you use words in sentences about things people you know have done, the words are easier to remember.

b Funny sentences – a funny image can help the word stay in your memory.

c Sentences that explain the word – these make the meaning clear, like the examples in dictionaries.

Here are some of my latest examples. Can you guess which types they are?

1 I prefer **plain** T-shirts to ones with writing or pictures on them.

2 Your skin gets **sweaty** when you're hot or exercise a lot.

3 My baby brother always wipes his nose on his **sleeve**.

4 The giraffe couldn't **zip up** his jacket because it was too long!

5 A **checkered** pattern is a pattern of squares of different colors.

6 I thought I saw a zebra – but it was a horse in a black and white **striped** T-shirt.

So ... that's all from me today. Don't forget to share some example sentences of your own. You can post them below!

2 **Match Ela's examples 1–6 with types a–c.**

1 ______ 4 ______

2 ______ 5 ______

3 ______ 6 ______

SHAPE IT!

3 **Choose five words from the box and write an example sentence for each one. Use all of Ela's types (a–c) at least once.**

baggy	charge
fashion victim	fold
hang up	high-heeled
leather	not go with
polka-dot	updates

1 ______________________

2 ______________________

3 ______________________

4 ______________________

5 ______________________

4 **Tell your partner your sentences from Exercise 3. Which types (a–c) are they? Which sentences are your favorites and why?**

2 What can you change?

LEARNING OUTCOMES

I can ...

- understand texts about international exchanges and a mystery object
- explain how to use something
- write an opinion essay
- understand how to use *used to* and *would* for past habits, the simple past, and the past perfect with *never, ever, already, by* (*then*), *by the time*
- talk about changes and parts of objects
- practice learning new words by using them in different situations, identify key words to understand audio texts, and help my classmates improve their writing
- make a history exhibition

Start It!

1 Look at the photo. Do you know what this animal is and how it changes?

2 Before you watch, how do you think cities change over time?

3 Which two events changed the city of Seoul? Watch and check.

4 How has your town or city changed?

Watch video 2.1

p25

Grammar in Action 2.2

p27

Grammar in Action 2.3

p28

Everyday English 2.4

VOCABULARY
Phrasal Verbs: Changes

1 **Which of the phrases a–l describes picture 1? Which phrase describes picture 2?**

a **settle down** in a new school
b **look forward to** the weekend
c **sign up** for French classes
d **try out** a new restaurant
e **turn out** well
f **move out** of a house
g **move to** a new school
h **go back** to the beginning
i **end up** in the wrong place
j **go through** a hard time
k **do without** the Internet
l **turn down** an invitation

1

2

2.01 2 **Match definitions 1–12 with phrasal verbs a–l from Exercise 1. Then listen, check, and repeat.**

1 feel happy about something in the future b
2 not have something
3 finally be in a place/situation
4 experience
5 stop living in a particular place
6 try something new
7 start to feel happy in a new place/situation
8 return
9 join an organized activity
10 say no to something
11 have a particular result
12 change to

2.02 3 **Listen to six conversations and complete the sentences using the correct form of the phrasal verbs from Exercise 1.**

1 He decides to ______________ for classes.
2 Molly ______________ the game.
Andre ______________ the invitation.
3 Tom ______________ a hard time now.
He ______________ in his new school.
4 Jo asks Ed to ______________ to the beginning.
5 They're going to ______________ the restaurant.
6 In the end, the party ______________ well.

LEARN TO LEARN
Using Words in Different Situations
Using new words in different situations helps you remember them.

4 **Think of different situations for the phrasal verbs in Exercise 1.**

What can you look forward to?

A party ... the end of exams ...

Use It!

5 **Think of questions using the phrasal verbs in Exercise 1. Ask and answer.**

Have you tried out a new restaurant recently?

Yes. We went to a great Italian restaurant last week.

Explore It!

Guess the correct answer.
How many students study in a foreign country every year?
a 2 million b 5 million c 11 million
Find out a fact about students in your country. Write a question for your partner.

A+ EXCHANGES – DISCOVER A NEW WORLD AND A NEW YOU!

Student Testimonials

LUCY

I love school here – it's so different from the U.S.A. Students have almost no homework and very few exams. At my school, we don't even have school subjects. We study topics and do projects instead. It's a great way to learn.

This experience has really helped me become more confident. I didn't use to be adventurous, but I've tried a lot of new things since I arrived here eight months ago. For example, I went on a reindeer safari on my birthday, and I've been going ice-swimming every Saturday. Plus, I've made a lot of friends. Finns are very cool people.

It hasn't all been easy. Winter is very hard because it's really dark – there are only three or four hours of light every day. The good thing is that you can see the beautiful Northern Lights.

If you get the opportunity to study abroad, don't turn it down, especially not if you can come to Finland!

BEN

Last year, I spent six wonderful months in Mexico. I used to dream about living in a different country, so when I discovered A+ Exchanges, I signed up immediately. It was an absolutely incredible experience. I loved the mix of local, European, and African cultures, and the people were really outgoing.

Of course, I went through some ups and downs at first, especially dealing with a different school system. For example, many Mexican schools have two schedules. Some students start school at 7:30 a.m., and some – like me – start at 2 p.m. We would finish at 8 p.m.! Also, I didn't speak much Spanish when I arrived, so it was really difficult to follow lessons. But my classmates would always help me, and I improved a lot.

I felt a bit homesick from time to time, but now I feel like I have two homes. In fact, I've decided to go to college there. I'm really looking forward to going back.

READING

A Brochure

1 **Look at the photos. Which show Finland? Which show Mexico? What do you think it is like to live there?**

2.03 **2** **Read the brochure. Write *L* (Lucy) or *B* (Ben).**

Which person …

1 has been abroad for more than half a year? ___
2 found the country's education system difficult? ___
3 has changed in a positive way? ___
4 found part of the year difficult because of the light? ___
5 likes the variety of cultures? ___
6 can do something better than they used to do? ___

3 **Find words in the brochure that mean …**

1 happy to try new things (Lucy). ________
2 from the nearby area (Ben). ________
3 friendly and sociable (Ben). ________
4 a mix of good and bad experiences (Ben). ________
5 missing your family (Ben). ________

4 **Read the sentences and write *T* (true), *F* (false), or *DS* (doesn't say).**

1 In Finland, students never take exams. ___
2 Students have long breaks in Finland. ___
3 Lucy has been ice-swimming more than once. ___
4 Ben never wanted to leave the U.S.A. ___
5 Mexican students don't all finish school at the same time. ___
6 Ben wants to go back home soon. ___

Voice It!

5 **Discuss the questions.**

1 Can you think of a country you would like to go on an exchange to?
2 Why would you like to visit that country?
3 What do you think would be difficult about living there?

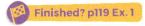

Finished? p119 Ex. 1

GRAMMAR IN ACTION

Used To, *Would*, and Simple Past

Watch video 2.2
What did her grandmother use to write on?
What did she use to do outdoors?

	Used To / Would	Simple Past
+	I [1] used **to** dream about living in a different country. My classmates [2] ______ always help me.	I **went** on a reindeer safari.
–	I **didn't** [3] ______ **to** be adventurous.	I **didn't speak** much Spanish.
?	**Did** Lucy **use to** be adventurous?	**Did** Ben **learn** a lot of Spanish?

Pronunciation p141

1 **Complete the examples in the chart above with one word in each blank. Use the brochure on page 24 to help you.**

2 **Complete the rules with *used to*/*would* or *the simple past*.**

1. We use ______ to talk about situations that continued and actions that happened more than once in the past.
2. We use ______ to talk about things that happened only once.

3 **Complete the text with *used to* and the verbs in parentheses.**

My grandfather's childhood was different from mine. When he was a boy, he never [1] used to have (have) many toys, but he [2] ______ (have) a lot of time. He [3] ______ (love) playing outside. Sometimes, his friends [4] ______ (play) outside all day – they [5] ______ (go) out early and then they [6] ______ (come) home late at night. I think it [7] ______ (be) safer for children then.

Get It Right!

We use ***would*** with repeated past actions, not situations.

We would ride our bikes after school.

NOT ~~We would live in Texas.~~

4 **Circle the correct words. Sometimes both are possible.**

1. More people *would* / *used to* live in the country than in cities. Now it's the opposite.
2. In the past, TV channels *would* / *used to* stop at night.
3. Some people *didn't use to* / *wouldn't* smile in photos because their teeth were bad.
4. Many people *would* / *used to* think that the Earth was flat.

5 **Complete the sentences with *used to*, *didn't use to*, or the simple past and the verbs in parentheses.**

1. For his birthday, Aidan got (get) a new bike. He loved it.
2. Ada ______ (like) apples much, but now she does.
3. I ______ (end up) in the wrong place yesterday because I didn't have a map.
4. When Bill was younger, he ______ (turn down) invitations all the time because he was so shy.

Use It!

6 **Write questions for a partner about their parents' lives with *used to* or the simple past.**

1. what toys / play with ______
2. study English / at school ______
3. how / meet ______

7 **Ask and answer the questions.**

What toys did your parents use to play with?

I think they used to play with wooden toys, and they would often play outside.

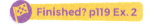

Finished? p119 Ex. 2

VOCABULARY AND LISTENING

Parts of Objects

1 Look at the photos. Which objects do you recognize?

2.08 **2 Match the words in the box with parts of the objects 1–10. Then listen, check, and repeat.**

button		cover		handle		lens	1	plug	
cord		display		key		lid		strap	

2.09 **3 Circle the correct words. Then listen and check.**

1 When you carry a backpack, do you use one *strap* / *cord* or both? Why?

2 Do you always put the *handle* / *lid* back on the peanut butter jar after using it?

3 How often do you clean the *key* / *lens* of the camera on your phone?

4 Without looking, can you remember what is on the *cover* / *display* of this book?

5 Can you name six objects that have an on/off *plug* / *button*?

6 Do you take your phone charger *cord* / *display* with you when you go out?

Use It!

4 Ask and answer the questions in Exercise 3. Are your answers similar or different?

A Game Show

2.10 **5 Listen to a game show about retro objects. Which three objects in Exercise 1 are mentioned?**

LEARN TO LEARN

Identifying Key Words

Identifying key words before you listen can help you understand what you hear.

6 Read the parts of the sentences and underline the key words.

1 Joey pushes the buzzer too early because he …
  a can't wait to play.
  b doesn't understand the rules.

2 Nicola guesses the first object correctly because she …
  a has seen one before.
  b has heard of it before.

3 People had fax machines …
  a in their houses.
  b in their workplaces.

4 People used lava lamps …
  a instead of lightbulbs.
  b because they were attractive.

2.10 **7 Listen again and circle the correct options to complete the sentences in Exercise 6.**

Voice It!

8 Discuss the questions.

1 Do you know any retro objects that have come back in style?

2 What do you think of them?

GRAMMAR IN ACTION

Past Perfect with *Never, Ever, Already, By (Then), By the Time*

Watch video 2.3
Where did she go last week?
When were 3-D printers first developed?

+	This was before anyone **had** [1] ___ever___ **heard** of printers. They**'d** [2] ______ **gone** out of style **by the time** you were born.
-	**I'd heard** of fax machines before, but **I'd** [3] ______ **seen** one. I **hadn't started** yet.
?	**Had** you **ever seen** a digital watch before then?

1 **Complete the examples in the chart above with *already*, *ever*, or *never*.**

2 **Circle the correct words to complete the rules.**

1 ***Already***, ***never***, and ***ever*** come *before* / *after* the main verb.

2 ***By the time*** means *before* / *after* something happened.

3 **Answer the questions. Use the past perfect and the words in parentheses.**

1 How did you know what would happen in the movie? (already / read / the book)

I knew because I had already read the book.

2 Why did you get lost? (never / be / there before)

______

3 Did you get a ticket for the concert? No, (by the time / I went online / they / sell out)

______

4 How was the party? (already / end / when we got there)

______

2.11 **4** **Complete the text with the simple past or the past perfect form of the verbs in parentheses. Then listen and check.**

Last year I [1] went (go) on an exchange to Moscow. I [2] ______ (never / travel) alone before, so I [3] ______ (feel) nervous at first. Before I [4] ______ (go), I [5] ______ (already / learn) to read the Russian alphabet, although I [6] ______ (not practice) speaking Russian. By the time I [7] ______ (leave), I [8] ______ (improve) a lot. Everybody in Moscow [9] ______ (be) really kind and friendly, but it [10] ______ (not be) easy to deal with the cold weather. I [11] ______ (not pack) enough warm clothes, so I had to buy some after I [12] ______ (arrive). Anyway, I can't wait to go back. I [13] ______ (not expect) to enjoy it so much before I actually [14] ______ (get) there, but in the end I really [15] ______ (do)!

Use It!

5 **Ask and answer the questions about the topics below. Use the past perfect.**

1 hear of / connected clothing?

2 see / a photo of 3-D printed clothes?

3 hear of / ice-swimming?

4 see / a photo of the Northern Lights?

Before you started using this book, had you ever heard of connected clothing?

No, I'd never heard of it, but now I want to know more! / Yes, I had. I'd already read about it online.

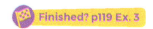

Finished? p119 Ex. 3

SPEAKING

Explaining How to Use Something

2.12 **1 Listen to the conversation. Which of the things in the box does the typewriter have?**

cord	display	keys	plug	speaker

JORGE What's that? [1] Is it some kind of computer?
MERI No, it's my grandpa's old typewriter.
JORGE Where's the display?
MERI There isn't one, and there's no plug or cord.
JORGE That's so old-school! How did it work?
MERI The paper would move as you typed. [2] ______________ press the keys hard, but not too fast, or they get stuck. Try it out!
JORGE [3] ______________
MERI That's it. Just imagine – people used to type books on these things!
JORGE No way! I can't even find the letters I want.
MERI You need to sign up for typing classes! They're in the same place as an ordinary keyboard.
JORGE Oh, no! [4] ______________ How do I go back? There's no "delete" key.
MERI [5] ______________ start all over again.
JORGE No, thanks! Anyway, how come your grandpa had this?
MERI He used to need it for work, but after a while he ended up buying a computer.
JORGE I'm not surprised! I'm glad they'd invented computers by the time I started school! I'd hate to do my homework on this!

2.12 **2 Complete the conversation with the phrases from the *Useful Language* box. Then listen again and check.**

Useful Language

Is it some kind of ...? I've messed it up.
Like this, you mean? What you do is, you ...
You'll have to ...

3 Complete the sentences with the phrases in the *Everyday English* box.

1 Barry's not here yet. ______________ – he's always late.
2 A Do I press this button here?
B ______________
3 Your new jacket's so ______________. My dad used to have one like that.
4 Oh, no! I've lost my homework! I'll have to do it ______________.

Watch video 2.4
Everyday English

all over again
I'm not surprised
old-school That's it.

PLAN

4 Choose an object on page 26. Take notes on how to use it in your notebook.

SPEAK

5 Practice the explanation with your partner. Remember to use past tenses, vocabulary from this unit, and phrases from the *Useful Language* and *Everyday English* boxes.

CHECK

6 Work with another pair. Listen to their explanation and complete the notes.

How does the object work? ______________

____

Do you understand how to use it? ______________

____

WRITING
An Opinion Essay

1 In what ways has life changed for teenagers in the last 30 years?

2 Read the essay. Does it mention any of your ideas in Exercise 1?

Are teenagers today more or less stressed than previous generations?

The world has changed a great deal in the last few decades, especially for teenagers, and not always in a positive way. In particular, people of my generation are a lot more stressed than teenagers in the past.

First, we are under enormous pressure to do well on exams. This means that we spend a lot of time studying. Young people didn't use to study as much because it wasn't always necessary to go to college. Therefore, they had more time to relax and hang out with friends.

Second, previous generations didn't have online profiles to worry about. In fact, young people 20 or 30 years ago hadn't even heard of "followers" and "likes" because social media hadn't been invented yet. For people of my age, it is almost impossible to do without social media. In addition, it can become extremely addictive.

In conclusion, I would say that teenagers today have more stressful lives than our parents did.

3 Complete the chart with the linkers from the *Useful Language* box. Look at the linkers in the essay to help you.

Order of Ideas	Connection Between Ideas
first	

Useful Language

first in addition in conclusion second therefore this means that

4 Complete the essay with the linkers from the *Useful Language* box. Do you agree with the writer? Sometimes there is more than one possible answer.

Are online games bad for you?

In my opinion, online games have many good points. 1 First, they improve your memory and your problem-solving skills. 2 ________, you can make friends. 3 ________, you play with people from around the world. 4 ________ you often have to communicate in English and 5 ________ your English improves. However, it's important to spend time with your friends offline. 6 ________, online games can be unhealthy, but only if you spend all your time playing them.

PLAN

5 Write an opinion essay. Look at the statement and take notes in your notebook.

Teenagers today have more freedom than in the past.

Do you agree or disagree with the statement?

Write two reasons for your opinion.

Give a summary of your opinion.

WRITE

6 Write your opinion essay. Remember to include *used to*, the simple past and past perfect, and phrases from the *Useful Language* box.

CHECK

7 Do you ...

- give your opinion?
- give reasons for your opinion?
- summarize your opinion?

Finished? p119 Ex. 4

HISTORY PROJECT

1 FASHION

Fashion is always changing, and old styles often come back into fashion, although few people look forward to seeing 1970s fashion again. If you watch TV shows from that decade, you will see that people used to wear pants that were tight at the top and wide at the bottom, flowery dresses, a lot of tight cotton T-shirts or shirts with big collars, and plenty of big round glasses. During the early 1970s, bright colors were extremely trendy, but by the end of the decade they had almost completely disappeared. Black, white, gray, and brown had replaced them, although people still wore enormous glasses.

2 TECHNOLOGY

It is hard to imagine dealing with the ups and downs of modern life without computers and smartphones. However, in the 1970s, there were very few computers, and the ones that existed were a lot bigger than those we have today. They were far slower, with simple displays and enormous buttons. Compared to the devices we use today, they also had very little memory. In fact, the computers on the Apollo spaceships that took men to the moon had less memory than some modern toasters. By the beginning of the 1970s, some companies had started to use computers in their offices, but it was extremely rare to see a computer in a house. In fact, most people had never used one, and some people had never seen one.

A History Exhibition

1 Look at the photos. What period in history do you think they are from?

2.13 2 Read the exhibit labels. Which one do you find most interesting? Why?

3 Complete the chart about exhibits 2 and 3.

	1	2	3
Area	Fashion	Technology	Music
Period	1970s		
Examples	pants (tight at top, wide at bottom), flowery dresses, big glasses, bright colors		
Changes Over Time	black, white, gray, brown became more popular		

3 MUSIC

Music has always been an important part of teenage identity, but in an age of streaming and downloading, it's easy to forget that it hasn't always been as available as it is today. In the 1970s, young music fans would spend hours in record shops looking for new music to buy. It wasn't only the music that was popular. The record covers were also important, and many of them became famous for their artwork. By the middle of the 1990s, CDs had become more popular than records. Nevertheless, people continued to collect records, and DJs still used to play them at dance clubs. Recently, they have come back into style, as many people prefer the sound of a record to the sound of a digital file.

PLAN

4 Make a history exhibition. Work in groups. Complete the steps below.

- Read the tips in *How to Schedule*.
- Decide which period in history you want to concentrate on (for example, the 19th century, the 1980s).
- Choose three areas you want to focus on.

entertainment | fashion | food and drink | house and home | school life | technology/communication | toys and games

- Decide who is going to research and write about which exhibit.

PRESENT

5 Present your history exhibition on a wall of your classroom. Remember to include a title for each label, vocabulary from this unit, *used to*, the simple past and past perfect, and the tips in *How to Schedule*.

CHECK

6 Read the other groups' history exhibitions. What areas are they focusing on? Which group's exhibition is most interesting?

How to Schedule

Ask your teacher how long you have to complete the project. Then decide together how long to spend on each of these stages:

1. looking for information and photos
2. writing draft texts for the labels
3. checking and correcting the drafts
4. writing the final labels and putting them on a poster with the photos

2 REVIEW

VOCABULARY

1 Complete the conversation with the correct form of a phrasal verb.

A How was your bike trip? Where did you go?

B Well, we wanted to [1] ______________ a new route. We were planning to bike to this old town near the ocean, but we got lost and [2] ______________ on a farm!

A Didn't you have a map with you?

B No, but the farmer helped us, so it [3] ______________ OK in the end. We found the town!

A Was it nice there?

B Beautiful. I'd love to [4] ______________ one day. How was your weekend?

A Not great. I was sick. My friends wanted me to go a concert. I'd said yes, and I [5] ______________ to it, but in the end I had to [6] ______________ them ______________.

2 Circle the correct words.

Did you know ...?

- The [1]*lids / straps* of plastic water bottles are made from a different plastic than the bottle is.
- If you change the [2]*lens / display* on your phone to black and white, it can become less addictive.
- On old trains, you couldn't open the doors with a [3]*button / plug*. You had to use a [4]*strap / handle*, like a normal door.

GRAMMAR IN ACTION

3 Complete the text with *used to*, *would*, or the simple past and the verb in parentheses. Sometimes there is more than one possible answer.

My dad's a writer now, although he [1] ______________ (not be). He [2] ______________ (be) a diplomat, so my family [3] ______________ (move) all the time. Once, we [4] ______________ (live) in three different countries in two years! I remember when we [5] ______________ (move) to Rio de Janeiro. I [6] ______________ (not know) any Portuguese at first, so the first week [7] ______________ (be) difficult. I used to take my lunch to the playground and then I [8] ______________ (eat) it alone. However, after a few days, my classmates [9] ______________ (start) to invite me to eat with them and I quickly [10] ______________ (make) friends.

4 Complete Diego's message to Tom with the past perfect form of the verbs in parentheses.

Tom, I'm so sorry I missed the wedding! I decided to take the car to the airport, but because I [1] ______________ (never / drive) there before, I got lost. Just the night before, I [2] ______________ (think), "I must leave early!," but then I completely forgot! Anyway, I got to the airport around ten o'clock. The plane [3] ______________ (not taken off), but by the time I finished checking in, the gate [4] ______________ (close). I tried to buy a ticket for the next flight, but they [5] ______________ (already / sell out)!

Self-Assessment

I can use phrasal verbs to talk about changes.

I can talk about parts of objects.

I can use *used to*, *would*, and the simple past.

I can use the past perfect with *never, ever, already, by* (*then*), *by the time*.

LEARN TO … HELP YOUR PARTNER IMPROVE THEIR WRITING

When you write something, ask your partner to check it. You can improve your writing this way.

1 Read the instructions for the writing task. Correct Edison's mistakes to help him improve.

WRITING TASK

Write about a favorite toy or game from your childhood.

- Write between 100 and 130 words.
- Use language from this unit.

Don't forget to use punctuation and check your spelling!

When I was little, I [1] ~~use~~ used to play with Lego® bricks all the time. I would [2] building ______ all kinds of things – cars, [3] airplaynes ______, houses. I even built a computer with keys and a display. After I finished one thing, I would keep it and then try out something else, but I once [4] used to build ______ a ship that I kept for weeks. [5] I've ______ never built anything like it before. However, I remember my mom [6] would be ______ really angry with me one day because I played with it in the bathroom and ended up damaging the sides of the bathtub. I still have a photo of it somewhere [7] , ______

Number of words: 107

2 Answer the questions in the checklist. Has Edison completed the task in Exercise 1?

Checklist		
	Edison's Writing	**Your Partner's Writing**
Has he/she …		
1 written about the topic?	Yes / No	Yes / No
2 written between 100 and 130 words?	Yes / No	Yes / No
3 used phrasal verbs for changes and words for parts of objects?	Yes / No	Yes / No
4 added details to make it interesting?	Yes / No	Yes / No
How well has he/she used …		
5 the simple past?	☹ 😐 ☺	☹ 😐 ☺
6 *used to* and *would*?	☹ 😐 ☺	☹ 😐 ☺
7 the past perfect?	☹ 😐 ☺	☹ 😐 ☺
8 punctuation?	☹ 😐 ☺	☹ 😐 ☺
9 correct spelling?	☹ 😐 ☺	☹ 😐 ☺
Other comments?	*I enjoyed the part about your mom being angry!*	

SHAPE IT!

3 Do the writing task in Exercise 1.

4 Answer the questions in the checklist for your partner's writing.

5 Tell your partner what you like and what they can improve.

3 What's usually on your plate?

LEARNING OUTCOMES

I can ...

- understand texts from an online forum and a cooking show
- give cooking instructions
- write a listicle
- understand how to use different future forms
- talk about cooking and quantities
- make adjectives from verbs, use diagrams, understand words from context by using the rest of the text, and set and achieve learning goals

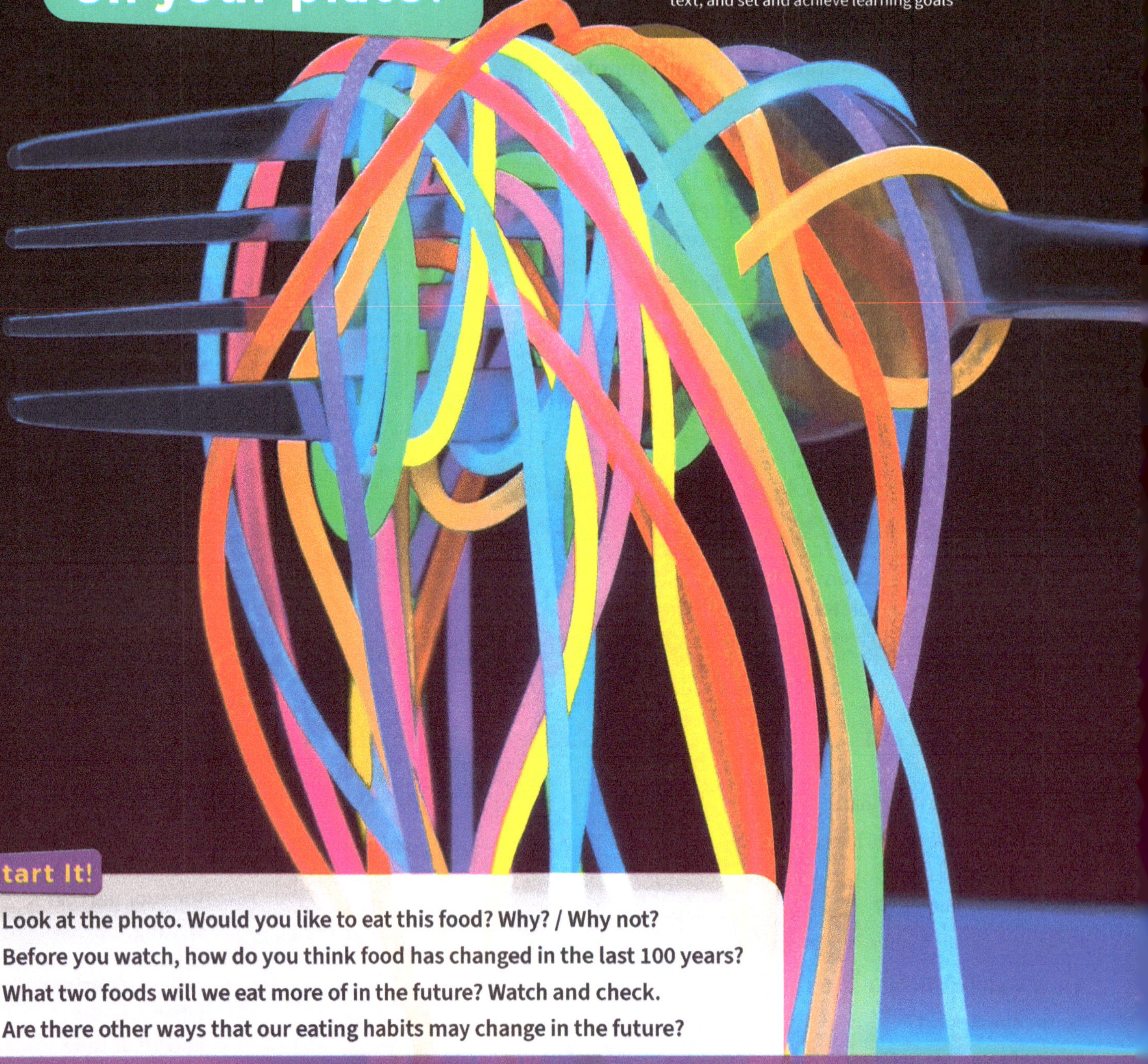

Start It!

1 Look at the photo. Would you like to eat this food? Why? / Why not?
2 Before you watch, how do you think food has changed in the last 100 years?
3 What two foods will we eat more of in the future? Watch and check.
4 Are there other ways that our eating habits may change in the future?

Watch video 3.1

p37

Grammar in Action 3.2

p39

Grammar in Action 3.3

p40

Everyday English 3.4

p42

Globetrotters 3.5

VOCABULARY
Cooking Verbs

1 **Match the verbs in the box with photos 1–12. Then listen, check, and repeat.** 3.01

bake	1	grate		roast	
boil		grill		season	
chop		overcook		slice	
fry		peel		spread	

2 **Circle the correct verbs to complete the instructions for making a homemade pizza. Then listen and check.** 3.02

[1]*Spread* / *Boil* the tomatoes and [2]*peel* / *grate* them. Then [3]*spread* / *chop* them into small pieces, put them in a pan, and [4]*spread* / *season* them with herbs and garlic. [5]*Slice* / *Roast* some bread. Then [6]*fry* / *spread* the tomatoes on the bread and [7]*grate* / *season* some cheese on top. [8]*Fry* / *Bake* it in the oven, but only for a few minutes – you don't want to [9]*overcook* / *peel* it!

3 **Circle the verb that does not go with each food.**

1 pepper:	chop	fry	spread
2 bread:	bake	roast	slice
3 chicken:	boil	overcook	grate
4 fish:	peel	grill	season

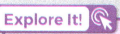

LEARN TO LEARN

Wordbuilding: Adjectives from Verbs

Learn the adjective form of new verbs. Sometimes the form is similar, for example, *bake* (v), *baked* (adj).

4 **Write the adjective forms of the verbs. Check your answers with a dictionary.**

bake baked	overcook ______
boil ______	peel ______
chop ______	roast ______
fry ______	season ______
grate ______	slice ______
grill ______	

5 **Which verbs in Exercise 1 usually go with the foods in the box?**

apple bread butter cake carrots cheese chicken egg fish jam orange pasta potatoes spinach steak

You can spread butter or jam on bread. You can have a fried egg.

Use It!

6 **Discuss the questions.**

1 Do you usually eat boiled, grilled, fried, baked, or roasted foods? Which are your favorites?
2 What can you cook?
3 Is it important to know how to cook? Why?

Explore It!

Guess the correct answer.

During the Chinese mid-autumn festival, people traditionally bake mooncakes. Which ingredient is baked inside them to symbolize the moon?

a chicken egg b ostrich egg c duck egg

Find another fact about a traditional food. Write a question for your partner.

Pronunciation p141

READING

An Online Forum

1 What types of food can you see in the photos? Which ones would you eat?

2 Read the forum and match comments 1–5 with photos a–e. 3.05

3 Read the forum again and match the future food solutions with the reasons.

Future Food Solution

1 ☐ jellyfish
2 ☐ lab food
3 ☐ smart fridges
4 ☐ 3-D printers
5 ☐ insects

Why It Solves the Problem

a better for the planet
b can reduce food waste
c a new food and we need these
d cheap and already popular in many places
e healthier and more convenient

4 Mark (✓) the reasons given for why people might not like future food.

a unusual in some cultures ☐
b sounds disgusting ☐
c could make humans sick ☐
d not much flavor ☐
e creates new environmental problems ☐

5 Match the words in **bold** in the forum with the meanings.

1 another possibility ______
2 the taste of something ______
3 not real ______
4 something special and good to eat ______
5 cooking instructions ______

CLASS 4C STUDY ROOM

Read the article about future food and add your comments. Professor Jones is coming to Friday's class and we're going to discuss your ideas.

1 c There isn't going to be enough food for everyone in the future because the population is growing, so we're going to need to be more adventurous and find new foods. I read that we could actually eat jellyfish, although many people won't like the idea. Jellyfish probably doesn't have much **flavor**, but if you season it and roast it, it might be tasty! *Abi*

2 ☐ We may eat **artificial** fish or meat grown in a laboratory in the future. I think the idea sounds disgusting, but scientists say it will be better for the planet. I'm definitely not going to eat lab burgers! *Carlos*

3 ☐ We throw away far too much food, often because we buy more than we need. I read about these cool apps that will tell us what's in the fridge and suggest **recipes** with the food we already have so we don't waste so much. I think they'll be really popular. *Jazmin*

4 ☐ One thing I'm not sure about is 3-D printed food. The idea that a printer will produce our food is a little strange. But people say it will be healthier and more convenient, and it might reduce pollution from transporting food products. *Marco*

5 ☐ Experts say that meat will be far more expensive in the future, so we're going to have to eat **alternative** types of food. Insects are cheaper than farm animals, so they may be a solution. Roasted grasshoppers are a popular snack in Mexico and fried tarantulas are a **delicacy** in Cambodia. In fact, a lot of cultures eat bugs, so why can't we? *Emma*

Voice It!

6 Discuss the questions.

1 Which of the ideas in the forum are your most and least favorite? Why?
2 What other future food solutions can you think of?

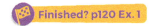

Finished? p120 Ex. 1

GRAMMAR IN ACTION
Future Forms

Watch video 3.2 What's happening this Saturday? Which workshop might he go to?

Present Tenses and *Be Going To* for Future Plans and Intentions
Friday's class **starts** at nine o'clock.
Professor Jones [1] ______ **coming** to Friday's class
and we**'re** [2] ______ discuss your ideas.

1 **Complete the examples in the chart above. Use the online forum on page 36 to help you.**

Get It Right!

We use the simple present for scheduled events in the future.

The movie starts at two o'clock. **NOT** ~~*The movie is starting at two o'clock.*~~

2 **Circle the correct words to complete the conversation.**

A [1]*Do you / Are you going to* watch the final tonight?

B Yeah. Kate [2]*comes / is coming* to my house to watch it.

A What time [3]*does it start / is it starting*?

B At 8 p.m., but she [4]*comes / is going to come* at 7 p.m.

Predictions with *Be Going To*, *Will*, and *May/Might*
The population is growing, so we [1] _'re going to_ need to find new foods. (a future prediction based on evidence)
We [2] ______ /**might** eat artificial fish or meat. (a future prediction we are not certain about)
Experts say that meat [3] ______ be far more expensive in the future. (a prediction we are certain about)

3 **Complete the examples in the chart above. Use the online forum on page 36 to help you.**

4 **Read the pamphlet. Complete the conversation with the simple present, present continuous, *be going to*, *will*, or *may/might* form of the verbs in parentheses.**

Come and have dinner in total darkness, Tuesday to Saturday, 8–10 p.m. Use your other senses to taste the food. Try new, unknown foods and guess what you're eating.

LUCAS Hey Milena, [1] _are_ you _coming_ (come) to Abi's birthday tomorrow?

MILENA Where [2] ______ you ______ (go)?

LUCAS To "Dining in the Dark." We [3] ______ (have) dinner in total darkness!

MILENA That's strange. Abi [4] ______ (not like) it!

LUCAS I'm sure she [5] ______ (love) it! It [6] ______ (be) different from anything she's done before.

MILENA But you [7] ______ (not be able to) see the food. You [8] ______ (eat) something you don't like.

LUCAS I know! We [9] ______ (have to) guess what we're eating!

MILENA What time [10] ______ it ______ (start)?

LUCAS At eight o'clock.

MILENA I'm not sure. I [11] ______ (come). I [12] ______ (tell) you later.

Use It!

5 **Write the questions. Use future forms. Then ask and answer.**

1 What / you / do / tomorrow?
What are you going to do tomorrow?

2 How old / you / be / in 2050?
______

3 What foods we / eat / in the future?
______

4 When / your next class / start?
______

What are you going to do tomorrow?

I'm not sure. I might go to the beach.

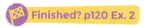

Finished? p120 Ex. 2

VOCABULARY AND LISTENING

Quantities

3.06 **1 Read the recipe and choose the correct photo 1–3. Then listen and repeat.**

1

2

3

How to Make Your Own Fruity Cereal

Mix the following ingredients in a bowl:

- a **cup of** cereal, like oats
- some **pieces of** strawberry
- some **slices of** banana
- some **chunks of** pineapple
- a **handful of** blueberries
- a **bag of** nuts
- a **pinch of** cinnamon
- a **sprinkle of** brown sugar

Serve with a **spoonful of** yogurt or a **splash of** milk.

Nutritious and delicious!

2 Complete the sentences with quantities from the recipe from Exercise 1 in the singular or plural form.

1. I have two _slices_ of toast for breakfast and coffee with ________ milk.
2. If your throat hurts, have ________ honey.
3. Season the pasta sauce with ________ salt and pepper.
4. I'm going to have a ________ of chips for lunch.
5. I love cookies with big ________ chocolate!
6. I make the best Greek salad. I put in ________ of olives, some ________ of feta cheese, and ________ oregano on top.

LEARN TO LEARN

Using Diagrams

Use diagrams to help remember new phrases.

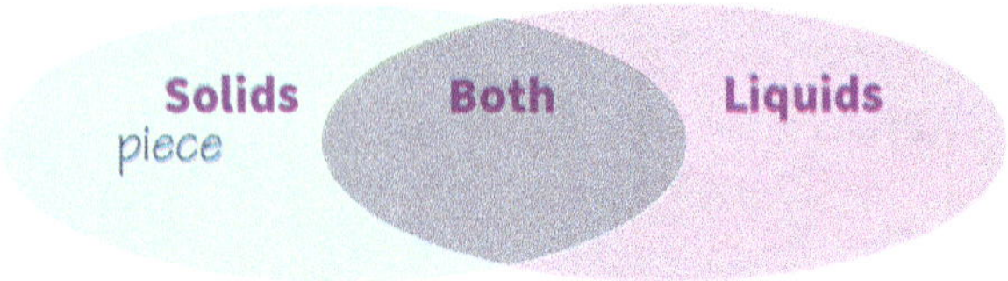

3 Add quantities in Exercise 1 to the diagram in your notebook.

Use It!

4 Think of a food you like and tell your partner the ingredients.

Pancakes … You need two cups of flour …

A Recipe

3.07 **5 Listen to the cooking show and write the quantities.**

Pear Smoothie	Ant Tacos
1 ________ orange juice	6 ________ ant larvae
2 ________ chopped pear	7 ________ chopped tomatoes
3 ________ cricket flour	8 ________ chopped chilies
4 ________ mango and pineapple	9 ________ salt and pepper
5 ________ lime juice	10 ________ chopped cilantro

3.07 **6 Listen again and circle the correct answers.**

1. Both of Anton's dishes ….
   a contain insects. c are Mexican.
   b are spicy.
2. By 2030 there will be … billion people in the world.
   a 5.5 b 6.5 c 8.5
3. Cricket flour will add … to the smoothie.
   a fruit flavor b vitamins c protein
4. Anton is going to … the ant larvae.
   a fry b boil c roast

GRAMMAR IN ACTION

Future Continuous and Future Perfect

Watch video 3.3
Who will be making our food in the future? What food was invented by accident?

	Future Continuous	Future Perfect
+	I [1] will be **making** a pear smoothie.	We [4] ______ **tasted** some very unusual dishes.
-	I [2] ______ **adding** milk or yogurt.	They [5] ______ **cooked** in time.
?	What [3] ______ you ______ **making** today?	[6] ______ you ______ **finished** by the end of the show?

1 **Complete the examples in the chart above with *will/won't be* or *will/won't have*.**

2 **Complete the sentences with the future continuous form of the verbs in the box.**

eat   not see   stay   ~~sleep~~

1 Don't call me at 8:30. I'll be sleeping .
2 Where ______ they ______ while they're on vacation?
3 I have exams next week. I ______ my friends.
4 ______ we ______ insects in 30 years?

3 **Complete the sentences with the future perfect form of the verbs in parentheses.**

1 I think scientists will have found (find) life on other planets by 2060.
2 I ______ (not finish) my exams by the end of May.
3 They ______ (not start) yet. It's only 7:30.

3.08 **4** **Complete the conversation with the future continuous or future perfect form of the verbs in parentheses. Then listen and check.**

ZOE How [1] will restaurants have changed (change) by 2030?
SAM I think they [2] ______ (become) more automatic. Instead of human chefs, machines [3] ______ (cook) your food and human waiters [4] ______ (not serve) the tables, robots will.
ZOE So humans [5] ______ (not work) in restaurants?
SAM That's right, but I think we [6] ______ (design) robots that look like humans by then.

Use it!

5 **Write sentences about your future. Use the future continuous or future perfect and the phrases in the box.**

In one year …   In 2050 …
On my 21st birthday …
By the end of this year …   By 2030 …
By the time I'm 25 …

In 2050, I'll be living in my own house.
By the time I'm 25, I'll have learned how to drive.

6 **Tell your partner your sentences about the future, but change some so that they are false. Can they guess which sentences are true and which are false?**

In 2050, I won't be living in my own house.

False?

Yes, it's false.

Finished? p120 Ex. 3

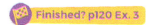

SPEAKING
Giving Instructions

3.09 **1 What can you see in the photo? What ingredients do you need to make it? Listen and check your answers.**

JOE Can you give me the recipe for your tasty Spanish omelet? I'm going to make it for the picnic tomorrow. It won't take forever, will it?

AMY No, it's a piece of cake! [1] You'll need two cooked potatoes, five eggs, salt, oil, and an onion.

JOE OK. Is that it?

AMY Yep, so [2] ________ slicing the potatoes. [3] ________ chop the onion.

JOE OK. Then what?

AMY Heat half a cup of oil in a pan and fry the potatoes and onions.

JOE That's a good bit of oil!

AMY Yeah, I know! [4] ________ frying, mix the eggs in a bowl. Then put everything together and add a pinch of salt. Heat a spoonful of oil in a smaller pan and pour in the mixture. Once the bottom part has cooked, [5] ________ flip the omelet and cook the other side.

JOE OK, I'll try.

AMY It's delicious! Your friends will all be asking for the recipe! Will you still be there at four?

JOE Yeah, but we'll have finished the omelet by then!

3.09 **2 Complete the conversation with the phrases from the *Useful Language* box. Then listen again and check.**

Useful Language

don't forget to … (+ verb)   Once that's done, …
start by … (+ *-ing*)   While that's … (+ *-ing*)
You'll need …

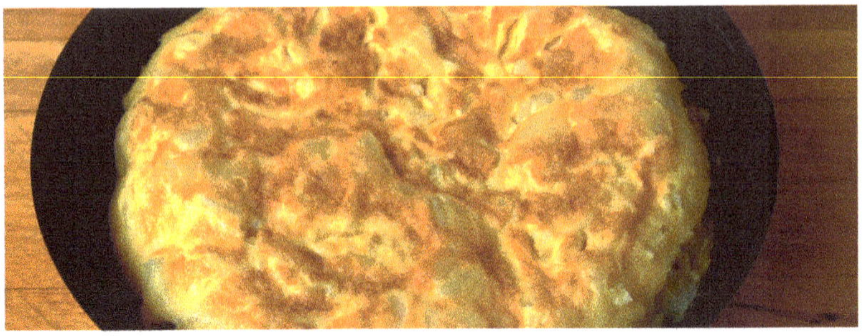

3 Match the words and phrases (1–4) with the words and phrases in the *Everyday English box*. How do you say these phrases in your language?

1 something that's easy
2 delicious
3 Is that everything?
4 a long time

Watch video 3.4
Everyday English

a piece of cake ☐   forever ☐
Is that it? ☐   tasty ☐

PLAN

4 Write about a recipe and the ingredients you need.

____

____

____

SPEAK

5 Practice explaining the recipe to your partner. Remember to use future forms, vocabulary from this unit, and phrases from the *Useful Language* and *Everyday English* boxes.

CHECK

6 Work with another pair. Listen to their conversation and complete the notes.

What was the recipe for? ________

____

What ingredients do you need?

____

____

Would you like to eat this food?

____

WRITING

A Listicle

1 What food can you see in the photos? Read Megan's listicle. Which of her predictions do you agree with?

2 The following are features of a good listicle. Which ones are in Megan's listicle?

1 an interesting title
2 a number in the title
3 short texts about the title, one for each number
4 some interesting predictions
5 photos

FIVE FOODS WE'LL ALL BE EATING IN 2070!

1 If there's one thing we'll still be eating in 50 years, it's pizza!
We've been eating pizza since the 19th century, so we're not going to stop now! In the future, toppings will change for sure, but pizza isn't going anywhere!

2 Tasty meat alternatives
With more humans on the planet, we'll need alternative sources of protein, such as insects. What could be tastier than a sprinkle of roasted ants on your salad?

3 Classics that will never die out!
Some classic British dishes, like fish and chips, will be around forever, although the fish will probably come from fish farms instead of the ocean.

4 Printed snacks
By 2070, we'll be printing most of our snacks with a 3-D printer. Impossible? Watch this space ...

5 Vegetarians and vegans
Vegetarian food is here to stay! In 2070 being vegetarian or vegan, and avoiding eggs, milk, and cheese, will be the norm!

3 Read Megan's listicle again and make two lists.

Food That Will Be the Same	Food That Will Be New
pizza	

4 Complete the *Useful Language* phrases with the words in the box. Check in Megan's listicle.

anywhere forever norm space stay

Useful Language

is here to [1] ____________
isn't going [2] ____________
Watch this [3] ____________
will be around [4] ____________
will be the [5] ____________

PLAN

5 Write your own listicle. Look at the questions and take notes.

What will people still be eating in 50 years?
____

What might we start eating in the future?
____

Which dishes will be around forever?
____

What food is unusual now but will be normal in the future?
____

WRITE

6 Write a listicle about your future food predictions. Remember to include future forms, vocabulary from this unit, and phrases from the *Useful Language* box.

CHECK

7 Do you ...

- explain what we will or might be eating in the future?
- explain what will be normal in the future?
- make any other predictions?

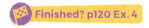

Finished? p120 Ex. 4

AROUND THE WORLD

Globetrotters

Watch video 3.5
Food in Japan

- What food is usually associated with your country or culture?
- Can you explain what *kaiseki* and *wagashi* are?
- How is Western food influencing Japanese food traditions?

READING
An Article

3.10 **1** **Look at the photos. What can you see? What do they tell you about food in Australia? Read the article and check your ideas.**

A TASTE OF *Australia*

A country's food is influenced by its inhabitants, geography, climate, and wildlife, and Australia is no exception.

Traditional Australia

For thousands of years, the indigenous people of Australia have eaten plants and animals from the land or ocean. Traditional Aboriginal food, or "bush tucker," includes crocodile, emu, and snake. Examples that are still eaten today include kangaroo, macadamia nuts, and witchetty grubs. These tasty insect larvae are roasted on the fire or grilled on the barbecue!

Multicultural Australia

Since the first Europeans arrived in Australia over 200 years ago, people have been moving to the country from all over the world. As a result, Australian cuisine is multicultural and includes British, Italian, Greek, and Asian food. Popular dishes are fish and chips, roasted lamb, and dim sum, as well as traditional favorites such as kangaroo, seafood pizza, and fried shark. The warm, sunny climate means plenty of fresh fruit and vegetables and barbecues to grill meat or fish outside.

Tomorrow's Australia

Desert Food

Australia has built the first farm in the world that can grow fruit and vegetables in a desert. The enormous solar-powered greenhouse only needs sunshine and seawater to work, and Australia has plenty of both. The solar panels create enough energy to transform the saltwater into fresh water, which is used to water the tomato plants. It's strange to think that in the future we might be eating food that is grown in the desert.

Ugly Food

Around a quarter of the fruit and vegetables around the world is thrown away before it gets to the supermarkets because people believe it's too "ugly" to sell. However, some Australian supermarkets are trying to sell this food. They tell their customers that even though the food looks odd, it tastes exactly the same as perfectly formed fruit and vegetables. There are a lot of advantages to eating this ugly food. It's less expensive for customers, farmers sell more of their produce, and we reduce food waste.

Voice It!

2 **Discuss the questions.**

1. People need to be open-minded to eat foods from other cultures or to change ways of getting food. How have people in Australia been open-minded about food?
2. What are the benefits of being open-minded about food?
3. How open-minded are you?

LEARN TO LEARN

Understanding Words from Context

When you see new words, use the rest of the sentence to help you understand them. Guess what the new word means and then check it in a dictionary.

3 **Find the words in the article and guess the meaning. Then check in a dictionary or with your teacher.**

New Word	What the Other Words Tell Me	What I Think It Means
indigenous	It's an adjective that describes people who have lived in Australia for a long time.	original, first
witchetty grubs		
multicultural		
shark		
solar-powered		
greenhouse		

4 **Find words in the article that mean …**

1 something not included in a group (introduction). ______
2 delicious (traditional Australia). ______
3 a style of cooking (multicultural Australia). ______
4 strange (ugly food). ______

Explore It!

Guess the correct answer.

What will you not find on a pizza in Australia?

a emu b kangaroo c koala d crocodile

Find another fact about Australian food. Write a question for your partner to answer.

SHAPE IT!

CULTURE PROJECT

A Poster

A poster presents information about a topic in a visually interesting way. Make a poster about a type of food from around the world.

Teacher's Resource Bank

3 REVIEW

VOCABULARY

1 **Circle the correct verbs.**

1. *Season* / *Peel* the orange before you eat it.
2. Is there any butter to *spread* / *grate* on my toast?
3. Let's *roast* / *fry* a chicken in the oven.
4. Can I borrow a knife to *grill* / *slice* the tomato?
5. Jose *bakes* / *chops* his own bread. It's great!

2 **Match the quantities with the photos. Then think of another example for each quantity.**

bag	☐	______	pinch	☐	______
chunk	☐	______	slice	☐	______
cup	☐	______	splash	☐	______
handful	☐	______	spoonful	☐	______

1

2

3

4

5

6

7

8

GRAMMAR IN ACTION

3 **Circle the correct words to complete the conversation.**

MAURO What [1]*do you* / *are you going to* do this afternoon?

ANDREA We [2]*'re going* / *will go* to the movies. Juan and Allie [3]*come* / *are coming*, too.

MAURO What movie [4]*are you going to* / *will you* see?

ANDREA *The Scream Factor.*

MAURO But you hate horror movies!

ANDREA I know! [5]*I'm not enjoying* / *I'm not going to enjoy* the movie, but Allie wants to see it.

MAURO It [6]*might be* / *is* OK. Who knows, you [7]*won't* / *may* enjoy it.

ANDREA We'll see. Anyway, I have to go. It [8]*will start* / *starts* in 45 minutes.

4 **Complete the predictions with the future continuous or future perfect form of the verbs in parentheses. Which predictions do you agree / disagree with?**

In 10 years …

1. Ethiopian cuisine ______ (become) popular.
2. most people ______ (stop) eating meat.
3. we ______ (not buy) "ugly" fruit and vegetables.
4. we ______ (not go out) to restaurants. We ______ (order) food online to eat at home.

Self-Assessment

- I can talk about food preparation.
- I can talk about quantities of food.
- I can use future forms to talk about plans, intentions, and predictions.
- I can use the future continous and future perfect.

LEARN TO … SET AND ACHIEVE LEARNING GOALS

When you know what your English learning goals are, you can take steps to achieve them.

1 Read what Ada says about her learning goal. What is it? Has she achieved it yet?

In three weeks, I'm going to New Zealand with my brother. He doesn't speak English, so I'll need to book the hotels, order food, and ask directions. My goal is to learn enough travel English to do this. I've bought a book with useful phrases for tourists, and I've downloaded episodes of a podcast about New Zealand. I'm going to listen to one episode every week. I'm also going to learn one useful phrase from the book every day. Piece of cake!

2 Write Ada's answers to questions 2–4 in her action plan.

3 Read what Enzo says about his learning goal. Write his answers to questions 1 and 2 in his action plan.

One month from now we have a speaking exam. I want to get a good grade, but I'm not great at speaking – not like my sister. She speaks English really well!

4 Whose advice should Enzo take?

Why don't you practice with your sister? Ten minutes a day would help. **Ela**

I'd study a lot of vocabulary the night before. And don't sleep! **Hamid**

Look at the Everyday English phrases in our book. Use three of them every day. **Olga**

5 Use your answers in Exercise 4 to complete questions 3 and 4 of Enzo's action plan. Write one sentence about his goal for question 5.

SHAPE IT!

6 Think of an English learning goal. What are your answers to questions 1 to 5?

7 Tell your partner about your learning goal. Use the action plan to help you.

Action Plan		NAME: Ada	NAME: Enzo
1	What do I want to do?	learn enough travel English to book hotels, order food, and ask directions learn enough travel English	
2	How much time do I have?		
3	How am I going to do it?	a b	a b
4	How often am I going to do the things in 3?	a b	a b
5	What's my goal in one sentence?	By the time we go to New Zealand, I'll have learned enough travel English.	

4 How do you use your senses?

LEARNING OUTCOMES

I can ...

- understand texts about people who don't feel pain or fear, and artists who make sound effects
- make guesses and give clues about unfamiliar objects
- write an encyclopedia entry
- make deductions and express obligation, prohibition, necessity, and advice
- talk about senses and describe how things look, sound, and feel, etc.
- brainstorm, use visual clues when listening, and plan my homework
- create an infographic.

Start It!

1 Look at the photo. What different senses do you use when you go to the beach?
2 Before you watch, what do you think bats, dolphins, and submarines have in common?
3 Which animal has the best hearing and how does that help them? Watch and check.
4 Can you think of any other animals that have special senses?

Watch video 4.1

p49

Grammar in Action 4.2

p51

Grammar in Action 4.3

p52

Everyday English 4.4

VOCABULARY

The Five Senses

1 Match the words in bold with photos A–E. Answer the questions.

Have you ever …

1 seen a **durian**? ☐
2 touched a **snake**? ☐
3 played soccer on **artificial grass**? ☐
4 heard a **koala**? ☐
5 eaten a **banana split**? ☐

2 Match the questions in Exercise 1 with statements a–e. Which things did you already know?

a They **look like** friendly teddy bears, but when they cry they **sound** really angry. [4]
b It's made of plastic, but it can often **feel like** the real thing. ☐
c It **tastes** sweet and it looks really colorful, and it **sounds like** a great idea for a dessert! ☐
d They **look** wet and slimy, but when you **touch** their skin they **feel** cold and dry. ☐
e They **smell** terrible. In fact, they **smell like** dirty old socks and they don't **taste like** fruit, but many people say they're delicious. ☐

LEARN TO LEARN

Brainstorming

Brainstorming word groups can help you make vocabulary connections.

3 Complete each line with the words in bold from Exercise 2. Add three or more words or phrases that you associate with them.

a the ears: sound, sounds like, hear, listen to, music
b the eyes: ______
c the hands: ______
d the nose: ______
e the tongue: ______

4 Choose one group of words in Exercise 3. Say your extra words to your partner. Can they guess which group they belong to?

5 Complete the sentences with the correct form of words in bold from Exercise 2.

1 When my dad sleeps, he snores so much he sounds like a trumpet!
2 I tried some crocodile meat once. It ______ chicken.
3 The milk ______ bad and ______ a bit yellow, so she didn't taste it.
4 I love wearing my new winter coat. It ______ so soft and warm.
5 A It ______ a painting by Picasso.
B No, but it is.
6 Please ______ the wall. I've just painted it.

Use it!

6 Talk about the things in the box with words from Exercise 2. Compare with another pair. Do you have the same descriptions?

cell phones   fast food   graffiti   new clothes   rap music

Explore It!

Guess the correct answer.

Which human sense is the weakest?

a sight   b hearing   c touch   d taste   e smell

Find another interesting fact about the human senses. Write a question for your partner to answer.

READING

A Magazine Article

1 Imagine you couldn't feel pain or fear. Would your life be better or worse? Why?

4.01 2 Read the magazine article. Which problems does it mention?

No Pain, No Fear – NO WAY!

Jordy Cernik

Everybody knows what pain feels like. It's horrible. So imagine never feeling physical pain. You cut your finger – nothing. You break your leg – no pain at all. It must be wonderful, right? Wrong, because pain is the body's way of telling the brain that there's a problem. But some people, like Amy Campbell, can't feel pain. When she was born, Amy looked like an ordinary baby, but after a few months, her parents realized something was wrong and thought she had developmental problems. She would chew her tongue and bite her fingers, but she never cried. By the time she was a teenager, she had broken both arms and a leg – all without feeling a thing. It also doesn't matter if the air feels hot or cold, Amy can't feel the weather. But, like any young person, she has friends, hobbies (she plays the guitar), dreams, and ambitions. She just has to be very careful. You may think her life can't be easy, but Amy is optimistic about her future. She says her condition affects what she can do but not who she is inside.

When Jordy Cernik tells people he feels no fear, they usually think he can't be serious. Having no fear might sound like a joke, but it's not. During his 20s and 30s, Jordy had to have operations to remove his adrenal glands. Some time later, he realized that these operations had had a strange effect – he couldn't feel any fear. He did a parachute jump but didn't feel scared at all. He finds rollercoasters boring. Some people imagine it must be great not to feel fear, but there are disadvantages to not having any adrenaline. Adrenaline is a natural painkiller, so Jordy now feels more pain than ordinary people. It also means he doesn't feel excited about anything. Jordy now does "scary" challenges to raise money for charity. Doctors think he could be the only person in the world who feels no fear, but knowledge about his condition may help them understand more common problems like anxiety.

3 EXAM **Choose the correct option.**

1 Pain is important because it tells the brain
- A you're all right.
- B there's a problem.
- C to go to the doctor.
- D to do scary things.

2 Amy Campbell and Jordy Cernik are examples of people who
- A experience life differently.
- B feel no pain.
- C feel no fear.
- D feel no pain or fear.

3 Fear and physical pain
- A prevent us from enjoying life.
- B are only feelings.
- C are always bad.
- D are necessary.

4 **Find words in the article that mean …**

1 to bite something many times with your teeth (Amy). ________

2 the things you want to achieve (Amy). ________

3 a chemical produced by the body (Jordy). ________

4 a chemical or drug that stops pain (Jordy). ________

5 the feeling of being very worried (Jordy). ________

Voice It!

5 **Why do people enjoying doing things like riding on rollercoasters?**

Finished? p121 Ex. 1

GRAMMAR IN ACTION
Modals of Deduction and Possibility

Watch video 4.2
Why is Andy an amazing athlete? How does he know when he's near the edge of the pool?

100% Certain	It [1] must **be** wonderful.
Possible	Having no fear [2] ________ **sound like** a joke, but it's not. Knowledge about his condition [3] ________ **help** them understand more common problems. Doctors think he [4] ________ **be** the only person in the world who feels no fear.
100% Impossible	He [5] ________ **be** serious.

1 **Complete the examples in the chart above. Use the magazine article on page 48 to help you.**

4.02 **2** **Circle the correct words. Then listen and check.**

1 This drink *must* / *can't* have a lot of sugar in it. It tastes really sweet.
2 Don't touch that snake! It *might* / *can't* be poisonous.
3 This milk *must* / *can't* be really old. It smells disgusting.
4 It looks like a painting by Monet, but it *may* / *can't* be. It was painted after he died.
5 A What instrument is that? It sounds like a violin.
  B Maybe, or it *can't* / *could* be a viola.
6 This jacket *must* / *can't* be very warm in winter. It feels like a blanket!

4.03 **3** **Complete the conversation with *must*, *can't*, or *might*. Then listen and check.**

MARTÍN What are you listening to? It's so loud!
LIZ It's Beethoven. I think it's beautiful.
MARTÍN You [1] must be joking! I thought you hated classical music.
LIZ Well, that's because I hadn't really listened to any before. Did you know Beethoven became deaf when he was still really young?
MARTÍN Wow, that [2] ________ be easy for anyone, but it [3] ________ be absolutely terrible for a musician. You should turn it down, though. The neighbors [4] ________ be home.
LIZ They [5] ________ be. The lights are off and their car's not there. Anyway, I'm sure they'd prefer Beethoven to the heavy metal you always play. They [6] ________ hate that! Every time you put it on they start banging on the wall.

4 **Write sentences about this situation with the verbs and phrases in the boxes. Use *must*, *can't*, *may*, *might*, or *could*.**

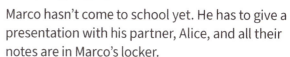

Why isn't Marco here? Our presentation starts in five minutes.

Marco hasn't come to school yet. He has to give a presentation with his partner, Alice, and all their notes are in Marco's locker.

be come feel have

a cold in bed late nervous soon very relaxed worried

Marco might be in bed. Alice must feel worried.
____
____
____

Use It!

5 **Look at the photos. What do you think they are?**

It could/might/can't/must be …

It looks like (a) …

1 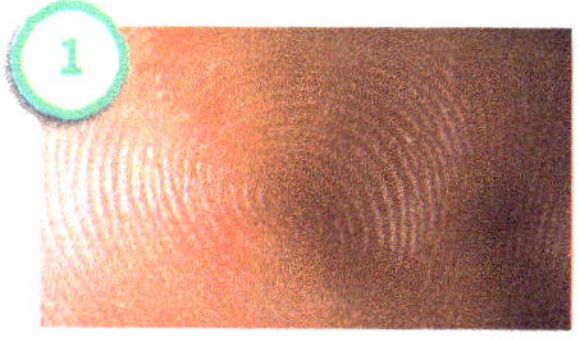

2 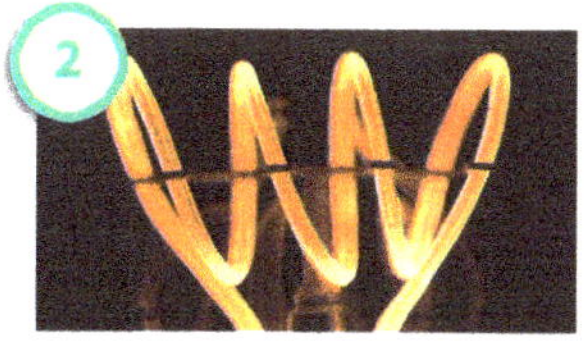

3 

4 

Finished? p121 Ex. 2

VOCABULARY AND LISTENING

Describing Texture, Sound, Taste, Etc.

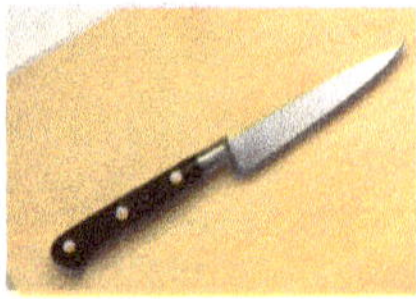

1 a sharp knife

2 a ________ umbrella

3 a ________ chameleon

4 ________ skin

5 a ________ chili pepper

6 a ________ road

7 a ________ grapefruit

8 ________ balloons

9 a ________ skunk

10 a ________ heartbeat

4.04 **1 Complete the photo labels with the words in the box. Then listen, check, and repeat.**

colorful faint rough ~~sharp~~ shiny
smelly smooth sour spicy transparent

2 In your notebooks, complete the chart with the words from Exercise 1.

Feel	Look	Smell	Sound	Taste
	colorful			

Use It!

3 Use words in Exercise 1 to describe the things in the box. Can your partner guess the item?

a cat's tongue a chili pepper a lemon a magazine
a new coin a pencil old shoes stars whisper

It's shiny and silver. *A new coin!*

An Interview

4 Foley artists create sound effects for movies. What sound effects do you think these items make?

a

two coconut halves

b

shredded newspaper and a plastic bag

c

cellophane

d

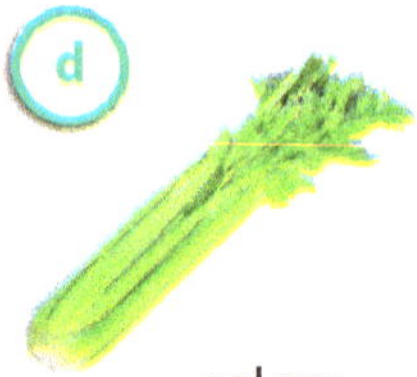

celery

e

rice and a metal tray

I think the coconut halves could be the sound of …

LEARN TO LEARN

Using Visual Clues When Listening

Use photos, instructions, etc., to help you understand what you are hearing.

4.05 **5 Listen to the interview with James Ford, a Foley artist. Were your answers to Exercise 4 correct?**

4.05 **6 Listen again and circle the correct words.**

1 It's important to *never* / *sometimes* have total silence in a movie.
2 The interviewer thinks the second effect is made with *newspaper* / *grass*.
3 Foley artists used to make *more* / *fewer* sounds.
4 James *made some* / *didn't make any* of the explosion sounds in his last movie.
5 To become a Foley artist, formal training is *necessary* / *unnecessary*.

Voice It!

7 Do you think the job of a Foley artist will disappear in the future? Why / Why not?

Watch video 4.3
What is she giving advice about? What three things do you need to do?

GRAMMAR IN ACTION

Obligation, Prohibition, Necessity, and Advice

	Obligation	Prohibition
+	They **must** sound natural.	
–	These days we [1] don't **have to** make them all.	You **must not** speak loudly in the library.
?	[2] ______ you **have to** work hard?	

	Necessity	Advice
+	We [3] ______ **to** experiment a lot.	We [5] ______ listen to one more effect. You **ought to** practice listening.
–	You **don't need** [4] ______ have any formal training.	You **shouldn't** do that.
?	**Do** you **need to** be creative?	**Should** we listen again?

Pronunciation p141

1 **Complete the chart above. Write one word in each blank.**

2 **Circle the correct words.**

7 TIPS FOR TAKING CARE OF YOUR EYES

1 Most of us [1]*must not* / *need to* use computers every day, but too much screen time can be bad for your eyes.
2 You [2]*ought to* / *shouldn't* spend more than about 20 minutes looking at a screen without taking a break.
3 You [3]*should* / *shouldn't* avoid using your phone in the dark. If you want to read, you [4]*ought to* / *have to* read a book.
4 Some people [5]*don't have to* / *must not* wear glasses, but if you do, you [6]*should* / *ought not to* keep the lenses clean.
5 Buy a good pair of sunglasses: everybody [7]*needs to* / *must not* protect their eyes from bright sunlight.
6 Don't forget about diet, either. It [8]*ought to* / *must not* include a lot of green vegetables and fatty fish.
7 Finally, everybody [9]*doesn't have to* / *should* have an eye exam once a year.

Past Obligation

In the past, Foley artists [1] ______ create all the effects.
I **didn't** [2] ______ make those sounds.
[3] ______ your parents ______ study English at school?

3 **Complete the chart above with the correct form of *have to*.**

Get It Right!
We don't use **must** in the past, only **had to**.

4 **Match 1-4 with a-d. Then listen and check.** (4.08)

1 She didn't have to study hard for the exam [d]
2 Billy didn't have to get up early this morning [ ]
3 Mia had to go to the dentist [ ]
4 I got all the answers wrong, [ ]

a because it's a holiday.
b so I had to do the exercise again.
c because she had a toothache.
d because she's really good at English.

5 **Complete the text with the correct form of *have to*.**

These days most people have a camera on their phone. In the past, you [1] had to be rich to own a camera. When you took a photo, the people [2] ______ stand still. The photographer [3] ______ be careful because photos were expensive. Now, we [4] ______ worry because we can take a ton.

Use It!

6 **Take notes and compare with a partner.**

- something you had to do in the past
- something you ought to do soon

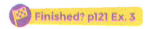

Finished? p121 Ex. 3

SPEAKING

Making Guesses and Giving Clues

1 (4.09) **Look at the photo. What are *tabi*? Listen and find out.**

ED Hey, do you want to see something cool?
ZOE Sure, why not? Wow! What are those?
ED They're called *tabi*. They're from Japan. [1]Guess what they are.
ZOE Well, they're [2] ________ of clothing. They look like gloves, but they can't be, can they?
ED Nope. They're definitely not gloves.
ZOE They're in the shape of an "L," so I guess [3] ________ socks.
ED Bingo!
ZOE But why is the big toe separate from the other toes?
ED I'm not telling you. Try to figure it out yourself.
ZOE Hmm. Perhaps [4] ________ traditional. Maybe Japanese people wear rings on their big toes?
ED No, that's not it. [5] ________ again.
ZOE No, I give up!
ED It's so that they can wear them with sandals with straps. The strap goes between the big toe and the others.
ZOE Oh, that's a smart idea! They must be nice and warm to wear.
ED I guess so. I haven't tried them on yet.

2 (4.09) **Complete the conversation with phrases from the *Useful Language* box. Then listen again and check.**

Useful Language

Guess again.
Guess what it is / they are.
I guess they must be …
Perhaps it's something (+ *adjective*)
They're definitely some kind of …

3 **Complete the conversations with the phrases in the *Everyday English* box.**

1 A Want to watch a movie? B ________
2 It's ________ today. Let's have a picnic!
3 A Is the answer 23? B ________
4 A Chinese must be hard to learn. B ________
5 A One more guess? B No – ________

Watch video 4.4
Everyday English

Bingo! I give up! I guess so.
nice and warm/hot, etc. Sure, why not?

PLAN

4 **Write about something from your country that might be new or strange to a foreigner, for example, a kind of food or an item of clothing. How would you describe it?**

Topic: ________
Description: ________
Purpose: ________

SPEAK

5 **Practice describing something from your country to your partner. Remember to use vocabulary from this unit.**

CHECK

6 **Work with another pair. Listen to their conversation and complete the notes.**

What did you hear about? ________
____
How was it described? ________
____

WRITING
An Encyclopedia Entry

1 **Look at the photos. What do you think the thing attached to the man's head does? Read the encyclopedia entry and check your ideas.**

1 ☐ Neil Harbisson was born on July 27, 1984.

2 ☐ Neil Harbisson is known as the world's first cyborg artist. He has been color blind since birth and has a special antenna connected to his skull that lets him "hear" colors as different vibrations in his head.

3 ☐ Neil was born in Belfast and grew up in Barcelona. At the age of 16, he started to make black and white art. In 2004, scientists developed his special camera and attached it to his head. With the camera, Neil can "hear" 360 colors, including some that are invisible to the human eye. In 2004, when he had to get a new passport, the UK passport office said no at first because he didn't look like a human. However, they finally accepted his application. He must be the only official cyborg in the world.

4 ☐ Neil now makes colorful art, including "sound portraits" of famous people and geometric paintings. He has had exhibitions all around the world.

5 ☐ According to Neil, all human skin sounds orange.

2 **Match headings a–e with paragraphs 1–5.**

a Artwork
b Other Information
c Introduction
d Name and Date of Birth
e Life

3 **Are the sentences *T* (true) or *F* (false)?**

1 Neil has always lived in the same place. ___
2 Neil doesn't always wear his antenna. ___
3 Neil can experience colors that ordinary humans can't see. ___
4 Neil couldn't get a new British passport. ___
5 People in many countries have seen Neil's art. ___

4 **Complete the sentences with the phrases from the *Useful Language* box.**

1 Stefani Joanne Angelina Germanotta ________ Lady Gaga.
2 She ________ March 28, 1986 ________ New York City.
3 ________ four she began to learn to play the piano.
4 She makes energetic pop music, ________ songs like *Bad Romance* and *Alejandro*.
5 ________ Lady Gaga, you can teach yourself art.

Useful Language

According to …	and grew up in …
At the age of …	including …
… is known as …	… was born on …

PLAN

5 **These artists all have a physical difference. Choose one and take notes.**

photographer Roesie Percy
chef Adam Cole
rapper Sean Forbes

Name and date of birth: ________

____

Their life: ________

____

Their work: ________

____

WRITE

6 **Write your encyclopedia entry. Remember to include five paragraphs, vocabulary from this unit, and phrases from the *Useful Language* box.**

CHECK

7 **Do you …**

- include information about the person's life?
- include information about the person's work?

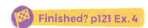

Finished? p121 Ex. 4

SCIENCE PROJECT

An Infographic

1 **Work in pairs. Can you answer the questions?**

1. Which continents do elephants live on?
2. How do they know where they are going?
3. How strong is their trunk (their long nose)?
4. What do they use their ears for?

2 **Read the infographic and check your answers to Exercise 1.**

How to Research

3 **Which of these things should you do when you research? Mark (✓) the correct answers.**

1. Decide the main information you want before doing research. ✓
2. Use questions in search engines, e.g., *How well can elephants see?*
3. Read articles from start to finish.
4. Read the contents list of articles or the titles of sections and then decide what you need to read.
5. Make sure the information is fact and not opinion.
6. Only check information on one site.
7. Take notes as you read.

Elephants and

Elephants' eyes are on the side of their head and have three eyelids, one above the eye and one below, like humans, and an almost transparent one they use to keep dust, dirt, and water out. However, their eyes aren't very strong. They normally use their trunks to know where they are going. In fact, the leader of a group of elephants is sometimes blind.

Elephants can hear extremely well because they have big ears. They can hear faint sounds, including the calls of elephants up to 1.5 km away. Their ears are about 1/6 of the size of their bodies. They also use them to keep cool.

Elephants have to move their trunk around and smell the air all the time in order to find water, so they have an excellent sense of smell. They can detect water up to 12 km away.

Elephants use their rough trunks to explore the environment and care for their young. They also use them to fight. The trunk can lift objects that weigh up to 250 kg. They can also sense tiny vibrations in the ground with their feet. Scientists think this must be the reason why many survived the Asian Tsunami of 2004. They felt the vibrations of the earthquake and moved to higher ground.

Their **Amazing** Senses

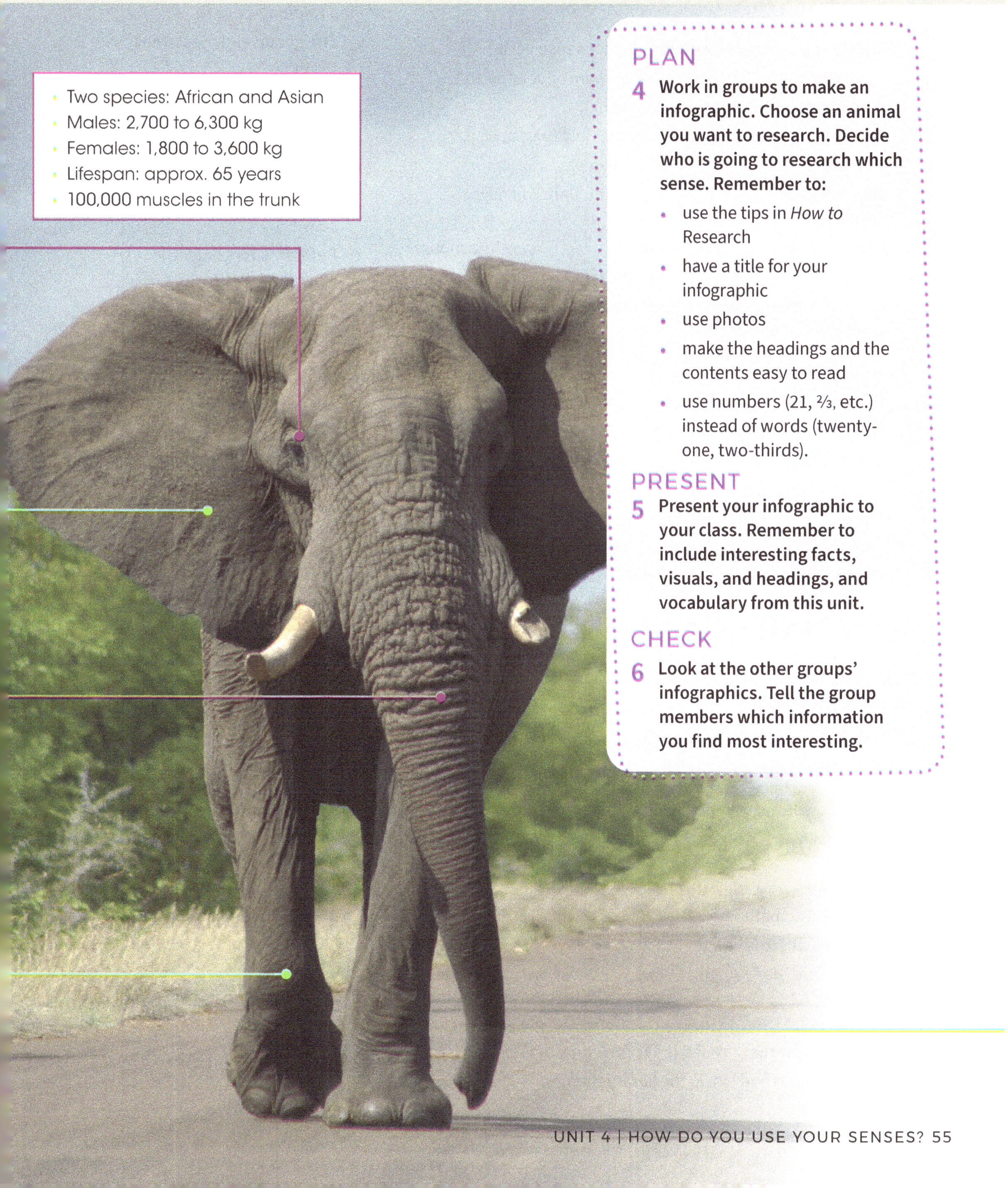

- Two species: African and Asian
- Males: 2,700 to 6,300 kg
- Females: 1,800 to 3,600 kg
- Lifespan: approx. 65 years
- 100,000 muscles in the trunk

PLAN

4 Work in groups to make an infographic. Choose an animal you want to research. Decide who is going to research which sense. Remember to:

- use the tips in *How to* Research
- have a title for your infographic
- use photos
- make the headings and the contents easy to read
- use numbers (21, ⅔, etc.) instead of words (twenty-one, two-thirds).

PRESENT

5 Present your infographic to your class. Remember to include interesting facts, visuals, and headings, and vocabulary from this unit.

CHECK

6 Look at the other groups' infographics. Tell the group members which information you find most interesting.

4 REVIEW

VOCABULARY

1 Complete the sentences with the correct sense verb.

1 A Do you ________________ your mom or your dad?
B My mom – I have the same eyes as her.
2 This coffee ________________ incredibly sweet.
3 Your perfume ________________ roses.
4 Your forehead ________________ hot, Dan. You might have a fever.
5 Listen! Do you hear that noise? It ________________ a mouse.
6 Ouch! I ________________ a cactus!
7 I've just started to learn the guitar. I ________________ very good yet, but one day I will.

2 Circle the correct words.

1 I don't like *spicy* / *smooth* food much – it burns my mouth.
2 I heard a very *transparent* / *faint* sound in the distance.
3 Are they new shoes? They're so *smelly* / *shiny* – I love them!
4 Be careful with that knife! It's really *sharp* / *faint*.
5 The pictures in that book are really *sour* / *colorful*.
6 These glasses are not completely *smelly* / *transparent*. You can't see the eyes of the person wearing them.

GRAMMAR IN ACTION

3 Complete the conversation with *must*, *might*, and *can't* and phrases from the box.

be doing that	be right	be studying	be wrong
have basketball practice	know the answer		

A What did you answer for question 10? I put 65.5.
B I put 75.3. We [1] ________________ both ________________.
One of us [2] ________________.
A Why don't we ask Tim? He [3] ________________.
He's good at math.
B Sure, but where is he?
A I'm not sure. He [4] ________________ in the library or he [5] ________________.
B No, he [6] ________________. Basketball practice is on Tuesday and today is Wednesday.
A OK, let's try to find him in the library then.

4 Match 1–5 with a–e. Complete the sentences with *have/has to*, *don't/doesn't have to*, *must/must not*, or *had to/didn't have to*.

1 Eric got up early yesterday because he ________________ ☐
2 This seat is reserved for older people, so you ________________ ☐
3 I have a lot to do tomorrow, so I really ________________ ☐
4 My friend had his car, so we ________________ ☐
5 Before visitors enter the exhibition, they ________________ ☐

a sit there.
b start work at 7 a.m.
c take the bus.
d put their bags in a locker.
e go to bed soon.

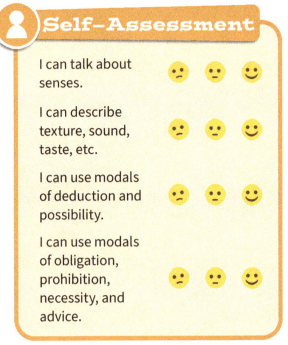

Self-Assessment

I can talk about senses.	☹	😐	☺
I can describe texture, sound, taste, etc.	☹	😐	☺
I can use modals of deduction and possibility.	☹	😐	☺
I can use modals of obligation, prohibition, necessity, and advice.	☹	😐	☺

LEARN TO ... PLAN YOUR HOMEWORK

When you have a lot of homework to do, it's important to decide what order to do it in and when to do it.

1 Ask and answer questions 1–4 in the pamphlet with a partner. Are your answers similar or different?

Feeling Stressed about Homework?

With our useful advice, you don't need to panic!

How often have you ...

1 forgotten what you had to do for homework?
2 handed in a piece of homework late because you didn't start it on time?
3 started when you were too tired?
4 done the quick or easy homework first and then not had time for more difficult things?

If you answered "often" or "always," then you really need our help!

a Decide when you need to start your homework and give yourself enough time.
b When you ought to start but don't want to, tell yourself, "I'll just do five minutes." Once you start, it's easy to continue.
c You should think about how difficult a piece of homework is and how much time it needs.
d When you get your homework, write it down immediately and always in the same place.

Now use our homework planner and start planning!

2 Match advice a–d with the problems in questions 1–4.

1 ______ 2 ______ 3 ______ 4 ______

3 Helen is planning her homework. What should she do first and last on Saturday? Why?

Homework Planner **Student's Name:** Helen

1 What is the subject and homework task?	2 When do I have to hand the homework in?	3 From 1–5, how easy/difficult is it? 1= very easy, 5= very difficult	4 How much time do I need to do it?	5 What day am I going to do it?	6 On each day, what am I going to do first, second, etc.?
math, p38 exercises 6–9	Monday	3	45 minutes	Saturday	
history, essay	Monday	5	1 1/2 hours	Saturday	
science, p67 exercises 3 and 4	Monday	4	1 hour	Saturday	
geography, project	Wednesday	4	2 1/2 hours	Sunday	

SHAPE IT!

4 Think about the homework you have to do this week. Use the homework planner to plan it.

5 What amazes you?

LEARNING OUTCOMES

I can ...

- understand texts about smart cities and a virtual reality tour
- express surprise and disbelief
- write a competition entry
- understand how to use the passive and question tags
- use verbs related to processes and extreme adjectives
- learn verbs with prepositions, listen for specific information, skim read to understand the general idea, and use a presentation plan

Start It!

1 Look at the photo of the Northern Lights. What does it look like?
2 Before you watch, can you think of any natural wonders?
3 What does a waterfall in Yosemite National Park look like? Watch and check.
4 Which is your favorite natural wonder? Why?

Watch video 5.1

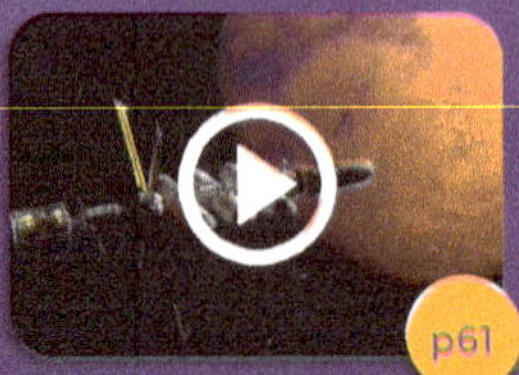
p61

Grammar in Action 5.2

p63

Grammar in Action 5.3

p64

Everyday English 5.4

p66

Globetrotters 5.5

VOCABULARY
Processes

1 (5.01) **Read about three amazing animals. Listen and repeat the words in bold.**

2 **Match the words in bold in the text with definitions a–l.**

a make something exist *create*
b make something come nearer ________
c get a new quality/ability ________
d take somewhere ________
e find the size ________
f join ________
g bring together ________
h make something ________
i give ________
j find the answer ________
k share information ________
l use too much ________

Bees **measure** distances between new flowers and their hive. They **communicate** this information by dancing for other bees, which then **collect** the nectar and **deliver** it to the hive. Nectar and pollen **supply** the nutrients bees need to live.

Spiders **create** webs to **attract** as well as catch insects. The silk they **produce** is five times as strong as steel, but they have to wait for the wind to **connect** the end of the first line to something nearby. Spiders don't **waste** any silk: they sometimes eat their webs when they have finished with them.

Crows **solve** problems to get food. In some cities they **develop** the ability to read traffic lights; they wait for the red light, place a walnut in the road, then fly up and wait for a car to drive over the nut and break it open.

LEARN TO LEARN
Learning Verbs with Prepositions
Learn verbs with the prepositions they take. This helps you use them correctly.

3 **Complete each sentence with a preposition (*to* or *with*).**

1 Insects are **attracted** *to* spider webs.
2 Spiders **connect** their webs ______ something nearby.
3 Bees **communicate** ______ each other by dancing.
4 Bees collect nectar and **deliver** it ______ other bees.
5 Nectar **supplies** bees ______ nutrients.

4 **Circle the correct words.**

1 Which puzzle has six sides and is difficult to *solve* / *deliver*?
2 Which North American country *measures* / *supplies* length in inches and feet, not centimeters and meters?
3 Which country *produces* / *attracts* the most movies every year?
4 What's the name of the tunnel that *wastes* / *connects* the UK with France?
5 How do dolphins *communicate* / *develop* with each other?
6 Which animals *create* / *collect* nuts for the winter?

Use It!

5 **Discuss the questions in Exercise 4.**

Explore It!

Guess the correct answer.

Bees beat their wings very fast, but how many times per second?

a 100 b 200 c 300

Find another interesting fact about birds or insects. Write a question for your partner to answer.

READING

A Webzine Article

5.02 **1** **Look at the photo. What do you think a smart city is? Read the webzine article and check your ideas.**

2 **Match headings a–d with paragraphs 1–4.**

a Soon to Become a Reality

b Greener Streets

c Everything Will Be Connected

d More Choices for Citizens

3 **Read the webzine article again and discuss the questions.**

1 How will the IOT make urban life better?

2 What will 3-D printers be able to do?

3 How will food be delivered to our homes?

4 How will we be healthier?

5 Why won't electricity be wasted?

6 What percentage of people will be living in rural areas by 2050?

4 **Find words in the webzine article that mean …**

1 the people living in a place (paragraph 1). ______

2 belonging or relating to a city or town (paragraph 1). ______

3 a small flying machine without a pilot (paragraph 2). ______

4 to stop something from happening (paragraph 3). ______

5 the people who live in a particular place (paragraph 4). ______

Voice It!

5 **Discuss the questions.**

1 What disadvantages might there be to living in a smart city? Think of three ideas.

2 Would you like to live in a smart city? Tell your partner and explain your reasons.

Finished? p122 Ex. 1

SMART CITIES OF THE FUTURE

1 ☐ Electric cars, drone deliveries, houses that communicate with you when you're out. Are you impressed by this image of city life? If so, you're not alone. Scientists and engineers around the world are developing a huge digital web called the Internet of Things (IOT) that will make all of this possible. Soon, billions of devices will be connected by the IOT. It will collect all sorts of data – information about the weather, the traffic, population movement, our shopping, the places we visit, even our health. This information will be used to make urban life better for everyone. Welcome to smart cities, the cities of the future.

2 ☐ In smart cities, we'll have more free time. For example, imagine you're feeling hungry on the way home but don't want to cook. All you'll need to do is send a message to your 3-D printer and tell it to print something tasty for you. Or, if you prefer, order takeout, and within minutes a delicious pizza is delivered by a drone. Smart citizens will be healthier, too. Our fridges will remind us when it's time to buy fresh fruit and vegetables, while devices on our bodies will measure our levels of fitness. The data they collect will be supplied to our doctors and we'll be told to visit them as soon as anything is wrong, so we won't be surprised by unexpected health problems.

3 ☐ Smart cities will also be better for the environment because electricity won't be wasted in them. Imagine you forget to turn the lights off when you go out. Don't worry – your house will do it for you. What's more, streetlights will only be switched on when you walk past them and cars will communicate with traffic lights to prevent traffic jams, saving both time and energy.

4 ☐ When the first cities were built thousands of years ago, their inhabitants couldn't have realized how different urban life would become, but smart cities are almost here. Will everything and everyone soon be connected by the IOT? Probably not, but by 2050, more than 70 percent of us will be living in a city, and we'll definitely be even more connected than we are today.

GRAMMAR IN ACTION

The Passive

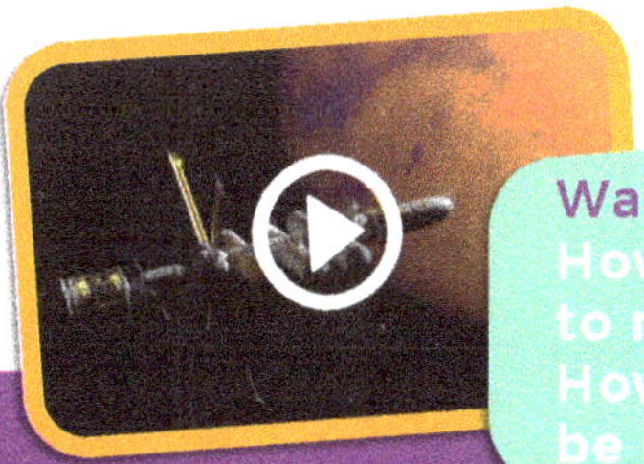

Watch video 5.2
How did people listen to music in the past?
How will our clothes be made in the future?

	Present	Past	Future
+	A delicious pizza [1] is **delivered** by a drone.	The first cities [3] ______ **built** thousands of years ago.	Billions of devices [4] ______ **connected** by the IOT.
–	Time and energy **aren't wasted**.	Hieroglyphics **weren't understood** until 1822.	We [5] ______ **surprised** by unexpected health problems.
?	[2] ______ you **impressed** by this image of city life?	When **was** the Internet **invented**?	[6] ______ everything and everyone soon ______ **connected** by the IOT?

1 **Complete the examples in the chart above. Use the webzine article on page 60 to help you.**

2 **Rewrite the sentences with a passive form of the verb in bold and *by*.**

1 Millions of people will **see** the solar eclipse.
The solar eclipse will be seen by millions of people.

2 Lightning **strikes** 240,000 people every year.
______

3 The Romans **didn't invent** Roman letters.
______

4 Elizabeth Magie **invented** Monopoly.
______

3 **Complete the text with passive forms of the verbs in the box.**

build bury make not lift place pull use ~~visit~~

The Pyramids of Giza in Egypt [1] are visited by millions of tourists every year. When they [2] ______, about 5,500 years ago, great kings called pharaohs [3] ______ inside them. What we don't know is how the pyramids [4] ______. More than two million blocks of stone [5] ______ for each one, but nobody knows how each stone [6] ______ in the correct position. Clearly, they [7] ______ by hand because they were too heavy. [8] ______ they ______ by ropes or did people push them by hand?

5.03 **4** **Complete the conversation with the future passive form of the verbs in parentheses. Then listen and check.**

A I was reading a blog that said in the future many jobs [1] will be done (do) by robots.
B Really? Like what?
A Well, food [2] ______ (serve) by them in restaurants, houses [3] ______ (build) by them – and in some schools, classes [4] ______ (teach) by them.
B Robot teachers! That will be strange. But [5] ______ all humans ______ (replace) by robots?
A I don't think so. The blog said most operations [6] ______ (not do) by robots – human doctors and surgeons will still do those.
B What about sports? [7] ______ human baseball players ______ (replace) completely?
A I don't think so, but who knows?
B I hope not because that's what I want to be!

Use It!

5 **Discuss the questions.**

1 Will all classes be taught by robots?
2 Will all shopping be done online?

Some classes will be taught by robots, but not all of them.

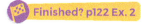

Finished? p122 Ex. 2

VOCABULARY AND LISTENING

A Virtual Reality Tour

1

2

3

1 Look at photos 1–3. Do you know where these places are?

5.04 2 Listen to the virtual tour and check your answers to Exercise 1.

LEARN TO LEARN

Listening for Specific Information

Knowing what kind of information we are listening for can help us hear it.

3 Read the sentences and decide if the missing information is a year, a measurement, or a number.

1 There are seven New Wonders of the Natural World. a number

2 A major sports event took place in South Africa in ______ . ______

3 The top of Table Mountain is ______ wide. ______

4 The biggest Komodo dragons are ______ long. ______

5 There are approximately ______ Komodo dragons on Komodo Island. ______

6 ______ smaller waterfalls make up Iguazu Falls. ______

7 The water falls up to ______ . ______

5.04 4 Listen again and complete the sentences from Exercise 3.

Extreme Adjectives

5.05 5 Replace the underlined words in the text with the words in the box. Then listen and check.

awful	boiling	deafening	enormous	fascinating
freezing	gorgeous	marvelous	~~stunning~~	terrifying

The Sahara Desert looks [1]<u>very beautiful</u> stunning. I've been learning about it in class. It's [2]<u>very interesting</u> ______ . At 9.2 million km^2, it's [3]<u>very big</u> ______ . The sand dunes are [4]<u>very beautiful</u> ______ . It would be [5]<u>very good</u> ______ to visit it one day, but it would be [6]<u>very scary</u> ______ to get lost there without water. During the day it's [7]<u>very hot</u> ______ , but at night it can be [8]<u>very cold</u> ______ . Sometimes there are sandstorms with [9]<u>very loud</u> ______ winds. It must be [10]<u>very bad</u> ______ to be caught in one.

Get It Right!

We don't use **very** with extreme adjectives, but we can use **really** or **absolutely**.

We don't use **absolutely** with regular adjectives, only with extreme adjectives.

Use It!

6 Discuss the questions.

1 Where can you find stunning scenery in your country?
2 Which is worse, boiling hot or freezing cold weather? Why?
3 Would you prefer to live in a gorgeous, tiny house or an ugly, enormous house? Why?

There is an enormous waterfall in my country. The noise is deafening when you stand next to it.

GRAMMAR IN ACTION
Question Tags

Watch video 5.3
What is his vlog about?
What was he most impressed by?

	Positive Sentence + Negative Tag	Negative Sentence + Positive Tag
To Be	It**'s** Cape Town, **isn't** it?	It **isn't** Sydney, [1] ______ it?
Modal Verbs	The speech **will** be recorded, **won't** it?	You **won't** be eaten, [2] ______ you?
Simple Present	You **speak** German, **don't** you?	We **don't have** a test, [3] ______ we?
Simple Past	Linda **went** home early, **didn't** she?	You **didn't tell** anyone our secret, **did** you?
Auxiliary *To Have*	Class **has** ended, **hasn't** it?	Ivan **hasn't** arrived yet, **has** he?

1 Complete the examples in the chart.

2 Match the sentences with the question tags.

1 You're a student here, [c]
2 The flowers are beautiful, [ ]
3 You've seen this movie already, [ ]
4 He's going to Iceland, [ ]
5 They bought tickets, [ ]
6 We can park here, [ ]
7 Your dog won't bite me, [ ]
8 They exercise every morning, [ ]

a didn't they?
b haven't you?
c aren't you?
d isn't he?
e can't we?
f don't they?
g will it?
h aren't they?

3 Complete the sentences with the correct question tag.

1 That tour was very good, wasn't it?
2 Insects are interesting, ______?
3 It's not very hot in here, ______?
4 We can't hear each other very well, ______?
5 They'll swim with sharks, ______?

4 Match the sentences in Exercise 3 with responses a–e. Complete the responses with the adjectives in the box.

deafening fascinating freezing marvelous ~~terrifying~~

a [5] Yes, it will be terrifying.
b [ ] No, it's absolutely ______.
c [ ] No – the music is ______.
d [ ] It was ______.
e [ ] Yes, they're really ______.

Get It Right!

In question tags, we use the auxiliary **do** with **have to**.

I don't have to buy a ticket, do I? **NOT** ~~*I don't have to buy a ticket, have to I?*~~

Use It!

5 Discuss the questions with question tags.

1 Do you speak any other foreign languages?
2 What's the weather going to be like this weekend?
3 When is the next vacation?

You studied French, didn't you?

Yes, I did.

Finished? p122 Ex. 3

SPEAKING

Expressing Surprise and Disbelief

5.06 **1 What do you know about the building in the picture? Listen to the conversation. What do you learn about it?**

ANGELA So, Ryan, how was your trip to Rome?

RYAN Oh, man, you should go. It's absolutely stunning. There's so much history and so many amazing buildings there. I loved it.

ANGELA Where was your favorite place?

RYAN I'd say it was the Coliseum.

ANGELA That's where the gladiators used to fight, isn't it?

RYAN Sometimes they would fight with animals, too. Bears, lions, elephants.

ANGELA You [1] can't be serious. With animals?

RYAN Yep. On one occasion, over 10,000 animals were killed in a single day.

ANGELA [2] ________________ me? That's awful!

RYAN And they used to have sea battles there.

ANGELA I find [3] ________________. How was that done?

RYAN They would fill the stadium with water from the aqueducts. There were real ships and everything.

ANGELA: [4] ________________? That's fascinating.

RYAN Wanna see a photo of me dressed as a gladiator outside?

ANGELA OK, sure. Wow! Is that you? I can't [5] ________________ wore that!

RYAN I look terrifying, don't I?

ANGELA Um, not exactly. You look sweaty. It must've been really hot there.

RYAN It was. It was boiling.

5.06 **2 Complete the conversation with the phrases from the *Useful Language* box. Then listen again and check.**

Useful Language

Are you kidding me? I can't believe you actually …
I find that hard to believe. Seriously?
You can't be serious.

Watch video 5.4
Everyday English

… and everything I'd say it was …
Oh, man Um, not exactly Wanna …?

3 Complete the conversations with the phrases in the *Everyday English* box.

1 A What's the best place you've ever been to?
B ________________ Iceland.

2 A How was the movie?
B ________________, I loved it!

3 A The exam was easy, wasn't it?
B ________________. I thought it was pretty hard.

4 A Jack's house is enormous, isn't it?
B I know! It has a pool ________________.

5 A ________________ have a picnic tomorrow?
B I can't, sorry. I'm busy.

PLAN

4 Write about an amazing place you have been to. Think of three interesting things about it.

SPEAK

5 Practice the conversation. Describe your amazing place and ask your partner about their place. Remember to use the passive, question tags, and phrases from the *Useful Language* and *Everyday English* boxes.

CHECK

6 Work with another pair. Listen to their conversation and take notes.

What place did they talk about?

____

What was interesting about it?

____

____

Would you like to visit it?

____

____

WRITING
A Competition Entry

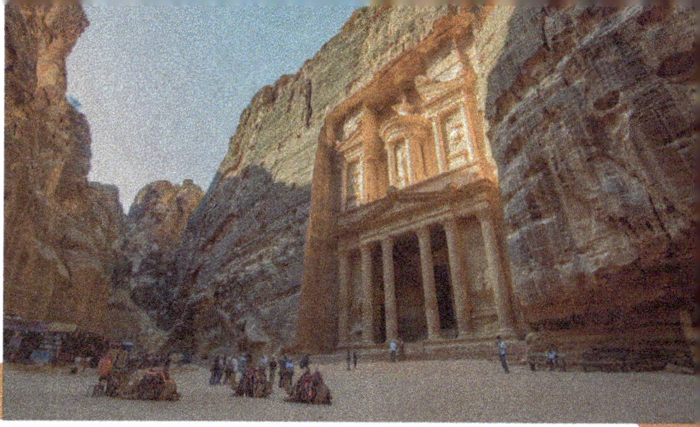

1 **Look at the photo. What do you think the building is? Read the competition entry and check your ideas.**

The Most Incredible Place I've Ever Visited

1 ☐ I've been to a lot of amazing places, but the one that impressed me the most was Petra, an ancient city in Jordan. I visited it last summer with my family. We all loved it.

2 ☐ Petra is fascinating. The first buildings were built over 2,000 years ago. At one time it was inhabited by 30,000 people. A lot of it was carved out of the rock of the mountains. In fact, it is sometimes known as "the Rose City" because of the color of the rock.

3 ☐ The highlight of a visit to Petra is the Treasury. Nobody is sure why it was built, but archaeologists think that a king was buried there or that it was a place for important documents. When the sun shines on the front of the building, it's really stunning. I'm absolutely certain that it will still be visited hundreds of years in the future.

4 ☐ I think Petra deserves to win because it is so beautiful, especially the Treasury. Without a doubt, it's one of the most incredible places in the world.

GO GLOBAL
Tell us about the most incredible place you've ever visited to win two plane tickets!

2 **Read the entry again. Match topics a–d with paragraphs 1–4.**

a the reason why the place should win
b introduction
c detailed description of part of the place
d general description of the place

3 **Match 1–5 with the phrases from the *Useful Language* box a–e with a similar meaning.**

1 for me, the … that was the best was … ☐
2 It's certain that … ☐
3 I'm completely sure that … ☐
4 … should win because … ☐
5 When you go to …, the best part is … ☐

Useful Language

a … deserves to win because …
b I'm absolutely certain that …
c The highlight of a visit to … is …
d the … that impressed me the most was …
e Without a doubt, …

4 **Discuss the questions.**

1 What is unusual about the way Petra was built?
2 What do people think the Treasury was built for?
3 List all the extreme adjectives in the entry.

PLAN

5 **Think of the most incredible place you have visited. Research it and take notes for a competition entry in your notebook.**

What is the place?
How would you describe the place?
Why did it impress you?
Why should it win the competition?

WRITE

6 **Write your competition entry. Remember to include the four paragraphs from Exercise 2, the passive, extreme adjectives, and phrases from the *Useful Language* box.**

CHECK

7 **Do you …**

- give a description of the place?
- say why it impressed you?
- explain why you think the place should win?

Pronunciation p142

Finished? p122 Ex. 4

AROUND THE WORLD

READING
A Travel Blog

1 **Look at the blog. How long did the writer travel? What did he see?**

5.09 2 **Read Scott's blog for Day 1. Which activities can you do in Meghalaya?**

Globetrotters
Watch video 5.5
Extreme Homes

- What can make a place difficult to live in?
- Why is it difficult to live in these places: Atacama Desert, Siberia, and Lake Titicaca?
- What's unusual about Matera?

Voice It!

3 **Discuss the questions.**

1 How do you think Scott showed respect for the people and the environment during his visit?
2 If tourists visited your town or neighborhood, how would you want them to show respect?
3 How can you show respect to people and your environment where you live?

SCOTT THE EXPLORER
BLOGGING MY WAY AROUND INDIA

DAY 1

Hi, everyone! This week I'm in Meghalaya in northeast India, the wettest place on Earth. I've only been here for a day, but I love the place already. It's really cloudy, but when the clouds lift the scenery is stunning: beautiful mountains covered by gorgeous green forests. The people are really friendly, and there are tons of things to do – you can go to festivals, explore caves, see waterfalls, visit a bird sanctuary, cross living root bridges, go hiking, and so much more. I can't wait! This blog will be updated while I'm here, so make sure you check out my posts!

DAY 2

This morning I went to the marvelous Siju Bird Sanctuary, where a lot of endangered birds are protected. I even saw one of the rare peacock pheasants. Check out the photo! After that I tried *jadoh*, a local dish of rice and meat. Rice is traditionally eaten several times a day here, and it was delicious. In the afternoon, I wanted to explore the capital, Shillong, where I'm staying, but it started raining heavily, so I stayed inside and relaxed. Tomorrow I'm going to visit the Krem Lymput cave. I'm really excited – I've never been in a cave before!

DAY 3

OK, I've just gotten back from the cave tour. It wasn't my favorite experience! The guide was great. He explained everything really clearly – how old the cave is, how it was made, and so on, and the cave was beautiful, but at times I was really scared. It's over six kilometers long, with some enormous rooms, but most of it was narrow, dark, and wet. I had to carry a flashlight and walk really carefully. It was terrifying! Anyway, I'm safely back in the hostel now. More from me tomorrow!

DAY 4

Today I saw the Nongkrem dance festival. This colorful festival is celebrated by the Khasi people, who are one of the main groups of people in Meghalaya. They have an incredibly fascinating society. Women have a very

LEARN TO LEARN

Skimming for Gist

Often you want to understand the general idea of a text, not the details. To do this you can "skim" the text, which means to read it very quickly.

4 Skim the rest of the blog and discuss with a partner. How did Scott feel about the things he saw?

5.10 **5 Now read the rest of Scott's blog. Discuss the questions.**

1 What problem did Scott have on Day 2?
2 Do you think Scott will visit any more caves in the future? Why / Why not?
3 What is unusual about births in Khasi society?
4 Why didn't Scott post anything on Day 5?
5 How are living root bridges made?

6 Find adverbs in the travel blog that mean ...

1 in a traditional way (day 2). ______
2 a lot (day 2). ______
3 in a way that is easy to understand (day 3). ______
4 extremely (day 4). ______
5 in the end (day 6). ______

Explore It!

Guess the correct answer.

Meghalaya is the wettest place on Earth, but where is the driest?

a The Atacama Desert in Chile
b Dry Valleys in Antarctica
c Lake Eyre in Australia

Find another interesting fact about an extreme place on Earth. Write a question for your partner to answer.

important role in Meghalaya society. For example, the birth of a boy is not a special occasion but the birth of a girl is celebrated by everyone, children take their mother's surname, and when parents die, the youngest daughter gets their house.

DAY 5

DAY 6

I'm back! I didn't write anything yesterday because I was hiking in the mountains overnight. I saw some incredible views and crossed one of the famous tree root bridges. These bridges are created by hand. People tie the roots of young trees together and help them to grow slowly across rivers. The process takes many years, but eventually the roots are strong enough for people to walk on. Check out the picture I took! Anyway, the time here has gone so fast. I'd love to stay longer, but tomorrow I have to leave. Thanks for reading!

SHAPE IT!

CULTURE PROJECT

A Travel Blog

A travel blog gives information and pictures about a visit to a fascinating destination. Make a travel blog about an interesting travel destination.

Teacher's Resource Bank

5 REVIEW

VOCABULARY

1 Complete the sentences with the correct form of the verbs in the box.

attract collect communicate connect create deliver develop measure produce solve supply waste

1 The postal worker ____________ seven letters to my house this morning.
2 The teacher ____________ the students' homework next Monday.
3 Scientists ____________ the Internet in the 1970s.
4 Most people ____________ a lot of plastic every day.
5 My car engine ____________ a lot of heat.
6 Electric lights ____________ different insects.
7 Walt Disney ____________ some of the world's most famous cartoon characters.
8 A stopwatch ____________ time.
9 A young mathematician ____________ the most difficult equation in history a few years ago.
10 Three different companies ____________ electricity to this city next year.
11 The Channel Tunnel ____________ the United Kingdom with France.
12 Pilots on international flights use English ____________ with each other.

2 Complete the sentences with the adjectives in the box.

awful boiling deafening enormous fascinating freezing terrifying

1 Turn that music down – it's ____________ !
2 Can you open the window? It's ____________ in here.
3 It was a bad movie – the actors were ____________ .
4 The Grand Canyon is 446 km long – it's ____________ .
5 Put your coat on. It's ____________ today.
6 I'm scared of spiders. They're ____________ .
7 The book was ____________ . I read it twice!

GRAMMAR IN ACTION

3 Rewrite sentences 1–5 from Exercise 1 as passive sentences.

1 ____________
2 ____________
3 ____________
4 ____________
5 ____________

4 Complete the conversation with the correct question tags.

A What are you looking for?
B My phone charger. It was here somewhere.
A You didn't put it in your bag, 1 ____________ ?
B No, I looked there. You don't have an extra one, 2 ____________ ?
A Sorry, no. You can buy a new one here, 3 ____________ ?
B I guess so. Wait! I put my wallet in my pocket, 4 ____________ ? Oh, here it is!

Self-Assessment

I can talk about processes.
I can use extreme adjectives.
I can use the passive.
I can use question tags.

LEARN TO ... USE A PRESENTATION PLAN

A presentation plan can help you prepare a presentation and make it clear and easy for the listener to understand.

1 **Read Roberto's notes. What is his presentation about? Circle a, b, or c.**

a a rainbow

b a total eclipse of the sun

c the Northern Lights

Presentation Plan

Introduce the presentation.		Today, I'm going to talk about ...
1 *What is it?*		a very special event in the sky!
2 *How does it happen?*		the sun is hidden by the moon, parts of the Earth are covered by its shadow
3 *Where and when can you see it?*	**Where?**	You need to be in the area covered by the moon's shadow.
	When?	about once every year and a half
4 *What other information can I give you?*		Never look directly at it! It's dangerous.
5 *Have I ever seen one?*	**Where?**	Yes, in Argentina
	When?	July 2, 2019
	What was it like?	absolutely stunning!

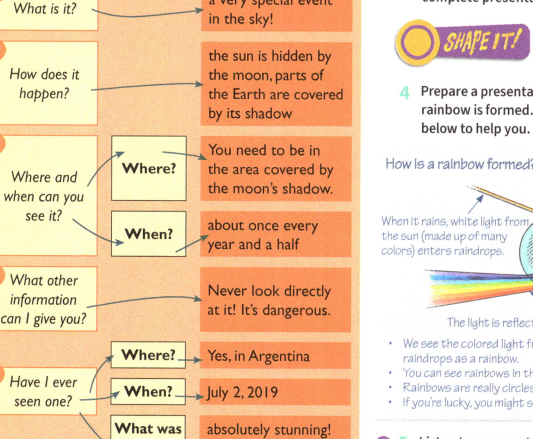

2 **Read the beginning of Roberto's presentation. Complete it with questions from the Presentation Plan.**

Good afternoon. Today, I'm going to talk about a total eclipse of the sun. Perhaps you've seen one. [1] What is it? *Well, it's a very special event in the sky.* [2] __________ *It happens when the sun is hidden by the moon and parts of the Earth are covered by its shadow.* [3] __________ *Well, you can only see it ...*

3 **Imagine you are doing Roberto's presentation together. Use the presentation plan to do the complete presentation.**

SHAPE IT!

4 **Prepare a presentation on how a rainbow is formed. Use the information below to help you.**

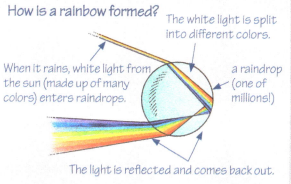

How is a rainbow formed?

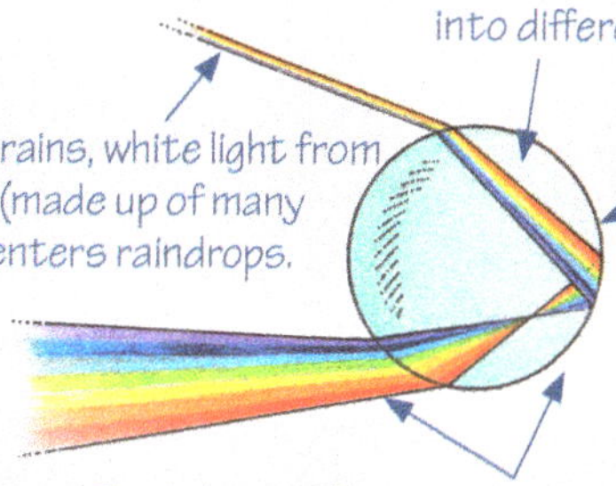

The white light is split into different colors.
When it rains, white light from the sun (made up of many colors) enters raindrops.
a raindrop (one of millions!)
The light is reflected and comes back out.

- We see the colored light from all the millions of raindrops as a rainbow.
- You can see rainbows in the sky opposite the sun.
- Rainbows are really circles, but we only see half.
- If you're lucky, you might see a double rainbow.

5 **Listen to your partner's presentation. Do they answer all the questions in the presentation plan?**

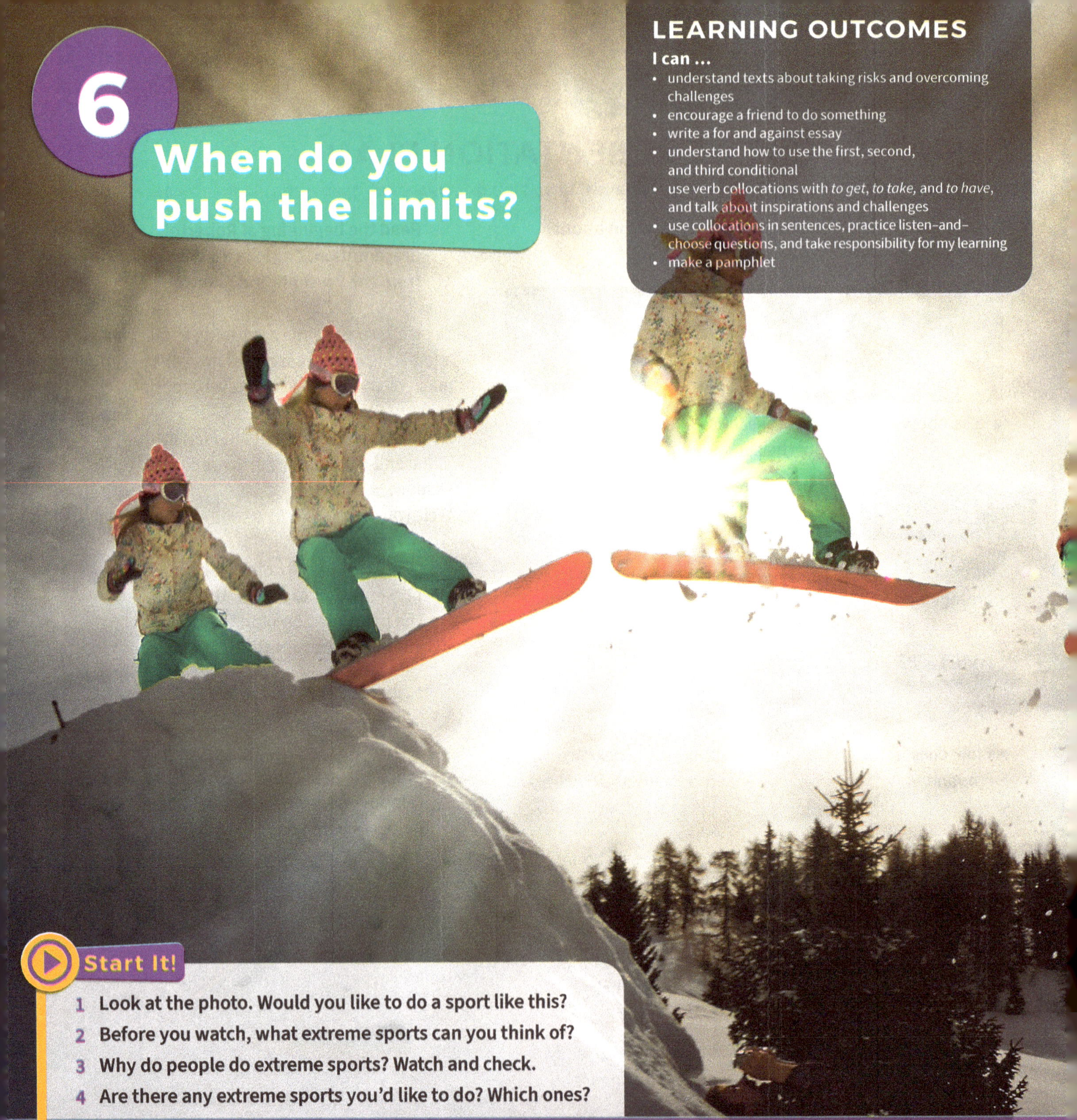

6 When do you push the limits?

LEARNING OUTCOMES

I can …

- understand texts about taking risks and overcoming challenges
- encourage a friend to do something
- write a for and against essay
- understand how to use the first, second, and third conditional
- use verb collocations with *to get*, *to take*, and *to have*, and talk about inspirations and challenges
- use collocations in sentences, practice listen-and-choose questions, and take responsibility for my learning
- make a pamphlet

Start It!

1 **Look at the photo. Would you like to do a sport like this?**
2 **Before you watch, what extreme sports can you think of?**
3 **Why do people do extreme sports? Watch and check.**
4 **Are there any extreme sports you'd like to do? Which ones?**

Watch video 6.1

p73

Grammar in Action 6.2

p75

Grammar in Action 6.3

p76

Everyday English 6.4

VOCABULARY

Verb Collocations with *To Get*, *To Take*, and *To Have*

6.01 **1** Read the quiz. Match the phrases in **bold** with definitions a–l. Listen and repeat the phrases.

a annoy somebody a lot get on my nerves
b become unhappy because something is not interesting ______
c do something that might be dangerous ______
d enjoy yourself ______
e be curious about something ______
f feel unsure about something ______
g get satisfaction from something ______
h have the possibility to do something ______
i not know where you are ______
j get a good feeling from something ______
k spending time with somebody so you learn more about them ______
l using the good things from a situation ______

1
A I **get bored** when I watch a movie I've seen before.
B I **take pleasure in** watching movies a second or third time.

2
A I like **taking advantage of** being in unknown places by myself to explore.
B I never walk around new places by myself in case I **get lost**.

3
A I **get a lot out of** extreme sports like skiing or waterskiing.
B I don't like to **take risks** and would never do extreme sports.

4
A I try new foods whenever I **have the chance**.
B I **have doubts** about trying new foods I've never eaten before.

5
A I like **getting to know** people who are exciting and unpredictable.
B People who are unpredictable sometimes **get on my nerves**.

6
A I **take an interest in** all kinds of fun activities, like going on theme park rides.
B I don't **have fun** on theme park rides. They scare me!

Did you choose more As or more Bs?
More As – You enjoy taking risks and like to experience new, exciting situations.
More Bs – You prefer not to take a lot of risks and enjoy being in a routine.

2 Read the quiz again. Circle the answers that are true for you.

3 Read the results at the bottom of the page. Do you agree with them?

LEARN TO LEARN

Using Collocations in Sentences

Collocations with *to get*, *to have*, and *to take* have a lot of meanings. Record these collocations in a sentence to remember the meaning.

4 Think of true sentences for the collocations in Exercise 1. Use *always*, *usually*, *sometimes*, *hardly ever*, *never*.

I sometimes get bored when I'm at home.

5 Compare your sentences with your partner. What other collocations do you know with *to get*, *to have*, and *to take*?

Use It!

6 Write questions with the collocations. Ask and answer the questions.

______
______
______
______

Have you ever had the chance to try an extreme sport?

Yes, I had the chance to try waterskiing last summer. I had a lot of fun!

Explore It!

Guess the correct answer.
How old was the oldest person to skydive?
a 89 b 102 c 110
Find another fact about an extreme sport. Write a question for your partner to answer.

Pronunciation p142

When Taking Risks Is a *Good Thing*

Everyone has to take risks sometimes, but many people think risks are negative, especially for teenagers. They connect risk-taking with dangerous behavior, such as riding a motorcycle too fast or looking at your phone while crossing the street. If this sounds like your parents, you might want to explain this to them. Taking risks can also be positive. Sometimes feeling scared or uncomfortable can help us experience new things and learn how to make good decisions. If more people understood this, they might see why teenagers sometimes need to take risks.

What Type of Risks Do You Like?

Surprises Would you be happy if your friends planned a surprise party for you? If the answer is yes, then you may enjoy unpredictable things. You get bored very easily and take pleasure in not knowing what's going to happen next.

Danger If you take an interest in activities such as skiing or parkour, you might enjoy danger. If you adore extreme sports or theme park rides, it's because risky situations produce a chemical in the brain called dopamine. Dopamine makes you feel happy and want to repeat an activity again to get the same feeling. That's why you want to go back on a rollercoaster ride as soon as it's finished.

New Experiences Alternatively, if you have fun trying new foods or discovering new places, you may be someone who gets a lot out of new experiences. This is important because if you didn't go to new places, you wouldn't learn new things about other cultures.

Healthy Risks

How would you feel if you had an audition for the school show? Auditions, trying out for a school sports team, or facing a school bully are situations that might make you feel scared. However, they also help you develop important skills such as how to solve problems, make good decisions, and become independent. Just think, you could be the world's best singer, lawyer, or volleyball player. But unless you take some risks, you'll never know.

READING

A Fact Sheet

6.04 **1 How do the people in the photos feel? How would you feel? Read the fact sheet and discuss your ideas.**

2 Read the fact sheet again and complete the chart.

Types of Risk-Taker	1 People who like unpredictable things. 2 People who like ______. 3 People who like ______.
Examples of Negative Risks	
Examples of Positive Risks	
Skills You Develop When You Take Risks	

3 Read the fact sheet again. Write *T* (true), *F* (false), or *DS* (doesn't say).

1. All risks are dangerous. F
2. Most parents don't want teenagers to take risks. ___
3. Some people like not knowing what will happen. ___
4. You have more dopamine in your brain when you feel bored. ___
5. Taking risks can teach us about other cultures. ___
6. There are advantages to scary situations. ___
7. If you don't take risks, you won't solve problems. ___

4 Find words in the fact sheet that mean …

1. something that can change suddenly (adj). ______
2. love (v). ______
3. involving the possibility of something bad happening (adj). ______
4. another possibility (adv). ______
5. not influenced or controlled by other people (adj). ______

Voice It!

5 Discuss the questions.

1. What type of risk-taker is most similar to you? Why?
2. What risky things have you done that aren't dangerous, e.g., having an audition?
3. How can taking risks help solve problems?

Finished? p123 Ex. 1

GRAMMAR IN ACTION

First and Second Conditional

Watch video 6.2
What did he try last week?
Did he like it?

	First Conditional	Second Conditional
+	**If** this [1] sounds (sound) like your parents, you **might want** to explain this to them.	If you **took** healthy risks, you **could become** more independent.
–	**Unless** you [2] ________ (take) some risks, you**'ll** never **know**.	**If** you [3] ________ (not go) to new places, you **wouldn't learn** new things about other cultures.
?	**Will** you **go** on all the rides **if** we **go** to the theme park?	**Would** you **be** happy if your friends [4] ________ (plan) a surprise party for you?

1 **Complete the examples in the chart above with the correct form of the verbs in parentheses. Use the fact sheet on page 72 to help you.**

Get It Right!

Unless has the same meaning as **if ... not** and **not ... if**.

I'll go to the beach unless it rains.

I'll go to the beach if it doesn't rain.

I won't go to the beach if it rains.

2 **Put the words in the correct order to make first conditional sentences.**

1 practice / you / won't / unless / get better at parkour / You / more
You won't get better at parkour unless you practice more.

2 from other cultures / if you / You might / try it / enjoy food
____

3 will you / doesn't rain, / go to / If it / the water park / ?
____

3 **Complete the second conditional sentences with the correct form of the verbs in parentheses.**

1 Would you learn to fly a plane if you had the chance? (would / have / learn)

2 If we ________ crazy things from time to time, life ________ boring. (could / be / not do)

3 I ________ frightened if I ________ in a forest at night. (wouldn't / get lost / be)

4 **Complete the first and second conditional sentences in the text with the correct form of the verbs in parentheses.**

If you [1] had (have) the chance, would you risk your life to save someone? If you thought about it carefully, you probably [2] ________ (not put) yourself in danger, but scientists say it's a natural impulse. For example, if we [3] ________ (see) someone in the water who couldn't swim, we would save them. In an emergency, unless we [4] ________ (stop) and [5] ________ (think) about it, the human body will react automatically.

Use It!

5 **Make first or second conditional questions with *you*. Ask and answer.**

1 If / not meet / friends / later / how / might / feel?
If you don't meet your friends later, how might you feel?

2 How / life / be different / not have / social media?
____

3 What / do this weekend / have some free time?
____

4 Which extreme sport / try / could choose?
____

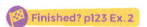

Finished? p123 Ex. 2

VOCABULARY AND LISTENING

Inspiration and Challenge

6.05 **1** **Read the nomination for an amazing athlete. Match the words in bold with definitions a–j.**

Send us your nominations for the most amazing athlete you know and we'll tell their story on our podcast.

- Which athlete [1]**inspires** you because they have [2]**overcome** an [3]**obstacle**?
- Did they show [4]**determination** and [5]**bravery**? How?
- How did friends or family [6]**support** and [7]**encourage** them?
- What was their biggest [8]**challenge**?
- What have they [9]**achieved**?
- Have they had any [10]**opportunities** to help other people?

a deal with a difficult situation successfully ☐

b finished something or reached a goal ☐

c give confidence to others and motivate them to do something ☐

d give emotional or practical help to others ☐

e makes someone feel they want to do something and can do it [1]

f no fear of dangerous or difficult things ☐

g situations or chances ☐

h something that requires a lot of hard work to be done (successfully) ☐

i the ability to continue trying to do something difficult ☐

j something that stops an action or makes progress difficult or slow ☐

Use It!

2 **Discuss the questions.**

1 Who or what inspires you?

2 What's the biggest obstacle you or someone you know has overcome?

3 Who encourages you to do your best?

A Podcast

6.06 **3** **Listen to the podcast. What big challenge did Bethany Hamilton overcome?**

LEARN TO LEARN

Listening and Choosing the Correct Option

Read all the options, check any unknown words, and cross out any options you know are not correct.

6.07 **4** **Listen and circle the correct option.**

1 When she was 13, Bethany …

a learned to surf. b had an accident.

c quit surfing.

- Check you understand *quit* (to stop something forever.)
- Option a isn't correct as she learned to surf when she was a young child.
- Option c isn't correct as she returned to surfing soon after the accident.
- The correct answer is option b.

6.06 **5** EXAM **Listen to the whole podcast again and circle the correct options.**

2 Bethany lost her arm

a in the ocean.

b in the hospital.

c three weeks after the accident.

3 It was … decision to return to surfing.

a Bethany's

b her family's

c a bad

4 Bethany competes

a in special competitions.

b only in the U.S.A.

c against other professional surfers.

5 Her book and movies

a are not true.

b teach people how to surf.

c inspire people to overcome challenges.

Voice It!

6 **What surprises you most about Bethany's story? What would you do in a similar situation?**

GRAMMAR IN ACTION
Third Conditional

Watch video 6.3
What is she thinking about?
Where would she have gone on vacation?

	Possible Situation in the Past	Imaginary Consequence
+	If it [1] had **happened** to me,	I **wouldn't** [2] ______ **returned** to the water.
-	If they [3] ______ **taken** her to the hospital right away,	she **would** [4] ______ **died**.
?	If it [5] ______ **happened** to you,	what [6] ______ you **have done**?

1 **Complete the examples in the chart.**

2 **Put the words in the correct order to make third conditional sentences.**

1 had seen / she wouldn't / in the water / If Bethany / the shark / have gone

______

2 Many people wouldn't / if she / a movie / have heard / hadn't made / about her bravery

______

6.08 3 **Complete the third conditional sentences about stories 1 and 2. Use the verbs in parentheses. Then listen and check.**

1 A child threw a ball onto the roof of a house.

a If the child hadn't thrown (not throw) the ball onto the roof, he wouldn't have started (not start) to cry.

b If the wind ______ (not blow) the ball off the roof, the child ______ (not get) his ball back.

2 It started to rain and we got out of the pool.

a If it ______ (not start) to rain, we ______ (stay) in the pool.

b If we ______ (stay) in the pool, we ______ (not go) to see a movie.

4 **Write a third conditional sentence for each situation.**

1 Alfie broke his leg when he went rock climbing.

If Alfie hadn't gone rock climbing, he wouldn't have broken his leg.

2 Four students got up late and missed the flight to France.

______

3 We didn't prepare enough food and the guests were hungry.

______

4 Oscar lived in Mexico and learned how to speak Spanish.

______

Use It!

5 **Complete the sentences about you.**

1 If I had been born in a different country ______.

2 If I hadn't gone to this school ______.

3 If I hadn't met my best friend ______.

Finished? p123 Ex. 3

SPEAKING

Encouraging a Friend to Do Something

1 6.09 **Listen to Mia and Jack's conversation. Which activities do they discuss?**

MIA Are you going to come whitewater rafting this weekend?
JACK I'm not sure. It looks a little scary to me.
MIA Oh, it's not really. I had so much fun when I went. [1] You'll never know unless you try, will you?
JACK But the water is so fast! It looks seriously deep and I'm not the world's best swimmer.
MIA Relax and [2] ______________________.
The instructors will keep you safe. They don't take any risks.
JACK Hmm, I'm still not sure.
MIA Well, what about paddle boarding? That's less risky.
JACK You've got to be kidding! I wouldn't dare stand up on the board in the middle of the ocean.
[3] ______________________ I fell in?
MIA Come on! It's easy!
[4] ______________________!
If you fall in, you just get back on the board.
JACK [5] ______________________, but I'm not like you. Water sports are a real challenge for me.

MIA Well, what if I practice with you?
JACK Hmm. That might help. OK, I'll come.
MIA Good for you! I promise
[6] ______________________
and you might even have fun! Let's go on Sunday.

2 6.09 **Complete the conversation with the phrases from the *Useful Language* box. Then listen and check.**

Useful Language

Encouraging
Don't worry, you'll be fine. You can do it!
You'll feel really proud afterward.
You'll never know unless you try …

Responding
That's easy for you to say … What if … ?

3 **Match the meanings (1–5) with the phrases in the *Everyday English* box.**

1 extremely
2 not very
3 That's great!
4 used to encourage someone to do something
5 You're not serious!

Watch video 6.4

Everyday English

Come on! ☐ Good for you! ☐ not really ☐
seriously ☐ You've got to be kidding! ☐

4 **How do you say the phrases in the *Everyday English* box in your language?**

PLAN

5 **Take notes in your notebook about something you want to encourage your partner to do. Use the ideas below or your own ideas.**

audition for a school show
try an extreme sport

SPEAK

6 **Practice trying to encourage your partner. Remember to use first, second, and third conditionals; vocabulary from this unit; and phrases from the *Useful Language* and *Everyday English* boxes.**

CHECK

7 **Work with another pair. Listen to their conversation and complete the notes.**

What did the other students encourage each other to do? ______________________

____

Would you try the things in their conversation?

____

____

WRITING

A For and Against Essay

1 **Think about a time when something went wrong for you. How did you feel? What did you learn?**

2 **Read the For and Against essay. Circle the best title.**

a Is It Always Bad When Things Go Wrong?

b Should We Try More New Things?

1 There are times when things go wrong. For example, you might lose a basketball game or fail an important exam. However, is it always negative when that happens?

2 On the one hand, when things go wrong, we feel bad. For instance, if we fail a French exam, we might have doubts about our ability to speak the language and lose confidence. Furthermore, we might think we don't have the skills to achieve our goals.

3 On the other hand, when we overcome a difficult situation, we feel good. If we think about what went wrong, we might solve the problem in the future, such as preparing for our next exam in a different way.

4 In conclusion, although it can feel negative when things go wrong, I personally believe that it is not always bad if we can learn something new. When we look for an opportunity to overcome the problem, we'll soon feel good again.

3 **Read the essay again and discuss the questions.**

1 How does the writer end the introduction? Why?

2 In which paragraph does the writer give their opinion?

3 Which paragraph talks about the negatives?

4 Which paragraph talks about the positives?

4 **Complete the *Useful Language* box with the phrases from the essay.**

Useful Language

introducing a new idea: Furthermore ...,
1 ______

introducing the opposite idea:
2 ______

giving an example: For example ...,
3 ______, 4 ______

giving an opinion:
5 ______

introducing a conclusion:
6 ______

PLAN

5 **Look at the for and against essay title. Take notes on your ideas and examples in your notebook. Decide what information to include in each paragraph.**

Should We Take Risks?

WRITE

6 **Write your for and against essay. Remember to include four paragraphs, conditional sentences, vocabulary from this unit, and phrases from the *Useful Language* box.**

CHECK

7 **Do you ...**

- include an introduction?
- talk about the negatives?
- talk about the positives?
- have a conclusion?

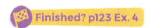

Finished? p123 Ex. 4

CITIZENSHIP PROJECT

A Pamphlet

1 **Look at the pamphlet. Which two things does it aim to do?**

a inform b warn c entertain d persuade

6.10 2 **Read the pamphlet and answer the questions.**

1 Who are the courses for?
2 Which activities can you do in each course?
3 On which course will you work in a team?
4 The courses are "unplugged." What does that mean?
5 Why might it be good to try one of the courses?

3 **Read the pamphlet again and find these features.**

1 title
2 introduction to get readers interested
3 details about the activities
4 phrases to persuade people to do the course

How to Motivate Yourself and Your Peers

4 **Match 1–4 with a–d to make tips about how to motivate yourself and your peers on a project.**

1 Be clear about what you have to do.
2 Don't give up when there's an obstacle.
3 Each person has a role.
4 Believe you can do the project.

a All projects have problems. Find a way to solve them.
b Divide up the work equally.
c Have confidence in yourself and your team.
d If you don't understand something, ask.

6.11 5 **Listen to students working in a team at the start of their project. Put tips 1–4 from Exercise 4 in the order you hear them.**

___, ___, ___, ___

ON COURSE TO CONFIDENCE!

Are you 14–18? Do you get bored during summer vacation? Do you like making friends, having fun, and doing a lot of exciting activities? If this sounds like you, then check out our courses and choose the one for you.

OUTDOOR SURVIVAL SKILLS

If you enjoy adventure and being outside in the fresh air, you will love this course. It's a great way to meet new people, as you will be working in teams on different activities such as navigation, building a fire, and cooking outdoors. Some of the activities are challenging, and you will have to work together and support each other to complete them.

WATER SPORTS

If your idea of fun is spending all day in the water, you will get a lot out of this course. You will have the chance to try everything from surfing and paddle boarding to scuba diving and whitewater rafting. If you've never tried water sports before, why not give them a try? You might be surprised at how much fun you have.

CLIMBING HIGH

One of our most popular courses is this confidence-building one. You will have the chance to go rock climbing and then rappel down again. You'll also go on a tree-top ropes course. If you'd like to learn a different skill, you could spend a day trying parkour.

Remember! All of our courses are unplugged, so leave your phones and other electronic devices at home. From day one you will discover that you don't have to be online to have fun.

We encourage you to take risks and try new things, so if you have never tried any of these sports, one of our courses is the perfect opportunity. Just think how good you'll feel if you overcome the fear to do something you've never done before!

PLAN

6 Work in groups. Make a list of courses for teenagers to build their confidence. Then choose two or three ideas and design a pamphlet to inform and persuade people to do them. Complete the steps below.

- Use the tips in *How to* Motivate Yourself and Your Peers.
- Draw a plan of the pamphlet.
- Decide who will prepare each section.
- Prepare your section with the features from Exercise 3.
- Show your section to someone else to check.
- Listen to your classmate's ideas and improve your section.
- Work together to make your pamphlet.

PRESENT

7 Present your pamphlet to your classmates. Remember to include information about the courses and the features from Exercise 3.

CHECK

8 Read your classmates' pamphlets. Decide which activities you would like to do from their pamphlets.

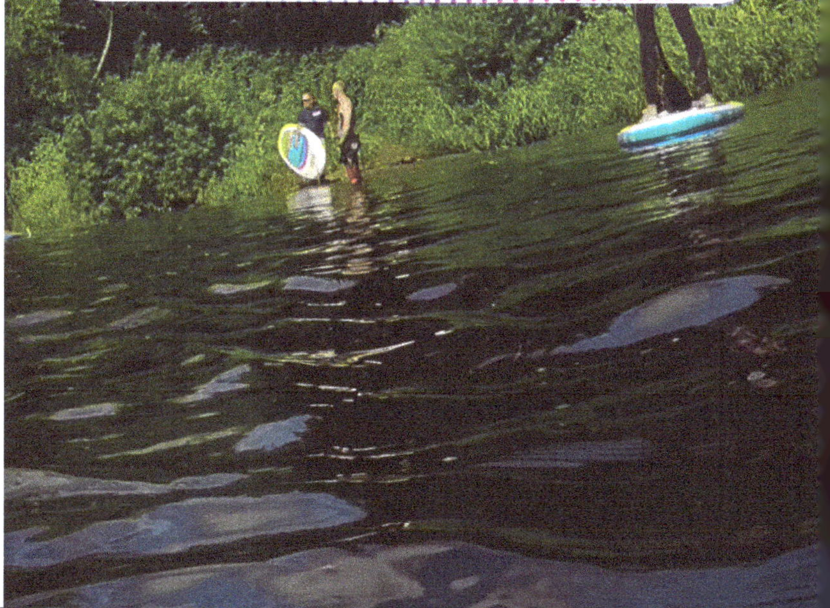

6 REVIEW

VOCABULARY

1 Circle the words that don't go with each verb.

1 get *a lot out of something / risks / lost*
2 take *pleasure in something / advantage of something / doubts*
3 have *on someone's nerves / the chance to do something / fun*
4 get *bored / to know someone / an interest in something*

2 Complete the sentences with the correct form of the words and phrases that don't go with the verbs from Exercise 1.

1 I had ______ before I went rafting because I'm not a strong swimmer.
2 It can be positive to take ______ because we learn to make decisions.
3 My brother has started to take ______ photography.
4 My sister really gets ______. She's always taking my things.

3 Complete the sentences with the words in the box.

achieved	bravery	determination
opportunity	overcome	supported

1 She was awarded a prize for her ______ in the fire.
2 My cousin finally ______ his dream to learn how to windsurf.
3 Do students have the ______ to go to music classes at your school?
4 My parents ______ my decision to do a bungee jump for charity.
5 He passed his final exams after a lot of hard work and ______.
6 Since I started swimming I have ______ my fear of deep water.

GRAMMAR IN ACTION

4 Complete the first and second conditional sentences about parkour with the correct form of the verbs in parentheses.

1 How quickly ______ I ______ (learn) if I practiced every day?
2 If you already ______ (do) exercise regularly, you may find it easy to learn.
3 If I ______ (watch) parkour videos online, will I learn some techniques?
4 If you ______ (train) every day for a month, you could learn to jump over walls.

5 Join the two sentences to make one third conditional sentence.

1 Mozart learned music as a young child. He wrote his first symphony when he was eight or nine.

______

2 Emma Watson studied drama as a child. She was Hermione in the Harry Potter movies.

______

3 The artist van Gogh moved to Paris. Van Gogh met his friend Paul Gauguin in Paris.

______

4 J.R.R. Tolkien wrote *The Lord of the Rings*. Peter Jackson made a movie trilogy of the book.

______

Self-Assessment

I can use collocations with *to get*, *to take*, and *to have*.

I can use nouns and verbs for inspiration and challenge.

I can use the first and second conditional.

I can use the third conditional.

LEARN TO ... TAKE RESPONSIBILITY FOR YOUR LEARNING

It's important to take responsibility for your own learning. This will help you learn inside and outside the classroom.

1 Do the quiz and find out your score. Do you agree with what it says about you? Discuss the results with a partner.

Are you taking responsibility for your learning?

	Always	Sometimes	Never
1 When you're in class, how often do you …			
a pay attention to the teacher's corrections?	☐	☐	☐
b try to help your partner speak and write better?	☐	☐	☐
c use spidergrams and presentation plans?	☐	☐	☐
2 When you want to learn new vocabulary, how often do you …			
a write example sentences?	☐	☐	☐
b make and use flashcards?	☐	☐	☐
c use a monolingual (only English) dictionary?	☐	☐	☐
3 Outside class, how often do you …			
a speak in English to other people?	☐	☐	☐
b watch TV series or movies in English?	☐	☐	☐
c read books or articles in English online?	☐	☐	☐
4 Thinking about technology, how often do you …			
a have English as the language on your phone and your apps?	☐	☐	☐
b use vocabulary learning apps?	☐	☐	☐
c listen to podcasts in English?	☐	☐	☐
5 If you were traveling in an English-speaking country, would you …			
a speak English in stores and restaurants?	☐	☐	☐
b try to understand signs in English?	☐	☐	☐
c ask for directions in English if you got lost?	☐	☐	☐

Extra Challenges!

- Write text messages to your friends in English.
- Send and receive voice messages with friends in English.
- Listen to music in English and look up the lyrics online.
- Read a "graded reader" – a famous book made easier for learners.

Points: always = 2, sometimes = 1, never = 0.

0–10 points: You aren't taking much responsibility for your learning yet, but if you try more ideas from the quiz, you'll soon become a better learner!

11–20 points: You're taking some responsibility for your learning, but there's a lot more you could do if you tried. Take advantage of what you've learned in this quiz to think about how to improve.

21–30 points: You're taking a lot of responsibility for your learning. That's great! Time for something new – try our extra challenges!

2 Look at the extra challenges. Which is the best idea? Write one more.

SHAPE IT!

3 Think about how to take responsibility for your learning. Choose three ideas and tell your partner what you have chosen and why.

I've chosen "read a graded reader" because I love books. If I'd known about them before, I'd have started one already!

7 Why are emotions important?

LEARNING OUTCOMES

I can ...

- understand texts about a growth mindset and reducing exam stress
- express sympathy and concern
- write an email reply
- understand gerunds and infinitives, and subject and object questions
- use adjectives that describe feelings and expressions with *heart* and *mind*
- personalize vocabulary, make fill-in-the-blank flashcards, learn synonyms and antonyms , and give my partner useful feedback

Start It!

1 Look at the photo. How does the girl feel?

2 Before you watch, what emotions do you associate with these colors: red, gray, purple, yellow?

3 What color can make you feel hungry? Watch and check.

4 What colors do you wear when you're happy and when you're sad?

Watch video 7.1

p85

Grammar in Action 7.2

p87

Grammar in Action 7.3

p88

Everyday English 7.4

p90

Globetrotters 7.5

VOCABULARY

Feelings

1 Read the pamphlet. Do you agree with it?

7.01 2 Match the words in **bold** in the pamphlet with definitions a–m. Listen, check, and repeat.

a happy [13]
b angry [ ]
c unhappy [ ]
d very silly [ ]
e feeling thanks [ ]
f not confident [ ]
g enthusiastic [ ]
h quiet and calm [ ]
i in emotional pain [ ]
j extremely happy [ ]
k finding something funny [ ]
l positive about the future [ ]
m pleased to achieve something [ ]

7.02 3 Listen and complete the sentences. Write one word in each blank.

1 Sally feels absolutely ________.
2 The boy feels ________.
3 Javier felt absolutely ________.
4 The girl feels really ________.
5 Mandy feels a little ________.

LEARN TO LEARN

Remembering Adjectives

Think about your personal experiences to help you remember new adjectives.

4 Do Part 1 in the pamphlet. Think of a sentence for each adjective and write it in your notebook.

I feel amused when I watch comedy movies.

5 In pairs, read out your sentences. Do you have similar or different ideas?

I feel satisfied when I score a goal in soccer.

Use It!

6 Now do Part 2 of the pamphlet. Tell your partner your plans.

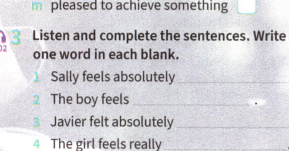

STAY POSITIVE!

For teenagers, life can be an emotional rollercoaster. Sometimes you're [1]**thrilled** to be alive; then you feel [2]**down** for no reason. You may feel [3]**insecure** about who you are or [4]**annoyed** with everyone on the planet. You might feel [5]**ridiculous** when you don't know something all your friends seem to know and [6]**hurt** that nobody seems to care how you feel. Of course, people do care, which is why we've created this exercise for developing positive emotions.

Part 1 For each word below (amused, etc.), think of a situation that helps you feel that emotion.

Part 2 Choose two positive emotions you want to focus on. In the chart, write something that will increase those emotions every day for a week.

I feel …	This week I will …
[7]**amused** when my best friend tells me jokes.	ask him to tell me some every day.
[8]**hopeful** when I make a wish.	make three wishes …
[9]**peaceful** when I walk on the beach.	
[10]**grateful** when people help me.	
[11]**eager** when I start a new art project.	
[12]**satisfied** when I've cleaned my room.	
[13]**glad** when my friends are happy.	

Explore It!

Guess the correct answer.

Complete the expression: *Laughter is the best …*

a communication. b exercise. c medicine.

Find out a fact about smiling. Write a question for your partner to answer.

READING

A Magazine Interview

1 **Read and answer the question at the beginning of the interview.**

7.03 2 **Read the interview and match the interviewer's questions a–d with 1–4. Then listen and check.**

a You had a fixed mindset?
b Malcolm, what exactly is a growth mindset?
c What advice would you give our readers?
d How can you develop a growth mindset?

3 **Read the interview again and circle the correct answers.**

1 Even if you have a fixed mindset, you …
  a never change.
  b are bad at math.
  c can change.
  d like taking tests.
2 People with a growth mindset …
  a think they can get better.
  b are good at everything.
  c are scared of failing.
  d don't have to learn new skills.
3 Malcolm …
  a wanted to learn the piano.
  b played the piano for several years.
  c learned to play the guitar easily.
  d slowly improved his guitar playing.
4 Malcolm encourages readers to …
  a learn from their mistakes.
  b wait before trying new things.
  c ignore their mistakes.
  d try one thing at a time.

4 **Find words in the interview that mean …**

1 a feeling or opinion (paragraph 1). ____________
2 not changing (paragraph 1). ____________
3 without purpose (paragraph 2). ____________
4 necessary (paragraph 4). ____________
5 not a success (paragraph 4). ____________

The Power of "Not Yet"

Imagine you've just failed an important math test. What do you think?

a I failed this test, but I can pass the next one if I study harder.
b I'm just not good at math. There's no point trying.

If you chose *a*, you have a growth mindset. People with a growth mindset are often happier and more successful. But if you chose *b*, don't worry – you can change. I spoke to psychologist Malcolm Adams to find out how.

1 ☐ A mindset is your attitude in life. Some people have a fixed mindset. These people often avoid trying new things because they're afraid of making mistakes. They refuse to try harder because they don't believe they can get better. On the other hand, people with a growth mindset believe they can improve with practice. They're eager to learn new skills and they're not afraid to fail sometimes. They often do well in life.

2 ☐ Let me tell you a story to explain this. When I was a kid, my parents made me learn the piano. I didn't like the piano, and it was really difficult. I remember feeling annoyed with myself whenever I made a mistake. After about a year, I stopped trying. I thought, "This is pointless. I don't have any musical talent."

3 ☐ Exactly. But later, in college, a friend said to me, "If you want to be good at something, you have to believe you can do it." So I thought, "OK, let's try again." I decided to learn the guitar, which I'd always adored. This time I told myself, "You can do it!" I practiced a lot. It was hard, but little by little I got better. I'll never forget playing for my friends for the first time. I was thrilled! My mindset had completely changed.

4 ☐ First, believe in yourself. Being positive is essential. Second, don't worry about making mistakes. A mistake isn't failure – it's an opportunity to learn. Finally, don't forget to use the power of "not yet." Never say, "I can't do this." Always remember to tell yourself, "I can – just not yet."

Voice It!

5 EXAM **Discuss the questions.**

1 Do you like to try new things? Why / Why not?
2 Where do you think you are on the scale for the activities in the box?

making art	playing music and singing
playing sports	speaking English

1	2	3
fixed mindset	a mixture of both	growth mindset

Finished? p124 Ex. 1

Watch video 7.2
Why does Claire inspire him?
What did he try last summer?

GRAMMAR IN ACTION
Gerunds and Infinitives (with *to*)

Gerunds		Infinitives (with *to*)	
As a Subject	[1] Being (**be**) positive is essential.	**To Explain Purpose**	I spoke to him [4] ______ (**find out**) how.
After Prepositions	They're afraid **of** [2] ______ (**make**) mistakes.	**After Adjectives**	They're **eager** [5] ______ (**learn**) new skills.
After Certain Verbs (avoid, enjoy, finish, mind, miss, practice, risk, suggest)	These people often **avoid** [3] ______ (**try**) new things.	**After Certain Verbs** (decide, hope, promise, refuse, want, would like)	They **refuse** [6] ______ (**try**) harder.

1 Complete the examples in the chart with the gerund or infinitive (with *to*) of the verbs in parentheses.

Get It Right!

Some verbs, including **like**, **love**, and **start**, can take the gerund or infinitive with no change in meaning.

He loves going/to go for walks.

Gerunds	Infinitives
I **remember feeling** annoyed. (= *I have a memory of a past action or event.*)	Always **remember to tell** yourself … (= *don't forget …*)
I'll never **forget playing** for my friends for the first time. (= *I won't forget that memory.*)	Don't **forget to use** the power of "not yet." (= *Don't forget to do this in the future.*)
I **stopped trying**. (= *I didn't do this anymore.*)	I **stopped to rest** for a few minutes. (= *I stopped what I was doing for a while.*)

2 Complete the text with the gerund or infinitive (with *to*) of the verbs in the box.

develop feel help (x2) increase ~~know~~ make say

THINK POSITIVE

You'll be glad [1] to know there are steps you can take [2] ______ a positive mindset. Psychologists suggest [3] ______ a list of activities that make you feel good and then doing one every day [4] ______ your positivity. [5] ______ others when they have a problem also makes us feel happier. Of course, it's important [6] ______ thank you to people for [7] ______ you. Try it! Everyone wants [8] ______ more satisfied with life.

3 Complete the questions with the gerund or infinitive (with *to*) of the verbs in parentheses.

1 Do you remember meeting (meet) your best friend?
2 When you're studying, how often do you stop ______ (take) a break?
3 What would happen if you forgot ______ (set) your alarm the night before an exam?
4 Would it be hard to stop ______ (use) your phone?
5 What things do you have to remember ______ (do) this weekend?
6 Think of two people you'll never forget ______ (meet) on your first day at school. Who are they?

Use It!

4 Ask and answer the questions in Exercise 3.

Finished? p124 Ex. 2

VOCABULARY AND LISTENING

Expressions with *Heart* and *Mind*

7.04 **1 Match the phrases in bold in the thought bubbles with definitions a–j. Then listen, check, and repeat.**

I have to [1]**learn by heart** so many facts for that exam, but I don't have time!

What am I going to study in college? I have to [2]**make up my mind** soon.

I set a reminder on my phone in case it [3]**slips my mind**.

[4]**I have something on my mind** about school. Who should I talk to?

I want to become an actor, but what will Dad say? It'll [5]**break his heart** if I don't study science.

Education is a subject that [6]**is close to my heart**, but I don't know if I'd be a good teacher or not!

I need to choose my degree carefully. I can't [7]**change my mind** later.

I know if I [8]**put my heart into** this project, I'll do well, but I'm so tired!

It's just [9]**crossed my mind** that Dan might be at the party.

I must [10]**bear in mind** we can't use a pencil for the exam. I don't want to fail for something silly like that!

a consider something important 10
b make an effort to do something
c thought of something
d make a decision
e memorize
f change a decision
g forget about something
h be worried about something
i make someone really sad
j be important to someone

LEARN TO LEARN

Fill-in-the-Blank Flashcards

Flashcards can help you learn expressions.

2 Make flashcards for some of the expressions in Exercise 1, leaving a blank for *heart* or *mind*. Write the missing word on the back. Then test your partner.

slip my ______

mind

Use It!

3 Choose six phrases from Exercise 1 and make sentences with the ideas in the box.

clothes	friends and family	going out

When I go out in the evening, I have to bear in mind what time my parents want me to come home.

A Conversation

4 Which of these things do you think can reduce exam stress?

1 studying late at night
2 studying with friends
3 drinking energy drinks
4 doing exercise
5 eating apples
6 making lists

7.05 **5 Listen to the conversation. Circle the things in Exercise 4 that the counselor recommends.**

7.05 **6 Listen again and discuss the questions.**

1 Why is Gavin so stressed?

He's worried he's going to fail his exams.

2 Why does the counselor suggest making a list?
3 Why does the counselor recommend eating apples and nuts?
4 Why doesn't Gavin want to go to bed early?
5 Why is it important for Gavin to do well in every subject?
6 What is Gavin going to ask his sister tonight?

7 Do you think the counselor's suggestions are useful?

GRAMMAR IN ACTION

Subject and Object Questions

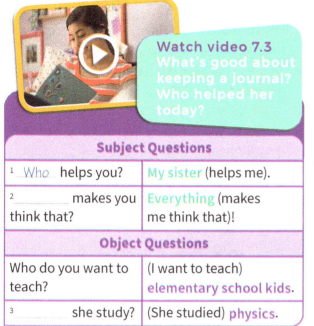

Watch video 7.3 What's good about keeping a journal? Who helped her today?

Subject Questions	
1 Who helps you?	My sister (helps me).
2 ______ makes you think that?	Everything (makes me think that)!
Object Questions	
Who do you want to teach?	(I want to teach) elementary school kids.
3 ______ she study?	(She studied) physics.

1 **Complete the examples in the chart above.**

2 **Circle the correct words to complete the rules.**

1. The words in green are *subjects / objects.* The ones in purple are *subjects / objects.*
2. *Subject / Object* questions always use a form of *do.*

3 **Complete the simple present questions with subject or object question forms.**

1. What do you do (do / you) on the weekend?
2. Who ______ (teach) you math?
3. Who ______ (send) you the most messages every day?
4. Which subjects ______ (put / you) your heart into?
5. Who ______ (help) you with your homework?
6. What ______ (happen) if you don't sleep enough?

4 **Complete the simple past questions with subject or object question forms.**

1. Who taught (teach) you English last year?
2. What ______ (eat / you) for breakfast today?
3. Who ______ (give) you presents for your birthday?
4. What presents ______ (give / they) you?
5. Which TV shows ______ (watch / you) yesterday?
6. Which country ______ (win) the last soccer World Cup?

5 **Ask and answer the questions in Exercises 2 and 3.**

6 7.06 **Complete the conversation with the correct subject or object question forms. Then listen and check.**

OWEN What's that?
ROSA It's a stress ball.
OWEN What [1] does it do (do / it)?
ROSA It helps you relax. Look, you squeeze it like this. It was a birthday present.
OWEN Wow, that feels great! Who [2] ______ (give) it to you?
ROSA My sister. She knows I get stressed out a lot so she thought it might help.
OWEN I want one.
ROSA You don't need one! You never get stressed.
OWEN That's not true. Who [3] ______ (tell) you that? I get stressed before exams.
ROSA Well, you could borrow this one if you like.
OWEN No, I'd prefer my own, thanks. Where [4] ______ (get / your sister) it?
ROSA Online, I think.
OWEN What site [5] ______ (use / she)? Do you know?
ROSA I'll ask her, but I'm sure you can get them in a lot of places. They've been around for years.
OWEN Really? Who [6] ______ (invent) them?
ROSA No idea. Let's look it up!

Use It!

7 **Ask and answer the questions.**

1. Who did you call/visit/help yesterday?
2. Who called/visited/helped you yesterday?

Pronunciation p142

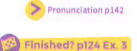

Finished? p124 Ex. 3

SPEAKING

Expressing Sympathy and Concern

1 What problems do brothers and sisters usually have?

7.10 2 Listen to the conversation. What is Jerry's problem?

PAULA Hey, Jerry. What's [1] the matter ? You look really down.

JERRY I am. It's my brother. He refuses to talk to me.

PAULA Really? That's not [2] ______________.
Why?

JERRY His tablet has stopped working. He thinks I took it without asking and broke it, but I didn't, I swear. Now, when I try to talk to him, he just walks away.

PAULA That's kind of harsh, isn't it?

JERRY The thing is, he ought to know I wouldn't take his stuff without permission. I feel really hurt.

PAULA I [3] ______________. It's horrible when someone doesn't believe you. But bear in mind he's taking his final exams at the moment. He's probably really stressed out about everything.

JERRY I guess you're right, but I hope he calms down soon.

PAULA Is there [4] ______________? I have an old tablet I could lend him.

JERRY That's kind of you, but you don't need to do that.

PAULA Don't mention it, but let me know if you change your mind. It'll [5] ______________.

7.10 3 Complete the conversation with the phrases from the *Useful Language* box. Then listen and check.

Useful Language

I can imagine. Is there anything I can do to help?
It'll be alright, you'll see. That's not very nice.
What's the matter?

4 Replace the phrases in **bold** with the phrases in the *Everyday English* box.

1 Do I need help? No, **that's a nice thing to offer,** but I'm fine. ______________

2 **I'm absolutely certain** my keys are here. I had them a few minutes ago. ______________

3 Your teacher gave you a talk for being two minutes late? That's **not fair**. ______________

4 Of course you're **totally nervous and worried**. It's your final exams! ______________

5 A Thanks for letting me use your desk.
B **No problem at all**. ______________

Watch video 7.4
Everyday English

kind of harsh Don't mention it. I swear
stressed out That's kind of you ...

PLAN

5 **Take notes about one of the problems you thought of in Exercise 1.**

____

SPEAK

6 **Explain the problem to your partner. Your partner should show sympathy. Remember to use gerunds and infinitives, vocabulary from this unit, and phrases from the *Useful Language* and *Everyday English* boxes.**

CHECK

7 **Work with another pair. Listen to their conversation and complete the notes.**

What problem did they talk about? ______________

How sympathetic did the conversation sound? ______________

WRITING
An Email Reply

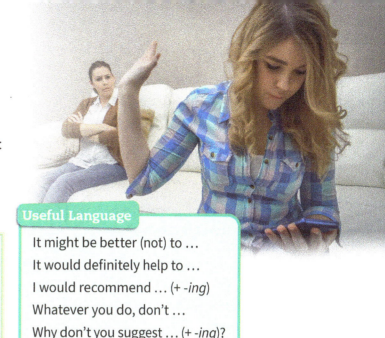

1 **Look at the photo of a teenager and her mom. What do you think is the problem?**

2 **Read the email to a teenage magazine and the reply. Who is asking for advice? Who is giving it?**

Dear Abby,

I want to follow my daughter on social media because I'm worried about who she might become friends with, but she says I can't because it would be "totally embarrassing" if I posted on her wall. I feel hurt by her reaction. You're a teenager – how can I change her mind?

Thanks,

Janelle

Dear Janelle,

I'm glad you wrote. First, this is a common problem, so don't feel down. Your daughter's reaction isn't unusual. It doesn't mean she doesn't love you, but she needs space.

I would recommend telling her why you are worried. It would definitely help to talk. Why don't you suggest following her, but promise not to post on her wall? If she isn't happy with that, it might be better not to follow her at all. Whatever you do, don't get annoyed with her and don't forget to tell her that you trust her.

Good luck, and let me know how it goes.

Abby

3 **How useful is Abby's advice?**

4 **Look at the *Useful Language* box. Find and underline the phrases in Abby's email.**

5 **Complete the mini-conversations with the phrases from the *Useful Language* box.**

1 A So the party starts at seven, right?
B Yes, but ______________, don't tell Pablo. It's a surprise.

2 A My best friend is stressed about her exams.
B ______________ joining a study group?

3 A Joe has to take his medicine.
B Yes, but ______________ not to wake him. He needs to rest, as well.

4 A What's a good way to get fit and have fun?
B ______________ joining a soccer team.

5 A Felix isn't talking to me.
B Well, ______________ say sorry.

Useful Language

It might be better (not) to …

It would definitely help to …

I would recommend … (+ *-ing*)

Whatever you do, don't …

Why don't you suggest … (+ *-ing*)?

PLAN

6 **Imagine you are Abby, and prepare a reply to an email from a worried parent. Choose one of the problems below. Think of three things that they should or shouldn't do.**

- My son never does his homework on time.
- His teachers are angry and I don't know what to do.
- My daughter refuses to help with the housework. She says she's too busy studying.

WRITE

7 **Write your email reply. Remember to include your ideas from Exercise 6, language from this unit, and phrases from the *Useful Language* box.**

CHECK

8 **Do you …**

- say what the person should do?
- say what the person should not do?
- think the advice is useful?

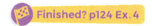

Finished? p124 Ex. 4

AROUND THE WORLD

Globetrotters

Watch video 7.5 Happiness Around the World

- What different things can make us happy?
- Are Costa Rica and Norway considered happy countries? Why?
- What do Ecuador and Bhutan have in common?

READING

A Report About Schools in Denmark

1 **What do you think is most important in making a school a happy place? Why?**

7.11 2 **Read the report and match paragraphs 1–5 with headings a–e. Listen and check your answers.**

a Enjoying *Hygge* Is for Everyone
b Conclusion
c Introduction
d Understanding Other People
e Learning with Others Builds a Better Society

Voice It!

3 **Discuss the questions.**

1 Which of the ideas in the report do you think is best for developing empathy? Why?
2 Why is empathy important in life?
3 What would you do differently based on the report?

The Happiest Children in the World

1 ☐

We have written this report to describe some of the reasons why Danish children are the happiest in the world. It is part of our school project, "Happier Students, Happier Societies."

2 ☐

One of the most important reasons Danish children are so happy is that they are taught empathy from a very young age. Empathy is the ability to imagine what it must be like to be another person. In preschool, Danish children learn to do this by studying facial expressions. They are shown pictures of the faces of other children showing anger, fear, sadness, etc. The preschool children say what they think the children in the pictures are feeling and try to imagine being them. Schoolchildren never stop learning about empathy. Even 15- and 16-year-olds continue to have one hour a week of empathy as a **required** subject.

3 ☐

Danish teenagers also have "class time." This is a special time when students come together to talk about any individual or group problems they are having. This could be a personal issue between two students or even something **unrelated** to school. During this time, everyone bears in mind the feelings of others and avoids criticizing anyone. The group tries to find a solution together. They do this in a peaceful environment, with everyone glad to take part. "Class time" is **connected** to *hygge*, a Danish word that is **tricky** to translate into English but means "relaxed and cozy."

4 ☐

In Danish schools, students with different **strengths** and weaknesses study together in mixed groups. This helps to develop their empathy by showing them that everyone has strong points, talents, and positive qualities. One student might find English difficult, for example, but be good at math. Another might find English easy but find it difficult to understand math. In a Danish school, these two students would help each other in class, and often between classes, as well. The system develops teamwork, respect, and collaboration. These are essential qualities for a successful, happy life both at school and in the adult world.

5 ☐

In summary, the main reason that Danish children are so happy is very simple: they develop empathy, and empathy increases happiness by making everyone feel included and understood. They do this in a number of different but connected ways: learning to read the feelings of others, discussing problems together, and working in mixed groups. We believe that introducing any one of these methods into our own school would be **straightforward** and would improve our school life a great deal. Imagine what we could achieve if we tried all three!

4 Read the report again and circle the correct answers.

1. This report was written by …
   - a teachers.
   - b students.
2. Preschool Danish children look at pictures of …
   - a themselves.
   - b children they don't know.
3. Danish teenagers …
   - a can study empathy if they want to.
   - b have to study empathy.
4. In "class time" students talk about …
   - a all kinds of problems.
   - b their individual problems.
5. In Danish schools, students with different abilities …
   - a help each other in class.
   - b help each other in and out of class.
6. To improve their own school, the writers suggest …
   - a trying all the ideas in the report.
   - b trying only one of the ideas.

LEARN TO LEARN

Synonyms and Antonyms

Learning words with similar and opposite meanings can help you increase your vocabulary quickly.

5 Complete the chart with words in bold from the report.

	joy	2 ______	related	difficult	6 ______	simple
Synonym	happiness	obligatory	3 ______	5 ______	strong points	7 ______
Antonym	1 sadness	optional	4 ______	easy	weaknesses	complicated

Explore It!

Guess the correct answer.

Which of these can make you happier?

- a smelling flowers
- b the color yellow
- c being outside

Find another interesting fact about happiness. Write a question for your partner to answer.

SHAPE IT!

CULTURE PROJECT

A Presentation

A presentation gives information in a clear, organized, and engaging way. Prepare a presentation on how to be happy.

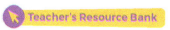

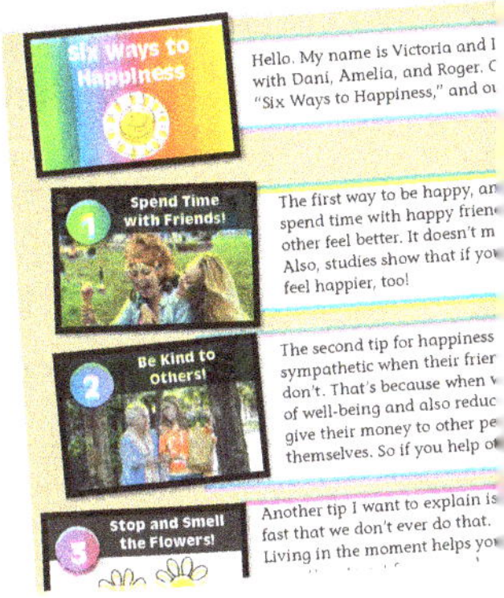

Teacher's Resource Bank

7 REVIEW

VOCABULARY

1 Circle the correct words.

Hi Lee,

How's it going? I've been in Mexico for a month. I'm [1]*glad / hopeful* I came to a town and not a city. It's more [2]*peaceful / grateful*. I've been practicing Spanish a lot – you know me, I'm [3]*eager / insecure* to learn! I felt [4]*satisfied / ridiculous* at first, but I'm improving. I'm [5]*thrilled / annoyed* when people understand me, although sometimes people are [6]*hurt / amused* by my mistakes. Mario has introduced me a lot of people. I'm really [7]*grateful / down* to him.

Anyway, how are you? Write back soon!

James

2 Complete each sentence with the correct form of an expression with *heart* or *mind*.

1. The party totally ______________________ . I'm afraid I can't go now.
2. Excuse me! I've ______________________ . I'll have pizza, not pasta.
3. My sister's great at ______________________ all sorts of facts and dates ______________________ .
4. Pollution is an issue that's really ______________________ . That's why I don't drive.
5. It takes me forever ______________________ about what to wear in the morning. I'd prefer a school uniform!
6. Can I talk to you? I have ______________________ . It's about my best friend.

GRAMMAR IN ACTION

3 Complete the sentences with the gerund or infinitive form of the verbs in parentheses.

1. I'm not shy about ______________ (give) presentations.
2. I was so glad ______________ (see) my cousin at the party.
3. I remember ______________ (feel) really insecure on my first day at school.
4. My baby brother is always amused at something. He never stops ______________ (laugh).
5. ______________ (keep) notes on new vocabulary is really important when you study.

4 Complete the subject and object questions with the correct form of the words in parentheses.

EMMA Happy birthday!

CARLOS Thanks, guys! This is amazing. Who [1] ______________________ (make) the cake?

TIM Emma did.

CARLOS It's delicious. What [2] ______________________ (put / you) in it, Emma?

EMMA Sorry – that's a secret! Anyway, what [3] ______________________ (you / think) of your birthday playlist?

CARLOS I love it. Who [4] ______________________ (make) it?

TIM Emma put it together.

CARLOS Who [5] ______________________ (choose) the song that's playing now? It's one of my favorites.

TIM That was me!

EMMA So tell us – what presents [6] ______________________ (get / you)?

CARLOS Some clothes and this fidget spinner.

TIM Who [7] ______________________ (give) you that?

CARLOS My cousin. He knows I collect them.

TIM What [8] ______________________ (want / you) to drink? Some juice, some soda? We have everything.

Self-Assessment

I can talk about feelings.

I can use expressions with *heart* and *mind*.

I can use gerunds and infinitives.

I can use subject and object questions.

LEARN TO ... GIVE YOUR PARTNER USEFUL FEEDBACK

You can help your partner improve their speaking by giving useful feedback. When you work together, they can help you improve, too.

1 **Match 1–5 with a–e to complete the advice about giving feedback.**

Giving your partner feedback can help them speak, but there are some important things to bear in mind.

1 Being positive is important, so always tell your partner
2 You don't want your partner to feel hurt, so
3 Remember to focus on their English and avoid
4 Feedback should be useful, so don't forget
5 Be honest. Don't say something is

a talking about unrelated things.
b to give ideas for how your partner can improve.
c say anything negative in a friendly way.
d better or worse than it really is.
e what you liked and what they did well.

2 **Look at the feedback that seven students have given Dario. Do they follow the advice in Exercise 1? Why / Why not?**

How was my presentation?

1 *You didn't speak very clearly. I couldn't hear what you were saying.*

2 *I'm glad you used a lot of the new vocabulary. That was nice!*

3 *I like your shoes.*

4 *You repeated some words a lot. I would recommend using synonyms next time.*

5 *You made some grammar mistakes but maybe because you were nervous.*

6 *That was absolutely the most awful presentation in history!*

7 *I think you'll sound more natural next time if you don't learn everything by heart.*

3 **Prepare a talk about a topic in the box.**

a happy memory
growth mindset
how to deal with exam stress
how to stay positive

SHAPE IT!

4 **Take turns giving your talks. While your partner is speaking, think about these things.**

- What do you like about their talk?
- What language do they use well?
- How can they improve next time?

5 **Give your partner useful feedback using the advice in Exercise 1. Is your partner's feedback on your own talk useful? How?**

8 What influences you?

LEARNING OUTCOMES

I can ...

- understand texts about online advertising and social media influencers
- recommend an online tool
- write an online product review
- understand how to use defining and non-defining relative clauses, and indefinite, reflexive, and reciprocal pronouns
- talk about advertising and use Internet verbs
- understand word building (nouns and verbs), how to answer open-ended questions, and work out the meaning of words.
- create a TV ad storyboard

Start It!

1 Look at the photo. Is there a place where you live where you can see a lot of ads like this?
2 Before you watch, think of all the different places where you can see ads.
3 What are the four important aspects of advertising? Watch and check.
4 What's your favorite ad? Why?

Watch video 8.1

p97

Grammar in Action 8.2

p99

Grammar in Action 8.3

p100

Everyday English 8.4

VOCABULARY
Advertising

8.01 **1 Read the story of an ad and put pictures a–f in the correct order. Then listen and repeat the words in bold.**

1 ___ 3 ___ 5 ___
2 ___ 4 ___ 6 ___

8.02 **2 Circle the correct words. Listen and check.**

1 I love watching funny *marketing companies / ads* online or on TV.
2 My dad always buys the same *brand / product* of toothpaste.
3 Sometimes it's not easy for *sellers / buyers* to decide which product they want.
4 I always look at *ad blockers / reviews* before I buy something new.
5 That ad *advertised / influenced* my decision to buy a new tablet.
6 At school we have to draw a simple design for a *logo / slogan* competition.

LEARN TO LEARN

Wordbuilding: Nouns and Verbs

When you learn a noun, check the verb form and record them in a chart.

3 Complete the chart.

Noun	Verb
advertisement (ad)	1 advertise
product	2
3	buy
review	4
5	block (an ad)
6	market
influencer	7
seller	8

4 Close your books. One person says a noun from the chart and the other says the matching verb.

ADVERTISING A PRODUCT

First, a company makes something to sell. This is the **product**. Then they create a **brand** to represent the product – this is a name and design that creates a product's identity. It is usually represented by a symbol, or **logo**. There is often a **slogan** (a short phrase that is easy to remember) linked to a brand.

Next an **ad**, or advertisement, is made to **advertise** the product. This could be a poster on the street or a short video on television or online that shows what the product is like. It is made by a **marketing company** to encourage or **influence** people to buy the product.

When the product goes on sale, the customer, or **buyer**, buys the product from a **seller**. Buyers sometimes write their opinions about the product in an online **review**. People who don't want to see online ads use an **ad blocker**, a computer program that stops ads from appearing on the screen.

Use It!

5 Read the questions and take notes.

1 Do you think ad blockers are a good idea? Why / Why not?
2 Do online reviews influence people to buy a product?
3 Which brand slogans or logos can you remember?

6 EXAM **Ask and answer the questions in Exercise 5.**

Explore It!

Guess the correct answer.

When you see a glass of milk in an ad, it probably isn't milk. What is it?

a paint b glue c yogurt

Find another trick that is used in ads to make products look good. Write a question for your partner to answer.

READING
A Report

8.03 **1** **What can you see in the photos? What do you think people do with the videos? Read the report and check your ideas.**

2 **Read the report again. What do the numbers refer to?**

1 31 percent ______
2 74 percent ______
3 600 million ______

3 **Which type of advertising do the sentences refer to: *I* (influencer), *UGC* (user-generated content), or *N* (native)?**

1 Customers can win prizes. ___
2 Customers share photos of themselves. ___
3 It doesn't look like advertising. ___
4 People buy the products to copy someone else. ___
5 Products are promoted by famous people. ___
6 There is a word that tells you it's an ad. ___

4 **Find words in the report that mean …**

1 people who follow someone online (I). ______
2 a planned series of activities to advertise a product (UGC). ______
3 something that has your name on it (UGC). ______
4 to stop (N). ______
5 paid advertising (N). ______

Voice It!

5 **Discuss the questions.**

1 Do you have a favorite social media influencer or vlogger?
2 Where have you seen native ads on social media?

Online Advertising

Social Media Influencers

One of the most successful types of advertising on social media is influencer advertising. Brands choose social media stars who have thousands of followers on their blog, YouTube channel, or Instagram to advertise their products. The stars talk positively about the products in a natural, personal way, which is different from the slogans in traditional ads. They might talk about a beauty product, play a song, or wear certain clothes in their videos, photos, or blogs. Many fans who want to copy their favorite social media stars go and buy the same products when they see them.

What influences us to buy a product?
Online Stores – 56%, Brand Websites – 34%, Blogs – 31%

User-Generated Content

Another technique used is user-generated content, or UGC. You may know a soft drink company whose ad campaign puts names on their bottles. Buyers took photos of themselves with their personalized bottle and shared them on social media. With UGC, the buyer becomes the person who advertises the brand, so, for example, they upload photos of themselves wearing clothes with the brand logo. Sometimes companies have competitions where you can win a prize for the best photo, and of course, it's free advertising for the brand.

Who gives you the best product information?
(Traditional Media) TV – 34%, Radio – 37%, Newspapers – 44%,
(UGC) Social Networking – 50%, Reviews – 68%, Conversations with Friends – 74

Native Advertising

Have you ever used an ad blocker so you don't see so many ads online? Ad blockers block some ads, but not native advertising. It's a type of advertising that you can't see because it looks exactly the same as a social platform or website. For example, on Facebook a native ad looks like a normal post with like, share, and comment buttons, or it could be a photo or video on Instagram. However, if you look closely, you will see the words "sponsored" or "paid post" next to it. The good thing about native advertising is that users don't feel like their favorite social media channels are full of ads, but some people don't like the idea of hidden ads.

Fact: more than 600 million people use ad blockers

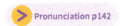

Pronunciation p142

Finished? p125 Ex. 1

GRAMMAR IN ACTION

Defining Relative Clauses

Watch video 8.2
What is he giving advice about?
What should you do with your phone?

Things	It's a type of advertising [1] *that* you can't see.
People	With UGC, the buyer becomes **the person** [2] ________ advertises the brand.
Places and Situations	Companies put ads in **places where** potential customers will see them. Sometimes companies have **competitions** [3] ________ you can win a prize.
Times	There was **a time when** ads were only in newspapers or on the radio.
Possessive	You may know **a soft drink company** [4] ________ ad campaign puts names on their bottles.

1 **Complete the examples in the chart above. Use the report on page 96 to help you.**

Get It Right!

When we use **who**, **that**, **where**, **when**, **which**, and **whose** in relative clauses, they're called relative pronouns. **What** is not a relative pronoun.

This is the ad that I saw. **NOT** ~~*This is the ad what I saw.*~~

2 **Circle the correct relative pronouns.**

1 The online advertising *who* / *that* most teens prefer is made by social media influencers.
2 Influencers *that* / *whose* channels have the most followers advertise a lot of products.
3 Some influencers *who* / *where* advertise products are paid a lot of money.
4 Many teens ignore the ads *that* / *who* they see on social networking sites.
5 Marketing companies look for sites online *that* / *where* they can advertise products.

Use It!

3 **Complete the sentences with the relative pronouns in the box and your own ideas.**

that	where	whose

1 A place ________ I go to relax is ________________________.
2 Someone ________ videos I have watched is ________________________.
3 The apps ________ I use most are ________________________.

Non-Defining Relative Clauses

Things	The **bottles, which** have names on them**,** become ads when shared on social media. Nowadays, companies often use **social media, where** ads don't look like traditional ads**,** to promote their products.
People	**Social media users, who** spend hours online every day**,** like and share ads for free.

4 **Join the sentences with with a non-defining relative clause and the relative pronoun in parentheses.**

1 Jo has her own vlog. Jo is older than me. (who)
Jo, who is older than me, has her own vlog.
2 We're going on vacation to the beach. Katia's family has a house at the beach. (where)
____
3 My phone takes excellent photos. My phone is really old. (which)
____
4 My friend plays the guitar well. His house is near the airport. (whose)
____

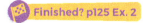

Finished? p125 Ex. 2

VOCABULARY AND LISTENING

Internet Verbs

8.06 **1 Match words 1–10 with definitions a–j. Then listen and repeat the words in bold.**

- I [1]**subscribe to** a YouTube channel about anime. They [2]**post** some awesome videos on it.
- If your Internet connection doesn't work, [3]**switch** your device **off** and then [4]**switch** it **on** again.
- My sister didn't [5]**build up** many followers on Twitter, so she [6]**shut down** her account.
- You should [7]**follow** Zoella. She [8]**vlogs** about tons of interesting things and I love her recipes.
- If people [9]**comment on** the post and what they write isn't very nice, we [10]**delete** it.

a choose to see the things someone uploads on social media 7
b close or stop something ☐
c increase the number of something ☐
d makes and shares videos online ☐
e put a message or image on social media ☐
f remove something ☐
g start something working ☐
h stop something working ☐
i write your opinion online ☐
j agree to regularly receive an online service or information about it ☐

Use It!

2 Ask and answer questions. Find three things you have in common.

commented on something	deleted something
followed someone	posted something
subscribed to a channel	vlogged about something

Have you ever followed someone on social media?

Yes, of course!

Who do you follow?

I follow all my friends and some celebrities online.

An Interview

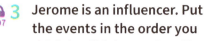

8.07 **3 Jerome is an influencer. Put the events in the order you think he did them. Then listen to the interview and check your answers.**

a ☐ He tried out and reviewed products.
b ☐ He commented on other posts.
c ☐ He got 10,000 followers.
d ☐ He posted videos every day.
e ☐ He set up his own YouTube channel.

LEARN TO LEARN

Open-Ended Questions

Read open-ended questions before you listen and think of possible answers. As you listen, take notes on important words, (names, numbers, etc.).

4 Discuss the questions in Exercise 5. Think of possible answers for each question.

Jerome wanted to talk about a hobby, teach people about something, or show people how to make something.

8.07 **5 Listen again and answer the questions.**

1 Why did Jerome start a YouTube channel?
because he wanted to talk about gaming
2 Why did he delete his videos at first?
______
3 What did his followers like about his vlogs?
______
4 Why did he almost shut down his account?
______
5 How did he solve the problem?
______
6 When did companies start to send him new games?
______
7 What advice does he give?
______

6 Would you like to be a social media influencer? Why / Why not?

GRAMMAR IN ACTION

Indefinite, Reflexive, and Reciprocal Pronouns

Indefinite Pronouns
Give them **something** new.
No one is interested in your selfies.
Do you have any advice for **anyone**?
There weren't any comments from [1] ______________ .
I think that's why **everyone** likes it so much.
Reflexive Pronouns
I tried out the game **myself**.
He saw the ad and bought **himself** a new T-shirt.
People are interested in [2] ______________ .
Reciprocal Pronouns
Some followers started arguing with **one another**.
They couldn't talk to **each other**.

Get It Right!

They looked at themselves in the mirror.
(Each person looked at himself/herself.)
They looked at each other/one another.
(They looked at the different people in the group.)

1 Complete the examples in the chart above.

2 Circle the correct indefinite pronouns.

1 Has *anybody* / *nobody* seen this funny video?
2 I've looked *everywhere* / *somewhere* for my phone, but I can't find it *anywhere* / *somewhere*.
3 *Anyone* / *No one* commented on *anything* / *everything* she said.
4 We're going *everywhere* / *somewhere* in the center of town for *everything* / *something* to eat.
5 Are you doing *anything* / *everything* special for your birthday?

3 Complete the sentences with reflexive pronouns.

1 She taught ______________ how to set up a website.
2 We really enjoyed ______________ at the party.
3 He's selfish. He only thinks about ______________ .
4 I love taking selfies of ______________ .

Watch video 8.3
How many followers do micro-influencers have? Why are they better than celebrity influencers?

4 Match 1–4 with a–d. Then make sentences with *each other* / *one another*.

1 My brother lives in the U.S.A., so we talk to
2 We talk a lot. We're always sending
3 We haven't seen
4 They don't understand

a and argue all the time.
b in ages.
c messages.
d with a webcam.

1 My brother lives in the U.S.A., so we talk to each other / one another with a webcam.
2 ______________
3 ______________
4 ______________

8.08 **5** Circle the correct words to complete the text. Then listen and check.

Ads are [1] *everywhere* / *anywhere*, but have you ever asked [2] *ourself* / *yourself* how advertising works? Marketing companies use techniques to make us buy things we don't even want. [3] *Everything* / *Nothing* is more effective than making us think that we are missing out on [4] *something* / *anything* that [5] *everyone* / *no one* else has and that we will be happier if we buy [6] *ourselves* / *themselves* something new. They also make us compare [7] *myself* / *ourselves* to others. For example, in a typical shampoo ad, two women look at [8] *themselves* / *each other*. One of them asks herself, "Why is her hair so beautiful?" When they talk to [9] *one another* / *themselves*, she discovers the secret: the incredible shampoo!

Use It!

6 Complete the sentences so they are true for you.

1 I have taught myself to ______________ .
2 I never go anywhere without ______________ .

Finished? p125 Ex. 3

SPEAKING

Recommending an Online Tool

8.09 **1 Listen to the conversation. What problem does Niall have? What does Ginny recommend?**

GINNY What's up, Niall?

NIALL I have to make a video for my technology project to advertise something and I don't have a clue what to do. [1] I don't know where to start ! Can you think of anything?

GINNY [2] ________ use a video creation tool. [3] ________ to make videos. I've used some great ones. There are tons of options online.

NIALL That sounds like a plan. What do I need to know?

GINNY Well, a video creation tool [4] ________ because it would provide you with a ready-made template.

NIALL [5] ________?

GINNY Yeah, you can teach yourself to do it, no problem.

NIALL Excellent! So I add my own text and images?

GINNY Well, you need to write your own text, but most video creation tools have a ready-made image bank, which is handy.

NIALL Great, I can use their images.

GINNY Yep and you can add music and a voiceover. [6] ________!

NIALL Sounds like a no-brainer. I'll check out the options online. Thanks, Ginny!

8.09 **2 Complete the conversation with the phrases from the *Useful Language* box. Then listen and check.**

Useful Language

I can't recommend it/them enough!
I don't know where to start!
Is it easy to use?
It's the best thing …
(It) would be ideal …
You really ought to …

3 Match the meanings (1–4) with the phrases in the *Everyday English* box. How do you say these phrases in your language?

1 useful
2 I have no idea.
3 What's the matter? / How are you?
4 obviously the right choice

Watch video 8.4
Everyday English

handy ☐ I don't have a clue. ☐
no-brainer ☐ What's up? ☐

PLAN

4 Take notes about an online tool you want to recommend. Use the ideas below or your own ideas.

an app a comic maker
a music video creator a presentation tool

____
____
____

SPEAK

5 Practice recommending the tool to your partner. Remember to use language from this unit and phrases from the *Useful Language* and *Everyday English* boxes.

CHECK

6 Work with another pair. Listen to their conversation and complete the notes.

What tool did they talk about? ________
____

What did they recommend about it? ________
____

WRITING

An Online Product Review

1 **Look at the photo. Which of the features in the box do you think the speaker has? Read the review and check.**

compact size   good price   good sound
lightweight   long-lasting battery
microphone   waterproof   wireless

Sounds Around ★★★★★

1 ☐ ***Sounds Around*** is a great new product. If you're looking for a wireless speaker with a cool design that is compact in size but big in sound quality, this is for you.

2 ☐ ***Sounds Around*** is designed to be used outside. You can take it everywhere, to the beach, camping, or to a pool party. It has all the features you need, it looks great, and is extremely tough. One of its best features is that it's waterproof. It also allows you to connect two devices at the same time, so you can choose to play music from either of them. The charging cord is included, but the one thing that's missing is a microphone, so you can't record yourself. However, the battery lasts for 10 hours, which is more than the wireless speakers offered by other brands.

3 ☐ ***Sounds Around*** offers the buyer an excellent range of features at an amazing price. In my opinion it's one of the best low-cost speakers. I can't recommend it enough!

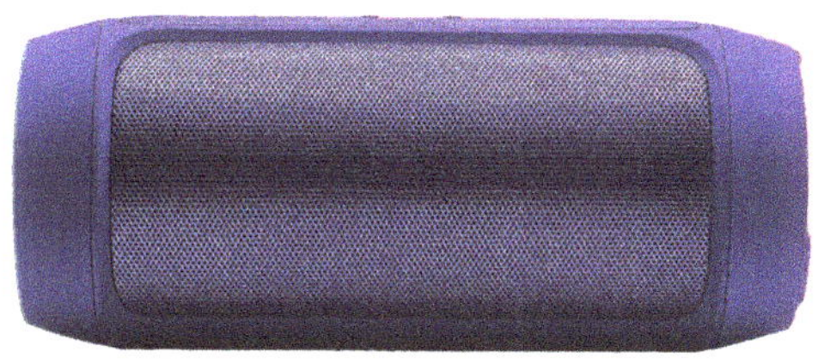

2 **Read the review again. Match topics a–c with paragraphs 1–3.**

a opinion
b short description
c specific features

3 **Discuss the questions.**

1 Where does the reviewer suggest taking the speaker?
2 What's the advantage of connecting to two devices at the same time?
3 What doesn't the reviewer like about the speaker?
4 Why is the battery better than that of other brands?

4 **Read the review again and complete the phrases in the *Useful Language* box.**

Useful Language

[1] ______________________ is included.
It allows you to [2] ______________________.
It is designed to be used [3] ______________________.
One of its best features is [4] ______________________.
The one thing that's missing is [5] ______________________.

PLAN

5 **Choose a product to review. Take notes in your notebook.**

- short description of the product
- design and specific features
- your opinion

WRITE

6 **Write your product review. Remember to include three paragraphs, language from this unit, and phrases from the *Useful Language* box.**

CHECK

7 **Do you …**

- give a star rating?
- say what you like and don't like?
- say whether you would buy it?

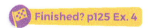

Finished? p125 Ex. 4

ART AND DESIGN PROJECT

A TV Ad Storyboard

1 Look at the pictures from an ad. What product does it advertise?

8.10 2 Work in pairs. Look at the pictures and guess the conversation for each one. Then listen and check.

8.10 3 Listen again and complete the chart.

Ad Features	Example
1 What's the problem?	Katia has a backpack that isn't waterproof. When it rains, everything gets wet.
2 What's the solution?	
3 What are the special features of the product?	
4 Who are the characters in the storyboard?	
5 What information does the narrator give?	
6 What's the slogan?	

How to Give Feedback

4 Feedback should be positive and useful. Complete the feedback phrases with the words in the box.

best how idea maybe positive work

1 The thing I liked ____________ was …
2 Some ____________ things were …
3 I really liked ____________ you …
4 … is a great ____________ .
5 ____________ you could …
6 … might ____________ , too.

1

20 seconds

The girl's things get wet in the rain. A friend talks about her special backpack.

3

15 seconds

The narrator describes the product.

2
20 seconds
The friend shows its special features.

4
10 seconds
The girl loves her new backpack.

PLAN

5 Work in groups to make a storyboard for a TV ad. Choose a product from the box or your own idea.

a new flavor of soft drink
a new perfume
personalized sneakers
sunglasses with headphones

Make a list of its features and the good things about its design. Then create an ad storyboard to advertise the product. Complete the steps below.

- Copy the chart in Exercise 3 and complete it with information about your product.
- Decide how many scenes your ad will have and what should happen in each scene.
- Draw a sketch of the scenes.
- Work together to write a conversation for the storyboard.
- Decide how to present the storyboard (act it out, video, poster, slide presentation).
- Practice your presentation.

PRESENT

6 Present your storyboard to your classmates. Remember to use information in Exercises 3 and 5.

CHECK

7 Look at your classmates' storyboard presentations. Give them motivating feedback with the phrases in *How to Give Feedback*. Which ad is your favorite?

8 REVIEW

VOCABULARY

1 **Complete the advertising facts with the words in the box.**

ad	ad blocker	advertise	
brand	buyer	influence	logo
marketing company	product		
review	seller	slogan	

Advertising Facts

An [1] ________________ is a video, song, or picture that tries to persuade you to buy a [2] ________________.

When you [3] ________________ something, you tell people about it to try to sell it.

A [4] ________________ is the name you call a product. It is often represented by a symbol or [5] ________________.

A [6] ________________ buys something from a [7] ________________. They sometimes give their opinions about the product in a [8] ________________.

When you [9] ________________ someone, you change how they think about something.

An [10] ________________ is a computer program that stops ads from appearing on screen.

A [11] ________________ is a business that encourages people to buy things.

A [12] ________________ is a short phrase used in an ad that is easy to remember.

2 **Circle the correct words.**

1 Are you going to *post* / *vlog* those photos online?
2 If you don't like comments, you can *subscribe to* / *delete* them.
3 How many people do you *build up* / *follow* online?
4 We have to *switch off* / *comment on* our phones at school.

GRAMMAR IN ACTION

3 **Join the sentences to make one sentence with a defining or non-defining relative clause.**

1 Pablo is Eva's cousin. Pablo does voiceovers.
____
2 She lent me a book. It didn't have the last page.
____
3 The movie was about Corfu. We went to Corfu on vacation.
____
4 My dad loves cars. He bought me a car magazine.
____
5 Luis is my friend. His sister is an influencer.
____

4 **Complete the comments with the words in the box.**

each other	everyone	everything
myself	ourselves	themselves

1 Sometimes images in ads make me feel bad about ________________.
2 When we see an ad, we should tell ________________ that it's not the real world.
3 ________________ sees ads, but that doesn't mean they believe ________________ they see.
4 Many ads show people enjoying ________________.
5 Some online ads encourage users to tell ________________ about new products.

Self-Assessment

I can talk about advertising.	☹	😐	☺
I can talk about the Internet.	☹	😐	☺
I can use defining and non-defining relative clauses.	☹	😐	☺
I can use indefinite, reflexive, and reciprocal pronouns.	☹	😐	☺

LEARN TO … WORK OUT THE MEANING OF NEW WORDS

You can work out the meaning of new words and phrases by using clues from the rest of the text.

1 Read the text quickly, ignoring the underlined words if you don't understand them. Do you think space advertising is a good idea?

Space Advertising

Imagine this. It's 2030 and you're gazing up at the night sky. The stars are twinkling and the moon is bright, but these days they're no longer alone. They've been joined by a lot of huge signs in the darkness, like the billboards you see at the sides of a road, advertising everything from soft drinks to vacations. This might sound like science fiction, but space ads will be with us sooner or later. In fact, a Russian company is already developing the technology to make it possible and wants to send up its first ads in the next few years.

They will be created by special satellites, like the ones that send and receive TV and Internet signals, only smaller. These satellites, arranged in groups to make the shapes of words or logos, will reflect light from the sun and will be visible at night from anywhere on Earth. For companies eager to advertise their products to buyers around the globe, this might seem like a dream come true. But ask yourself this: shouldn't we keep somewhere free from advertising? After all, ad blockers won't work in space.

2 Three students are working out the meaning of the underlined words. Which ones are they talking about?

1 *OK, it's a noun. They must be a kind of advertising sign, because it says you see them at the side of a road. What else? Well, I know "board" from "whiteboard"…*

______

2 *I think this phrase must be about when the ads will be sent up to space. I know "soon" and "late." They're both about time and they're opposites …*

______

3 *It's a verb, something that stars do. I think it's connected to their light because the sentence also says "and the moon is bright."*

______

3 Look at the word "gazing" in the text. Answer the questions to try to guess its meaning.

1 What is it? A verb, a noun, an adjective, or a phrase?
2 What does the rest of the sentence tell you about it?
3 Do you understand part(s) of the word or phrase?
4 What do you think it means?

SHAPE IT!

4 Choose five of the other underlined words or phrases. Answer the questions in Exercise 3 to try to guess their meaning.

5 Check the meanings in a dictionary or with your teacher. Were you correct? Did the questions in Exercise 3 help you?

9 What's new?

LEARNING OUTCOMES

I can ...

- understand a newspaper story and a news report
- tell an anecdote
- write a news story
- understand how to use reported statements, reported questions, and indirect questions
- use reporting verbs and adverbs of time and manner
- tell stories to remember new verbs, compare notes to improve listening, learn irregular adjective and noun pairs, and ask for help when I don't understand

Start It!

1 Look at the photo. What do you think the girls are telling each other?
2 Before you watch, why do people like stories?
3 How have Hollywood movies and the Internet changed storytelling? Watch and check.
4 Do you like stories with a moral? Why / Why not?

Watch video 9.1

p109

Grammar in Action 9.2

p111

Grammar in Action 9.3

p112

Everyday English 9.4

p114

Globetrotters 9.5

VOCABULARY
Reporting Verbs

1 Read news stories A–D. Which one is most interesting? Why?

9.01 2 Match the words in **bold** in the news stories with definitions a–l. Then listen, check, and repeat.

A A woman in Georgia, U.S.A. [1]**claimed** that she had thrown away jewelry worth $100,000. The garbage collection company agreed to look through nearly ten tons of trash to try to find a black bag with the jewelry. After three hours, they [2]**announced** that they had found it.

a told people officially 2
b said something was true even if it might not be

B A curator at a university in Australia who [3]**insisted** that he should open an old box in a store room [4]**discovered** that it contained an Egyptian mummy that he believes is 2,500 years old. Experts [5]**have confirmed** that the body is an adult and [6]**suggest** that it might be an important woman from ancient Egyptian society.

c have shown that something is true
d found something, especially for the first time
e said something firmly
f mention an idea for others to consider

C A family [7]**has complained** that their neighbors have stolen their cat. However, the neighbors [8]**deny** that they stole the cat and say that it was homeless and hungry, so they gave it food and a home. The neighbors say that the family [9]**refuses** to believe that the cat prefers to live with them!

g say something is not true
h says he/she/it will not do something
i has told someone that something is wrong

D A school in the north of England [10]**has apologized** for leaving a teenage student in London after a school trip to the capital city. The school [11]**admitted** that they made a mistake and [12]**promised** that it will never happen again.

j agreed that something was true
k has said sorry for something someone has done
l told someone you will certainly do something

LEARN TO LEARN
Telling Stories to Remember New Words

Use reporting verbs in stories to remember what they mean.

3 Work in pairs.

Student A: Tell your partner one of the stories in Exercise 1. Use reporting verbs, but change one fact.

Student B: Listen to your partner tell the story. What did they change?

Use It!

4 Read the options. Take notes on your answers.

Think of a time when you … something.

1 admitted to: yesterday - forgot my homework
2 denied: ______
3 promised to do: ______
4 apologized for: ______
5 refused to do: ______

5 Compare your answers. Which situations were the most difficult? Which were the easiest?

Yesterday, I admitted to forgetting my homework. That was hard!

Explore It!

Guess the correct answer.

In 2014, a French family found a Caravaggio painting in their house. Experts suggested it could be worth … million euros.

a 20 b 80 c 120

Find another interesting fact about something famous or valuable. Write a question for your partner to answer.

Pronunciation p142

READING

A Newspaper Story

9.04 **1 Read the newspaper story. Circle the best title.**

a The Twins Who Have Never Met

b The Twins Who Have Never Spent a Day Apart

c International Twins!

2 EXAM **Read the newspaper story again and circle the correct answers.**

1 Jonas and Santiago have …
  - a nothing in common.
  - b the same adoptive parents.
  - c a lot in common.
  - d the same school friends.

2 The orphanage … the boys …
  - a said … weren't twins.
  - b took … to Spain.
  - c gave … a blue sweatshirt.
  - d suggested … were twins.

3 The twins see each other …
  - a every day.
  - b as often as possible.
  - c only in the U.S.A.
  - d only on social media.

4 The boys were filmed …
  - a only in Spain.
  - b only in the U.S.A.
  - c in Spain and the U.S.A.
  - d separately.

3 Find words in the story that mean …

1 exactly the same (paragraph 1). ______

2 a home for children whose parents cannot care for them (paragraph 2). ______

3 taken into a different family and looked after (paragraph 2). ______

4 from the same family (paragraph 3). ______

(1) **Identical twins Jonas and Santiago look similar, sound similar, and even love the same things. But they live separate lives in different parts of the world and very nearly didn't discover that each other existed.**

(2) In 2004, Jonas and Santiago were left at an orphanage in Ghana, Africa, when they were babies. A few months later, both boys were adopted but by different families; Jonas by a couple from New York and Santiago by a Spanish family. Fortunately, both families went to collect their baby son at the adoption agency in Ghana on the same day and both had bought a new blue sweatshirt for him to wear. A woman at the adoption agency suggested that the babies looked extremely similar, and when the parents saw the two baby boys together in their blue sweatshirts, they agreed that they were exactly the same. The parents then discovered that the boys shared the same birthday, but the orphanage denied that they were twins.

(3) The four adoptive parents couldn't believe that the boys weren't related and insisted that they were going to do a DNA test, which confirmed that the boys were in fact identical twins. The parents promised to keep in touch and said that they would meet as soon as they could, which wasn't easy because Santiago lived in a small village in northern Spain and Jonas lived on the other side of the world in New York.

(4) However, in 2010 they finally met and although they couldn't speak the same language, there was a deep connection between the brothers.

A twin "can understand you when most people don't," Jonas said. "Like in weird situations when you feel a certain way, most people are like, 'What?' But your twin is like, 'Oh, yeah. Yeah, I get that.' I am like, 'Thank you, someone finally gets me.'"

(5) Since then, they have seen each other several times and speak online regularly. In an interview, Jonas explained that he had learned some Spanish phrases, such as how to ask for directions, and that Santiago's English had improved dramatically. In 2012, a Spanish movie director offered to make a movie about the boys' story. He suggested filming the boys together in both Spain and the U.S.A. He told the boys to act naturally while he filmed them, so we get to see the boys playing soccer in Spain and going skateboarding and to the movies in the U.S.A. Jonas admitted that being in a movie was "a bit strange" but "really fun," especially with his twin brother by his side.

Voice It!

4 Discuss the questions.

1 What is the most amazing thing about their story?

2 What would be difficult about living in a different country from your twin?

3 What would you ask Jonas or Santiago if you met them?

4 Would you like to be a twin? Why / Why not? (If you are a twin, what do / don't you like about it?)

Finished? p126 Ex. 1

GRAMMAR IN ACTION
Reported Speech: Verb Patterns

Watch video 9.2
Why did the visitors to the zoo complain? What did the zoo explain?

... (*that*) + independent clause	They **said** [1] *that* they would meet as soon as they could.
... + gerund	They **denied losing** the documents. They **admitted hiding** the truth. He **suggested** [2] ______ (film) the boys together in both countries.
... preposition + gerund	They **apologized for hiding** the truth. They **insisted on** [3] ______ (do) a DNA test.
... + infinitive (with *to*)	A Spanish movie director **offered to make** a movie about the boys' story. The parents **promised to keep** in touch. They **refused to believe** it. He **told** the boys [4] ______ (act) naturally. He **told** me **not to worry**.

1 **Complete the examples in the chart above. Use the story on page 108 to help you.**

Get It Right!

Other verbs that can be used with independent clauses include: **tell**, **insist**, **deny**, **suggest**, **explain**, **promise**, and **admit**. The word **that** is optional.

She suggested that the babies looked extremely similar.

Jonas admitted that being in a movie was a bit strange.

2 **Circle the correct words.**

The director has agreed [1]*that he makes* / *to make* another movie about twins Jonas and Santiago. He explained that the new movie [2]*had been* / *would be* about their lives as teenagers and he told us that the boys [3]*were* / *had been* more independent now and that they [4]*were starting* / *to start* to travel between the U.S.A. and Spain without their parents. He said that Jonas [5]*lived* / *had been living* with Santiago in Spain and [6]*to go* / *had been* to school with his brother.

3 **Complete the reported statements and commands.**

1 "I'll do my homework when the movie has ended."
He explained that he *would do his homework when the movie had ended.*

2 "'I'm going to play your song."
He promised me that he ______

3 "I didn't take my dad's tablet!"
She denied that she ______

4 "Don't watch this video!"
He told me ______

5 "We will come and meet you at the park."
They said that they ______

Use It!

4 **Read the conversation. Write offers, suggestions, and statements in reported speech in your notebook.**

SOFIA Let's go to the movies.
PAULA OK. Let me see what's on.
SOFIA What about *Horror Fair*?
PAULA Sounds good.
SOFIA How about we go at six o'clock?
PAULA Sure. I can buy the tickets online.

Sofia suggested going to the movies.

5 **Tell each other the offers, suggestions, and statements that Sofia and Paula made.**

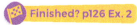

Finished? p126 Ex. 2

VOCABULARY AND LISTENING

A News Report

1 **Look at headlines a–c. What do you think the stories are about?**

a Sock Horror in Girl's Bedroom
b **The Bird that Came Back Speaking Another Language**
c Emergency in the Kitchen!

9.05 2 **Listen and put the stories in Exercise 1 in the order you hear them.**

1 ___ 2 ___ 3 ___

LEARN TO LEARN

Collaborative Listening

Talking about what you understood with a partner before listening a second time can help you find out what you missed.

3 **Tell your partner what you remember about each story. Do you remember the same information?**

9.05 4 **Listen again and answer the questions. Did talking to your partner in Exercise 3 help you?**

1 Where had the parrot been?
____
2 Why did Darren decide not to keep the parrot after he was found?
____
3 What mistake did the girls make?
____
4 What was the emergency?
____
5 Why did the English family make a phone call?
____
6 Why didn't the specialist touch the "lizard" immediately?
____

Adverbs of Time and Manner

5 **Read the blog. Which of the two news stories in the blog do you think was invented?**

If you read my blog **regularly**, you'll know I **occasionally** write about "unbelievable" news stories, like the one about the parrot that spoke Spanish **fluently**. **Nowadays**, there's so much information on the Internet that it's difficult to know if something is true or not. The other day, I was reading a story about a boy who had invented a robot to do his homework. It said he'd been **secretly** developing the technology in his bedroom, **patiently** trying out different designs. Cool idea, right? But the story got **gradually** more ridiculous. It said that one day the robot had offered to go to school, telling the boy he could stay in bed. **After a while**, I began to think, "This can't be true." **Eventually**, I realized it was a joke. It's **surprisingly** easy to believe "fake news"!

9.06 6 **Match the adverbs in bold in the blog with their definitions. Then listen, check, and repeat.**

1 little by little *gradually*
2 these days ___
3 sometimes but not often ___
4 in the end ___
5 in an unexpected way ___
6 without telling anyone ___
7 often ___
8 in a patient way ___
9 easily and well ___
10 after some time ___

Use It!

7 **Think of situations when people do things in these ways. Can your partner guess the verb and adverb?**

gradually: get better, move
regularly: go to bed late, not eat, practice
patiently: listen, sit, wait
secretly: gesture, speak, write

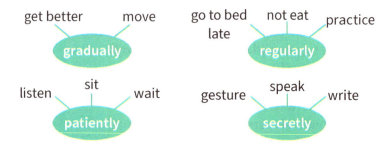

This happens before you play an important soccer match.

You practice regularly?

Yes!

GRAMMAR IN ACTION

Reported Questions

Watch video 9.3
What did the two friends want to see?
How did they get into the radio studio?

Direct Questions	Reported Questions
"What **are** your favorite stories?"	One of our listeners asked us [1] what our favorite stories **were**.
"Where **did** you **leave** the other sock?"	They **asked** (her) [2] ________ she**'d left** the other sock.
"**Can** we have the parrot back?"	The family asked him if they **could** have the parrot back.
"**Have** you ever **cooked** anything before?"	Their Italian friends asked them [3] ________ they'd ever **cooked** anything before.

1 Complete the examples in the chart above.

2 Put the words in the correct order to make sentences. Then, listen and check. 9.07

1. the boy / had / his homework / done / the teacher / if / asked / he
   The teacher asked the boy if he had done his homework.
2. doing / Laura / what / she / Jack / asked / was
   ____
3. we / where / the station / a man / was / asked
   ____
4. arrive / Tom / me / would / I / asked / what time
   ____

3 Rewrite the sentences as reported questions. Then listen and check. 9.08

1. "Who's the hero of the story?" Mikhail asked his sister.
   Mikhail asked his sister who the hero of the story was.
2. Ruben asked his friend, "Where did you hear that?"
   ____
3. "Will it rain later?" she asked.
   ____
4. "What are you reading?" Sally asked me.
   ____

Indirect Questions

Direct Questions	Indirect Questions
Where do you **want** to start?	**Could you tell me** [1] where you want to start?
How did he **learn** Spanish?	**Would you mind telling me** [2] ________ he **learned** Spanish?
Was anyone **hurt**?	**Do you know** [3] ________ anyone **was hurt**?

4 Complete the examples in the chart above.

5 Rewrite the questions in Exercise 3. Use indirect questions.

1. Could you tell me who the hero of the story is?
2. Would you mind telling me ________
3. Do you know ________
4. Could you tell me ________

Use It!

6 Write five direct questions in your notebook. Then swap questions with a partner. Flip a coin. For heads, write the question as a reported question. For tails, write the question as an indirect question.

What movies have you seen recently?
He asked me what movies I'd seen recently.
Could you tell me what movies you've seen recently?

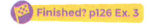

Finished? p126 Ex. 3

SPEAKING

Telling an Anecdote

9.09 **1 Look at the photo. What happened at the bowling alley? Listen to the conversation and check.**

JAMIE [1] *You'll never guess what happened* to me last night.
DULCE No, what? Tell me.
JAMIE [2] ______________ embarrassing! [3] ______________ was, my new classmates asked me if I wanted to go bowling with them. I said yes, and when we got there, they asked me how well I could bowl.
DULCE You didn't say you were any good, did you?
JAMIE Well, you know I'm a show-off! So, I said, "Just watch me!"
DULCE But you're terrible at bowling! I've seen you.
JAMIE Hey! I'm not that bad! So [4] ______________, I picked up the ball, put my fingers in the holes, went to bowl …
DULCE Let me guess. Your fingers got stuck.
JAMIE Completely! I swung the ball back carefully and then swung it forward and just kind of went flying with it. The next [5] ______________, I was on the floor!
DULCE What a fantastic first impression!
JAMIE And to make matters worse, I couldn't get my fingers out.
DULCE Oh, Jamie!

9.09 **2 Complete the conversation with the phrases from the *Useful Language* box. Listen and check.**

Useful Language

Basically, what happened was …
It was so (+ *adjective*) So, anyway, …
The next thing I knew …
You'll never guess what happened …

3 Match 1–5 with the words and phrases in the *Everyday English* box.

1 I disagree!
2 to make the situation even more unpleasant
3 someone who tries to make other people look at them
4 in a way
5 I think I know what you're going to say.

Watch video 9.4
Everyday English

Hey! ☐ Let me guess. ☐ show-off ☐
kind of ☐ to make matters worse ☐

PLAN

4 Take notes in your notebook on something embarrassing, funny, etc., that has happened to you.

- Introduce the anecdote.
- Decide which details are the most important.
- End the anecdote.

SPEAK

5 Practice telling the anecdote to your partner. Remember to use reported statements and questions, vocabulary from this unit, and phrases from the *Useful Language* and *Everyday English* boxes.

CHECK

6 Work with another pair. Listen to their conversation and complete the notes.

What kind of anecdote was it? ______________
____
What were the important details? ______________
____
How did the anecdote end? ______________
____

Free Ice Cream, Anyone?

Most of us expect to receive presents on our birthday. However, Jimmy Teng, or "Uncle Jimmy" is different. The ice-cream man from Singapore regularly gives away free ice cream on his birthday. He started the tradition on his 70th birthday when he offered to give away 700 ice-cream treats.

This year, Uncle Jimmy announced that he was going to give away 1,000 free ice-cream treats. Surprisingly, some customers insisted that they would pay for the ice cream. When asked why he did it, Mr. Teng explained that, nowadays, everyone in Singapore was stressed and he wanted to make them feel happy. He also admitted that sharing ice cream made him feel good, too. "I'm so happy," he said. "I wouldn't be this happy if I won the lottery!"

Uncle Jimmy, who has been an ice-cream man for over 15 years, has a lot of customers. When asked what his favorite flavor was, he answered "sweetcorn," and he explained that ice cream in Singapore was sometimes served with bread rather than a cone.

WRITING

A News Story

1 **Why would someone give away free ice cream? Read the news story and check.**

2 **Read the news story again and answer the questions.**

1 Who is the story about? ______
2 What happens? ______
3 When does it happen? ______

3 **Discuss the questions about the structure of the story.**

1 What does the headline tell us about the story? What doesn't it tell us?
2 What is the aim of the first sentence?
3 What do we learn in the first paragraph of the story?
4 When do we learn why the story happened?
5 Is the information in the third paragraph necessary or extra?
6 What effect does the direct speech have in the story?

4 **Complete the phrases in the *Useful Language* box with details from the news story.**

Useful Language

A man from [1] Singapore regularly gives away free ice cream...
He announced/explained/admitted that [2] ______
______
[3] "______," he said.
Surprisingly/Nowadays, etc., [4] ______
______
When asked ... he answered/explained/said [5] ______
______

PLAN

5 **Take notes on something special that someone has done to celebrate their birthday or find an interesting news story online.**

______
______
______
______

WRITE

6 **Write a news story about your idea in Exercise 5. Remember to include three paragraphs, language from this unit, and phrases from the *Useful Language* box.**

CHECK

7 **Do you ...**

- include an interesting headline?
- include some extra details in the third paragraph?
- include some direct speech?

Finished? p126 Ex. 4

AROUND THE WORLD

READING
A Story

1 Look at pictures A–D. What is happening in each one? Put them in order to make a story.

9.10 2 Were your ideas correct? Read the introduction about Maori storytelling and the story "How Maui Slowed the Sun."

Voice It!

3 Discuss the questions.
1 How did the men discuss their problems?
2 Why is it important to discuss issues before taking action?
3 How do you convince other people to listen to your opinion?

Globetrotters
Watch video 9.5
Stories on Stage

- Where do you think opera comes from?
- Where is it popular?
- What is *jingju* and what does it involve?
- What different skills do *jingju* performers need to have?

A

B

MAORI STORYTELLING

Storytelling is an essential part of the culture of the Maori people, the first inhabitants of Aotearoa (New Zealand). They didn't use to have a written language, so they learned stories by heart to remember their history. The Maori people still tell their stories, often in a traditional meeting place called a *marae*. The stories are accompanied by dance, songs, and chants. Here is one for you to enjoy.

How Maui Slowed the Sun

Long ago, the Sun used to move so quickly across the sky that the days were too short for people in the village to do all their work. The villager Maui, however, had a plan. He gathered his four brothers and said, "Why should the Sun control us? Let's catch him and make him go more slowly."

The brothers were worried. They asked Maui if it was really possible to get safely near the Sun. "The heat and flames will burn us!" they said. "We might die!" Maui held his grandfather's bone high, and said, "I have achieved many things that you thought were impossible. I have brought fire to the people, I have caught the greatest fish in the world. With this bone, and with your help, I will catch the Sun."

Everyone agreed to help him. Over the next five days, they made strong ropes to catch the Sun. When they were ready, the brothers set off to the east, where the Sun rises. They traveled during the night so that the Sun wouldn't see them approaching. Eventually, they arrived at an enormous deep hole in the ground. This was where the Sun slept.

While the Sun was still asleep, the brothers built a wall around the hole and hid behind it, waiting patiently. Maui told his brothers not to throw the ropes until he said so. After a while, the ground began to shake. The Sun was waking up! First came his burning hair, then his fiery eyes and his white-hot teeth.

"Now!" cried Maui. The brothers threw the ropes over the Sun. They tangled in his hair and trapped his

4 **Read the introduction and the story again. Write *T* (true) or *F* (false).**

1 The Maori have always written down their stories. F
2 It was impossible for the villagers to finish their work each day. ___
3 Maui had never done anything impressive before. ___
4 Only Maui's brothers helped make the ropes. ___
5 The Sun saw Maui and his brothers coming closer. ___
6 Maui hit the Sun more than once with the bone. ___

LEARN TO LEARN

Irregular Adjective and Noun Pairs

Learn adjectives and their related nouns to increase your vocabulary.

5 **Complete the chart with words from the story.**

Adjective	wide	1 ______	hot	3 ______	strong	5 ______
Noun	width	height	2 ______	length	4 ______	depth

C 

D 

huge, hot body. The men pulled on the ropes as strongly as they could.

"What are you doing?" the Sun cried angrily.

Maui jumped on the wall and lifted up his grandfather's bone. He smashed it with all his strength down on the head of the Sun, who screamed in pain.

"Are you trying to kill me?"

"No, but you must go more slowly," said Maui.

The Sun tried hard to escape, but again and again Maui hit him with the bone. The Sun gradually grew weaker, until at last he could only move slowly across the sky.

And that is why the days are now long enough for all our work, and why sometimes, if you look carefully, you can still see the ropes that connect the Sun to the Earth – shining through the clouds.

Explore It!

Guess the correct answer.

Aotearoa, the Maori name for New Zealand, means land of …

a the perfect sky.
b the long white cloud.
c the towering mountains.

Find another interesting fact about the Maori. Write a question for your partner to answer.

SHAPE IT!

CULTURE PROJECT

A Story

A traditional story shares events and values in a memorable way. Write a traditional story that you know about.

A Cornish Legend
The Legend of Tom Bawcock

Teacher's Resource Bank

9 REVIEW

VOCABULARY

1 **Match the reporting verbs in the box with the definitions.**

admit	apologize	complain	deny	discover	promise

Which reporting verb do we use to …

1 say that something is not true? ______
2 tell someone you're sorry? ______
3 find out information for the first time? ______
4 agree that something is true? ______
5 tell someone formally something is wrong? ______
6 tell someone you will certainly do something? ______

2 **Complete the sentences with the adverbs in the box.**

eventually	fluently	gradually	nowadays
regularly	secretly	surprisingly	

1 I ______ finished reading the book you recommended, but it took me ages.
2 I speak French ______ , mostly with my Canadian cousin – once a week.
3 Mike's family planned his birthday party ______ . He was very surprised!
4 The exam was ______ easy. I finished it really quickly.
5 My best friend speaks English ______ .
6 ______ I get along with my brother, but we didn't use to.
7 My English is improving ______ , but I need to learn more vocabulary.

GRAMMAR IN ACTION

3 **Complete the second sentences.**

1 "I'll help you with your homework."
Felipe offered ______
2 "Send me a message when you get there."
Shaun told me ______
3 "Why don't we meet at the new café?"
Ada suggested ______
4 "I promise I'll give you a ride."
She promised ______

4 **In your notebook, rewrite the direct questions as reported questions.**

1 "How often do you read the news online?" my sister asked me.
2 "How can I improve my English?" Vero asked her teacher.
3 "Have you seen what's happened in London?" Ian asked Jake.
4 "Will the museum be open tomorrow?" the tourist asked.

5 **In your notebook, rewrite the questions in Exercise 4 as indirect questions.**

Self-Assessment

I can use reporting verbs.
I can use adverbs of time and manner.
I can use reported statements.
I can use reported questions and indirect questions.

LEARN TO LEARN

LEARN TO … ASK FOR HELP WHEN YOU DON'T UNDERSTAND

There are different ways to ask English speakers for help and check you understand what they've said.

1 Read the problems people have understanding someone in English. Then discuss the questions.

We asked five language learners what problems they'd had understanding people in English. This is what they told us.

"For me, it's usually that the other person speaks too fast."

"The worst thing is when people use a lot of difficult words I don't know."

"I usually understand, more or less, but I don't understand all of the details."

"Sometimes I think I've understood someone, but then I realize I haven't at all!"

"My problem is that when I don't understand, I'm too shy to say. I just say 'yes' a lot!"

Have you had any of these problems? How did you solve them?

2 Read the conversations. Match phrases 1–5 with phrases with similar meanings a–e.

a Could you repeat that from the beginning? ___
b I want to make sure I've understood correctly. ___
c What's the meaning of that word? ___
d I didn't hear the last thing you said. ___
e What were your instructions? ___

1

JOSÉ: Sorry, Miss. I didn't understand. [1]**What did you say I had to do?**
TEACHER: I told you to compare the two pictures and discuss how similar they are.
JOSÉ: [2]**What does "similar" mean?**

2

ALISON: Excuse me, can you tell me how to get to the post office, please?
MAN: Sure. Go straight until you see a big building. It's across from that …
ALISON: [3]**I didn't catch that.** The big what?
MAN: Building.

3

GISELLE: Bea thought Juan had promised he would bring the food, but he hadn't! After a while, someone said –
JO: Wait, wait, wait! [4]**Can you start again, please?** I'm lost!
GISELLE: Sorry, sorry. What happened was that …

4

EVAN: Which bus do I need for Oxford Park?
WOMAN: You need two, actually. Take the 147 from here to Austen Square, cross the road, and then take the 29 from in front of the bank.
EVAN: OK, [5]**let me check I've got this right.** First, I take 147 to Austen Square?
WOMAN: That's right.

SHAPE IT!

3 Student A: choose one of the topics in the box below and explain it to Student B. Student B: use the phrases from the conversations and Exercise 2 to help you understand. Then swap roles.

how to get from your school to your house
the rules of a sport
the story of how Maui slowed the Sun

1 FINISHED?

1 Put the letters in order to make words to describe clothes and shoes.

1

flowery

2 P L O D T K O A ________

3 R I S T E D P ________

4 H I T G T ________

5 H D R C E C E K E ________

6

____

7
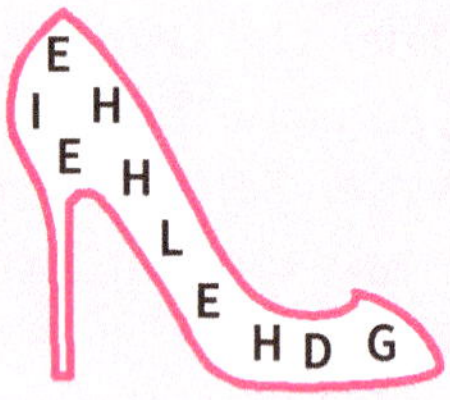

____

8

____

2 Match the texts with photos a–d.

1 I've just had a totally amazing time! I've been looking at all kinds of interesting animals, with a lot of fantastic colors. I haven't done anything like this before, but I'd like to do it again. I've told all my friends, and they want to do it with me next time. ________

2 We've just come back, and we've spent all our money. The good news is now I have a lot of really good clothes, so I don't need to do anything like this again for a long time! ________

3 I've been outside all day, and now I'm feeling pretty tired. I've being doing this since I was very young, and one day I want to train other people to do the same as me. ________

4 I've had a pretty bad experience. I haven't tasted anything so bad in a long time. And since I had it, I've been feeling really sick. My stomach has been hurting for ages. I'm never going back there, and I'm going to tell all my friends about it! ________

a

b

c

d

3 Complete the modifiers with vowels. Make sentences about you with the modifiers and the words in the box.

amazed	better	confused	good at
happier	happy	more interesting	
shocked	slow	slower	taller

1 absolutely
2 _xtr_m_ly
3 r_ _lly
4 t_t_lly
5 f_ _rly
6 pr_tty
7 _ l_t
8 _ l_ttl_
9 _ b_t

4 Put the letters in order to make verbs related to clothes and shoes.

1 WIGOHT GO WITH
2 MTCAH □□□□□
3 TIF □□□
4 WERTAUO □□□□ □□□
5 KOOLDOGONO □□□□ □□□□ □□
6 HAPNUG □□□□ □□
7 LOFD □□□□
8 PUPIZ □□□ □□
9 NUZPI □□□□□

2 FINISHED?

1 **Read the clues and complete the crossword.**

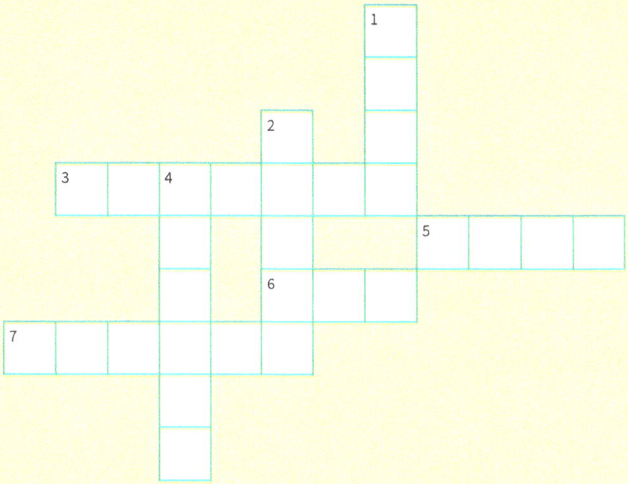

Across

3 I had to do … my phone for a week because it was broken.

5 Last week, I went … to my old elementary school to visit my teacher.

6 I feel bad. I hope I don't … up getting sick.

7 I've … up for piano lessons.

Down

1 I … through a difficult time when I started my new school, but now everything's OK.

2 Sara … out of her old apartment and went to live in a new one.

4 I … down three party invitations last month because I was so busy.

2 **Compare the pictures. How many sentences can you write about Stuart's life in the past with *used to*, *didn't use to*, and *would*? Use your imagination!**

When Stuart was a student, he used to live in an apartment.

3 **What movies had you seen by the time you were ten? Write as many as possible in two minutes.**

4 **Find words in the sentences that rhyme with parts of objects. Change them so the sentences make sense.**

1 Put the ~~kid~~ back or the pen will dry. lid

2 I've broken the sandal on my bag. ________

3 My computer needs a hug. ________

4 The Swiss play on that phone is really bright. ________

5 Don't get the camera pens dirty. ________

6 The map of my bag hurts my shoulder. It's too tight. ________

3 FINISHED?

1 Match the squares to make cooking verbs.

ro	ch	over	gri	sea	pe	sli	fr	ba	spre	gra	bo
y	son	te	ke	ll	il	ad	ast	cook	ce	el	op

2 Use the code to write the questions. Answer them so they are true for you.

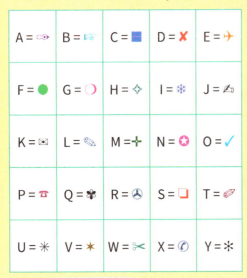

A = ⚭	B = ☞	C = ■	D = ✗	E = ✈
F = ●	G = ❍	H = ✧	I = ❄	J = ✍
K = ✉	L = ✎	M = ✢	N = ✪	O = ✓
P = ☎	Q = ✾	R = ✇	S = ❑	T = ✐
U = ✳	V = ✶	W = ✂	X = ✆	Y = ✻

1 ✗✓❄✪❍ ✐✧❄❑ ✈✶✈✪❄✪❍
What are you ______________________________?
____

2 ❍✓❄✪❍ ✐✓ ✗✓ ✪✈✆✐ ❑✳✢✢✈✇
What are you ______________________________?
____

3 ☎✈✓☎✎✈ ✂❄✎✎ ✐✇⚭✶✈✎ ❄✪ ✐✧✈ ●✳✐✳✇✈
How do you think ______________________________?
____

4 ✂✈⚭✐✧✈✇ ❍✓❄✪❍ ✐✓ ☞✈ ✎❄✉✈ ✐✓✢✓✇✇✓✂
What's the ______________________________?
____

3 Make sentences with the future continuous or future perfect form of the verbs in the box.

chat with friends do homework
have dinner listen to music
play sports sleep

At 5 p.m. I will / won't be …
At 7 p.m. …
By midnight I will / won't have …

____
____
____
____
____
____
____

4 Circle nine more quantities.

H	A	N	D	F	U	L	T	G	F	D
V	Y	D	B	E	H	E	E	D	G	X
S	P	R	I	N	K	L	E	C	C	O
L	K	J	K	C	O	I	C	P	E	W
E	A	S	A	W	U	S	V	I	A	E
E	J	P	D	F	B	P	I	E	C	E
P	Q	O	F	V	B	L	L	C	H	J
O	I	O	V	C	K	A	W	E	U	K
P	J	N	E	D	A	S	G	O	N	R
C	H	F	C	W	Y	H	N	D	K	N
Q	R	U	J	H	Q	B	G	G	R	T
W	S	L	I	C	E	H	T	I	O	M

4 FINISHED?

1 Can you figure out these riddles?

1 Sometimes they look like faces; sometimes they look like animals. They're always changing shape. Gray ones usually disappear after the rain.

____

2 It looks like a tear and it tastes a bit like an apple. It sounds the same as two things of the same size that are used together.

____

3 Mine sounds like a bird. Mary's latest one sounds like a famous pop song. We don't know what Dave's sounds like because he always has his phone on silent.

____

2 Look at the photos. In your notebook, describe the things and guess what they might be.

1

2

3

4
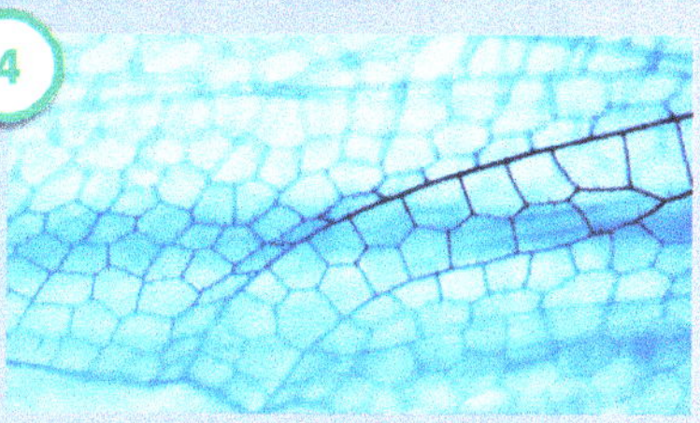

3 Imagine you do an unusual job. Write as many of these as possible in three minutes.

- things you had to do to get your job

- things you have to do every day in your job

Show your list to a partner. Can they guess the job?

4 Circle nine more adjectives.

R	U	Z	D	H	S	W	I	D	D	T	W
C	O	L	M	S	H	A	R	P	F	R	C
F	G	U	J	T	I	C	Y	L	S	A	O
N	A	X	G	H	N	A	B	U	M	V	L
B	V	I	D	H	Y	L	Q	S	E	U	O
S	K	L	N	D	E	F	E	B	L	H	R
P	M	P	R	T	K	M	U	Z	L	E	F
N	F	O	Z	G	S	P	I	C	Y	N	U
M	A	S	O	U	R	O	W	J	U	C	L
E	D	R	M	T	P	A	S	I	L	J	E
O	S	Q	U	G	H	T	V	Z	N	I	F
T	R	A	N	S	P	A	R	E	N	T	H

5 FINISHED?

1 **Put the letters in order to write two verbs to describe processes.**

1 eodseaptwlev develop, waste
2 uclertoplocced ___________
3 evaemrrilusede ___________
4 lepmtapmnicocsuyu ___________
5 toeercaslev ___________
6 toctacrenactnt ___________

2 **Mark is going to have an operation next week. Complete the sentences about who will be doing what. Put the sentences in order.**

a ☐ Next, the anesthetic ___________ (give) by Dr. Sanna.
b ☐ The second part of the operation ___________ (do) by Dr. Rees.
c ☐ First, his heart rate ___________ (measure) by Nurse Evans.
d ☐ Finally, he _________ (take) home by his family.
e ☐ Until he is completely better, he ___________ (visit) in the hospital by Dr. Jones.
f ☐ The first part of the operation ___________ (do) by Dr. Lansbury.

3 **How many sentences can you write that go in front of these question tags in three minutes?**

1 …, isn't it?
It's freezing today
2 …, doesn't she?
____
____
3 …, can't they?
____
____
4 …, would you?
____
____
5 …, are we?
____
____
6 …, haven't you?
____
____
7 …, will he?
____
____

4 **Circle nine more extreme adjectives.**

F	E	T	D	E	A	F	E	N	I	N	G
R	A	N	E	E	F	R	L	J	A	B	P
E	H	S	O	R	A	F	L	Q	M	O	U
E	D	S	C	R	R	U	I	J	Q	I	N
Z	R	W	T	I	M	I	A	U	J	L	D
I	E	J	J	U	N	O	F	F	I	I	Q
N	A	V	X	X	N	A	U	Y	R	N	B
G	W	V	F	Y	O	N	T	S	I	G	V
D	F	F	C	S	W	I	I	I	K	N	A
B	U	M	L	R	X	N	X	N	N	E	G
V	L	M	A	T	B	T	E	C	G	G	H
M	A	R	V	E	L	O	U	S	C	Z	D
A	B	L	Z	G	O	R	G	E	O	U	S

6 FINISHED?

1 **Read the clues and complete the crossword.**

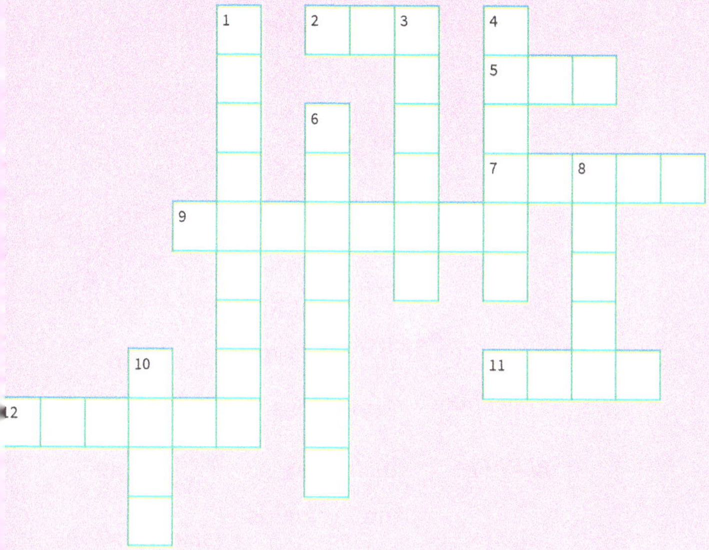

Across

2 I always have … with my friends.
5 I get a lot … of my English lessons.
7 We fell asleep because we got … with the TV show.
9 Do you take an … in soccer?
11 My dad always gets … when he's driving.
12 My grandfather never had the … to go to college.

Down

1 We have 30 minutes before our train arrives, so let's take … of it.
3 My annoying cousin really gets on my … .
4 I have … about whether my team will win tomorrow.
6 My grandmother takes a lot of … in looking at old photos.
8 It's important to take some … in life.
10 I got to … a lot of new people at summer camp last year.

2 **Match the jokes with the answers.**
Give each joke a score (one star = terrible, five stars = very funny).

1 If you dialed 08968 767 457 454 233 989 767 521 123, what would you get? ___
2 What would happen if you put your music in the fridge? ___
3 What word would become shorter if you added two more letters to it? ___
4 Where would a cow go if it wanted a vacation? ___
5 If you look in any dictionary, which word will always be spelled wrong? ___

a Mooooo York! ★★★★★

b A very tired finger! ☆☆☆☆☆

c Wrong. ★★★★★

d Short! ☆☆☆☆☆

e You'd get some really cool music! ★★★★★

3 **Complete the story with third conditional sentences and interesting information.**

1 If Sara hadn't gone to school that day, she wouldn't have met ______________________.
2 If she hadn't met ______________________ she wouldn't have found out ______________________.
3 If she hadn't ______________________.
4 If ______________________.
5 If ______________________.

4 **Put the letters in order to make verbs and nouns for inspiration and challenge.**

1 a c e e g h l l n *challenge*
2 y e b r a r v ______________
3 d t r i a i n o t n m e e ______________
4 o p r u i y t n t o p ______________
5 b t c e l a s o ______________
6 u p r t o p s ______________
7 n o r g e a u c e ______________
8 o e c m v r o e ______________
9 a e c v h e i ______________
10 e i n r i s p ______________

7 FINISHED?

1 Find the letters and then write them to make the first half of a message. Can you guess the second half?

1 satisfied (letter 2)
2 hopeful (letter 1)
3 peaceful (letter 5)
4 eager (letter 2)
5 glad (letter 2)
6 hurt (letter 4)
7 thrilled (letter 2)
8 annoyed (letter 5)
9 amused (letter 2)
10 ridiculous (letter 4)
11 insecure (letter 2)
12 down (letter 1)

a h _ _ _ _ _ _ _ _ _ _ _ is as important as
a _ _ _ _ _ _ _ _ _ _ _ _ _.

2 Four brothers each have a sister who is the complete opposite of them. Match the sentences halves to find out who the sisters are.

Jack keeps eating chocolate all day.
Emily avoids eating too much sugar.

Alex never stops	getting up early.
Thiago hopes	eating chocolate all day.
Charlie always forgets	to stay in the city forever.
Jacob doesn't mind	talking in class.
Jack keeps	to put his notebook in his bag.

Emily avoids	to get up late every day if she could.
Sara always remembers	to speak during most lessons.
Megan refuses	living in the country.
Olivia would love	to take all her books to class.
Mira misses	eating too much sugar.

3 How many pairs of subject and object questions can you write in three minutes using the ideas in the box?

Q: What did Al Zahrawi write?
A: One of the earliest books about medicine.
Q: Who wrote one of the earliest books about medicine?
A: Al Zahrawi.

invent
write
J.K. Rowling
the Ancient Egyptians
build
discover
Steve Jobs
one of the earliest books about medicine
gravity
the Italians
the Pyramids
the iPhone and the iPod
Isaac Newton
the Harry Potter stories
the Pyramids
pizza
Al Zahrawi

4 Put the letters in order and add *heart* or *mind* to make expressions.

yellow: put my (heart) into
blue: ______
red: ______
brown: ______
pink: ______
orange: ______
purple: ______
green: ______

N	M	T	P	I	T
G	E	U	O	Y	N
S	D	O	L	N	Y
C	H	C	E	E	H
I	S	Y	O	C	M
Y	O	S	M	G	A
S	P	T	N	B	Y
R	Y	R	E	L	A
M	L	S	S	R	B
E	I	M	A	O	E
M	E	N	E	'	B
O	A	B	S	M	K
T	I	R	D	O	Y

8 FINISHED?

1 Use the code to complete the questions. Answer them so they are true for you.

A	B	C	D	E	F	G	H	I	J	K	L	M	N	O	P	Q	R	S	T	U	V	W	X	Y	Z
8		24	11	19			12	14		22	17			18			2	26	13	21	6	10		4	

1 WHICH ADS DO YOU LIKE?
(10 12 14 24 12 / 8 11 26 / 11 18 / 4 18 21 / 17 14 22 19)

2 W _ _ C _   L O _ O _   _ O   _ O _   _ _ O W ?
(10 12 14 24 12 / 17 18 25 18 26 / 11 18 / 4 18 21 / 22 1 18 10)

3 _ O   _ O _   E V E _   W _ _ T E   _ E V _ E W _ ?
(11 18 / 4 18 21 / 19 6 19 2 / 10 2 14 13 19 / 2 19 6 14 19 10 26)

4 _ O   _ O _   _ _ E   A _   _ L O C _ E _ _ ?
(11 18 / 4 18 21 / 21 26 19 / 8 11 / 15 17 18 24 22 19 2 26)

5 W _ A T   _ _ _ L _ E _ C E _   _ O _   T O   _ _ _   A   _ _ O _ _ C T ?
(10 12 8 13 / 14 1 20 17 21 19 1 24 19 26 / 4 18 21 / 13 18 / 15 21 4 / 8 / 23 2 18 11 21 24 13)

6 W _ _ C _   _ L O _ A _ _   C A _   _ O _   _ E _ E _ _ E _ ?
(10 12 14 24 12 / 26 17 18 25 8 1 26 / 24 8 1 / 4 18 21 / 2 19 16 19 16 15 19 2)

2 Complete the sentences with a relative pronoun. Guess what each thing or person is. Use the scrambled words in the box to help you.

1 It's a feeling you have ________ someone has helped you. ______________
2 It's a word ________ goes with *have* and means "a good time." ______________
3 It describes a place ________ you can feel very calm and relaxed. ______________
4 It's a word ________ means "very interesting." ______________
5 It describes someone ________ feels angry. ______________
6 It's someone ________ products are bought by someone else. ______________

lgruafte
unf
lpeuafce
fganisctian
daneyon
relsle

3 Circle five pronouns in the wordsnake. Use them to complete the sentences so they are true for you.

temyselfonboanyonesetsomeoneoranysomethingeverynothingeach

The last time I ...
1 enjoyed ____________ was ______________________________.
2 didn't talk to ____________ for an hour was ______________________________.
3 helped ____________ was ______________________________.
4 forgot ____________ important was ______________________________.
5 had ____________ to eat and felt hungry was ______________________________.

4 Circle nine more Internet verbs.

I	A	V	X	E	W	N	H	L	M	U	P	E
R	D	E	L	E	T	E	B	E	P	W	P	C
S	P	K	P	O	S	T	C	B	K	A	N	O
U	W	O	T	E	G	W	R	C	S	U	S	M
B	O	G	Y	F	S	B	I	R	M	N	F	M
S	Q	G	O	N	B	E	U	T	S	P	O	E
C	Y	J	Z	L	L	U	A	I	C	D	L	N
R	E	W	S	E	V	E	I	C	L	H	L	T
I	Y	Y	T	H	X	X	T	L	H	Y	O	O
B	Y	E	U	S	S	H	U	T	D	O	W	N
E	C	D	H	X	K	O	S	H	K	U	S	G
T	S	W	I	T	C	H	O	F	F	K	P	C
O	I	P	Y	P	W	C	G	W	N	V	K	C

9 FINISHED?

1 **Match the squares to make reporting verbs.**

de	apolo	ann	con	com	ad	in	sug	re	pro
plain	mise	ny	ounce	gest	sist	mit	fuse	firm	gize

2 **Write examples of the following.**

A time when you …

1 suggested doing something different. ______

2 offered to help someone. ______

3 denied that you had done something and then admitted that you had done it. ______

4 promised to do something. ______

5 insisted that you did something. ______

6 told someone to do something. ______

3 **Imagine you are a famous athlete, pop star, or actor. Imagine indirect questions your fans might ask. How many can you list in three minutes?**

Lionel Messi

Could you tell me what your dream team would be?

______

4 **Complete the sentences with the adverbs in the box. What is the adverb in the boxed letters?**

after a while eventually fluently gradually ~~nowadays~~ patiently regularly secretly surprisingly

1 Most people *n* [*o*] *w a d a y s* have a cell phone.

2 I whispered __ [*c*] ____ to her.

[*c*]

3 ____ [ ] ____, the baby fell asleep.

4 The twins are ____ [ ] ____ different.

5 The teacher waited __ [ ] ____.

[*o*]

[*n*]

6 The rain ____ [ ] __ stopped.

7 Aroha spoke Maori [ ] ____.

8 English gets ____ [ ] __ easier.

9 The Olympics take place ____ [ ].

STARTER VOCABULARY BANK

Travel

accommodation

backpacking

resort

sightseeing

tourist attraction

trip

Music and Theater

audience	part	scene
lines	rehearsal	show

1 Are the sentences true or false?

1 An audience is all the actors in a play. ____
2 A resort is a store where you go to book a vacation. ____
3 The lines in a play are the words the actors speak. ____
4 Your accommodation is the plane, boat, etc., that takes you to your vacation. ____
5 Actors have rehearsals to practice their performance. ____

Ways of Communicating

describe	post	shout	translate	whisper
greet	shake hands	smile	wave	

2 Circle the correct words.

1 At the beginning of the trip, we were *posted* / *greeted* / *waved* by our tour guide.
2 I think he enjoyed the show because he was *shouting* / *waving* / *smiling*.
3 Alfonso will *describe* / *translate* / *whisper* all the tourist attractions we are going to see.
4 She plays the part of an angry teacher who *shouts* / *posts* / *smiles* at her students a lot.
5 In the first scene, two actors meet and *translate* / *shake hands* / *describe*.

LEARN TO LEARN

Personalizing Vocabulary

Writing personalized sentences helps you learn new words.

3 Choose four verbs from the list above and write sentences that are true for you. Then tell your partner.

1 ____
2 ____
3 ____
4 ____

Our teacher greets us every morning.

1 VOCABULARY BANK

Describing Clothes and Shoes

baggy

checkered

cotton

denim

flowery

high-heeled

leather

long-sleeved

plain

polka-dot

striped

tight

1 Is the adjective order correct or incorrect? Circle the correct answer.

1. We have to wear leather high-heeled shoes. *Correct / Incorrect*
2. Paul was wearing a red baggy T-shirt. *Correct / Incorrect*
3. Laura bought a flowery cotton blouse. *Correct / Incorrect*
4. I'd like a denim black jacket. *Correct / Incorrect*
5. The singer wore tight striped pants. *Correct / Incorrect*

Verbs Related to Clothes and Shoes

fit	go with	match	zip up
fold	hang up	unzip	
go out of style	look good on	wear out	

2 Circle the correct words.

1. I can't wear this polka-dot scarf. It doesn't *hang up / go with / fold* my coat.
2. This dress is a bit tight. It doesn't *match / unzip / fit* me any more.
3. I've had this sweater for years. It never seems to *wear out / look good on me / unzip me.*
4. Don't leave your jacket on the floor. *Hang it up / Do it up / Wear it out* in your closet.
5. You look great in that checkered shirt. It really *goes out of style / looks good on you / goes with you.*

LEARN TO LEARN

Categorizing

Recording new words in categories helps you remember their meaning.

3 Put the verbs related to clothes and shoes above in the correct categories. Compare with a partner.

Putting Clothes Away	
Ways of Saying That Clothes Look Good	fit
Reasons Not to Wear Clothes	
Putting On and Taking Off Clothes	

2 VOCABULARY BANK

Phrasal Verbs: Changes

do without	go back	look forward to	move to	sign up	turn down
end up	go through	move out	settle down	try out	turn out

1 Complete the statements with a phrasal verb from the list. Then put them in order from most true for you (1) to least true for you (5). Compare with a partner.

1 I would love to ______________ New York. ___
2 I never ______________ party invitations. ___
3 I always ______________ my English classes. ___
4 I like to ______________ new video games with my friends. ___
5 I would like to ______________ in one place for my whole life. ___

Parts of Objects

button

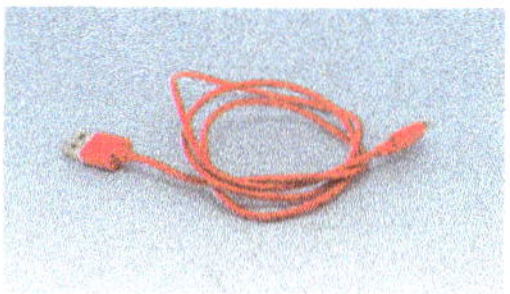
cord

cover

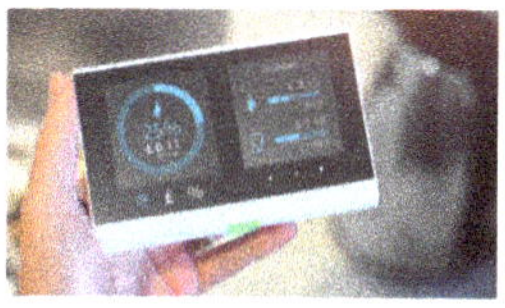
display

handle

key

lens

lid

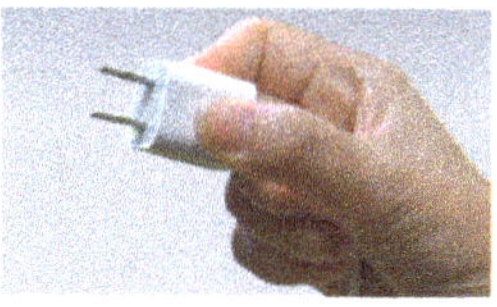
plug

strap

2 Use the clues to complete the puzzle.

1	l	e	n	s				I am made of glass. You look through me.
2								I am round. You press me to make an elevator come.
3								I am made of paper. I go on a book to protect it.
4								I am thin. You use me to fasten something.
5								I show information, for example, the time.

LEARN TO LEARN

Visualizing Words in Different Situations

Visualizing words in different situations helps you remember them.

3 Where would you find these parts of objects (1–4)? Use the objects from the box. Some may have more than one part. Then choose two more parts from the list above and think of objects that have them.

door	jam jar	keyboard	laptop	saucepan	shoe box	TV	vacuum cleaner

1 key ______________
2 handle ______________
3 lid ______________
4 plug ______________

3 VOCABULARY BANK

Cooking Verbs

bake

boil

chop

fry

grate

grill

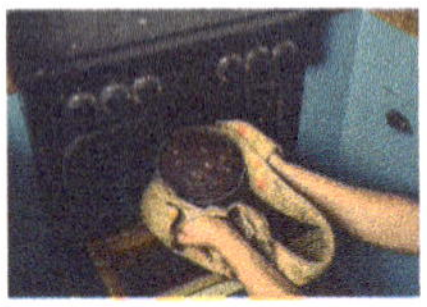
overcook

peel

roast

season

slice

spread

1 Put the verbs in the correct place so that this potato recipe makes sense.

First, [1]*overcook* the potatoes and [2]*peel* them into large pieces. Add two spoonfuls of oil and [3]*roast* them with some salt and pepper. [4]*Chop* the potatoes in the oven for 45 minutes, but be careful not to [5]*season* them!

1 ________ 2 ________ 3 ________ 4 ________ 5 ________

Quantities

a bag of	a cup of	a piece of	a slice of	a spoonful of
a chunk of	a handful of	a pinch of	a splash of	a sprinkle of

2 Match 1–5 with a–e.

1 This sauce isn't sweet enough. I'm going to add a spoonful of
2 I'm cooking tonight. We're having a lovely piece of
3 Grill the fish with a pinch of
4 I'm going to fry the potatoes with a splash of
5 The soup will be delicious because she's putting in a handful of

a sugar.
b oil.
c fresh herbs.
d beef.
e salt.

LEARN TO LEARN

Word Partners

When you learn new words, try to learn words that go with them so that you can use them in natural contexts.

3 Choose three quantities and think of four food items to go with each one. Compare with a partner.

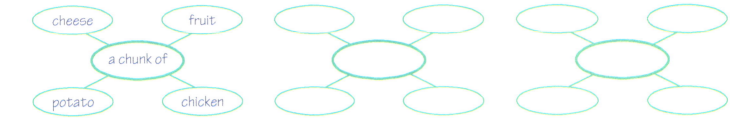

a chunk of: cheese, fruit, potato, chicken

4 VOCABULARY BANK

The Five Senses

feel	look	smell	sound	taste	touch
feel like	look like	smell like	sound like	taste like	

1 Complete the sentences with the words in the box.

a train delicious fresh bread icy stone

1 Has someone been baking? It smells like ________________ in here.
2 It's actually wood, but it's so cold, it feels like ________________.
3 I don't know what's in this dish, but it tastes ________________.
4 I heard a loud noise. It sounded a bit like ________________.
5 Be careful when you go outside. The pavement looks ________________.

Describing Texture, Sound, Taste, Etc.

colorful

faint

rough

sharp

shiny

smelly

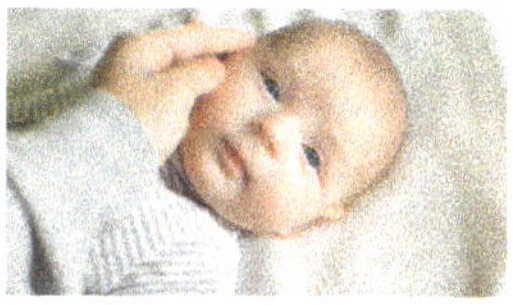
smooth

sour

spicy

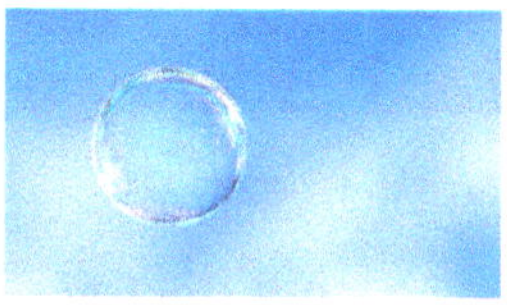
transparent

2 Match 1–5 with a–e.

1 You've worn that shirt for three days.
2 Be careful with that knife.
3 The noise can't be coming from this room.
4 Antonio washed his car yesterday.
5 I think it must be lemon juice.

a It tastes pretty sour.
b It's too faint.
c It must be a bit smelly.
d It looks very sharp.
e That's why it's so shiny.

LEARN TO LEARN

Using Your Senses

Using your senses can help you remember new words. Find objects that look, sound, taste, feel, or smell like the new words.

3 Choose three of the words from the list above and think of words connected to the senses.

shiny: shoes, hair, gold, metal, glass, car, clean

5 VOCABULARY BANK

Processes

attract	communicate	create	develop	produce	supply
collect	connect	deliver	measure	solve	waste

1 Match 1–5 with a–e.

1 The package was delivered
2 This course will help you to develop
3 The new factory will create
4 I need to collect
5 We hope the museum will attract

a hundreds of jobs.
b to the wrong house.
c more tourists to the area.
d some books from the library.
e your communication skills.

Extreme Adjectives

awful

boiling

deafening

enormous

fascinating

freezing

gorgeous

marvelous

stunning

terrifying

2 Put the letters in order to make extreme adjectives.

1 Before the electricity was connected, our house was *engefzir* in winter. ______
2 The crowd produced a *engafedni* noise. ______
3 They measured the bones and discovered that the creature was *eomosurn*. ______
4 It's *ufwal* to waste so much water. ______
5 She's able to communicate difficult ideas in a *nafsatingci* way. ______

LEARN TO LEARN

Personalizing New Vocabulary

Using personalized sentences helps you remember new vocabulary.

3 Choose four words from the list above and use them to write questions to ask your partner.

What is the most fascinating book you've ever read? *Treasure Island*

______
______
______
______

6 VOCABULARY BANK

Verb Collocations with *To Get*, *To Take*, and *To Have*

get a lot out of	get on my nerves	have fun	take an interest in
get bored	get to know	have the chance	take pleasure in
get lost	have doubts	take advantage of	take risks

1 Put the words in the correct order to make sentences.

1 better / know / to / I'd / her / get / like / to / . I think she's very interesting.

2 lot / Simon / course / got / a / of / the / out / . He said it was very useful.

3 the / at / picnic / you / did / fun / have / ? You certainly had good weather for it.

4 get / some / nerves / of / on / my / my / classmates / . They're really annoying.

Inspiration and Challenge

bravery (n)

challenge (n)

determination (n)

obstacle (n)

opportunity (n)

achieve (v)

encourage (v)

inspire (v)

overcome (v)

support (v)

2 Cross out the incorrect option in each sentence.

1 Harry managed to overcome the *problem* / *solution* / *obstacle*.
2 Mr. Olsen always tries to encourage his *students* / *children* / *happiness*.
3 Kristen has the determination to achieve her *salary* / *goals* / *ambition*.
4 I think we were all inspired by their *speech* / *bravery* / *disappointment*.

LEARN TO LEARN

Stress Patterns

Knowing the stress pattern of a word can help you pronounce it and recognize it when people say it.

3 Write the stress pattern for each word. The first one has been done for you.

1 bravery *Ooo* 2 encourage ______ 3 opportunity ______

7 VOCABULARY BANK

Feelings

amused

annoyed

down

eager

glad

grateful

hopeful

hurt

insecure

peaceful

ridiculous

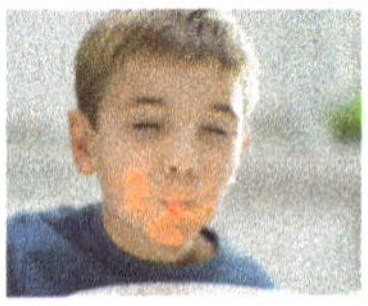
satisfied

thrilled

1 Complete the statements with the words in the box. Do you agree or disagree?

eager grateful insecure peaceful ridiculous

	Agree	Not Sure	Disagree
1 I feel ______ when friends remember my birthday.	☐	☐	☐
2 I feel a bit ______ about the future.	☐	☐	☐
3 I feel ______ in a hat.	☐	☐	☐
4 I am always ______ to try new experiences.	☐	☐	☐
5 I feel ______ when I am in the country.	☐	☐	☐

Expressions with *Heart* and *Mind*

be close to your heart
break someone's heart
learn by heart
bear in mind
change your mind
cross your mind
have something on your mind
make up your mind
put your heart into something
slip your mind

2 Circle the correct words.

1 Leaving my girlfriend behind in Australia *was close to my heart / broke my heart / changed my mind.*
2 I'm annoyed because you won't *make up your mind / learn by heart / cross your mind* about the party.
3 Winning was important to Max and he really *had it on his mind / bore it in mind / put his heart into it.*
4 I *changed my mind / crossed my mind / slipped my mind* about my project topic.

LEARN TO LEARN

Fill-in-the-Blank Flashcards

Using fill-in-the-blank flashcards can help you learn expressions.

3 Use the flashcards you made in class. Pick up a flashcard, look at the front, and make a sentence. Score two points for a correct sentence but lose a point if you look at the back.

I was going to go swimming but I ***changed my mind.***

8 VOCABULARY BANK

Advertising

ad	brand	logo	review
ad blocker	buyer	marketing company	seller
advertise	influence	product	slogan

1 Complete the sentences with a noun from the same word family as the verb.

1 They're looking for someone to buy their company. They want a __________.
2 Dan reviews hotels online. He writes __________.
3 They advertise on the London Underground. They have __________ there.
4 She has a factory that produces mugs. Its __________ is mugs.
5 I'm not influenced by celebrity vloggers. They don't have any __________ on me.

Internet Verbs

build up	delete	post	subscribe	switch on
comment on	follow	shut down	switch off	vlog

2 Use verbs from the list above to complete the questions. Ask and answer them.

1 Do you __________ anyone online?
2 What would influence you to __________ to an online magazine?
3 What subject does your favorite YouTuber __________ about?
4 Would you __________ an online comment if it upset a friend?
5 Do you ever __________ other people's posts?

LEARN TO LEARN

Collocations

When you learn a new verb, try to learn the nouns that go with it. This will help your English sound natural.

3 Match verbs 1–5 with nouns a–e to make collocations. Can you think of any other nouns that go with these verbs?

1 shut down	a followers
2 follow	b a post
3 build up	c a phone
4 switch off	d a vlogger
5 comment on	e an account

Reporting Verbs

admit	apologize	complain	deny	insist	refuse
announce	claim	confirm	discover	promise	suggest

1 Complete the sentences with the correct form of a reporting verb from the list above.

1 "I stole the money." She ______________ that she had stolen the money.
2 "The hotel was really dirty." My mother ______________ about the hotel.
3 "I'll definitely be back by nine o'clock." Samantha ______________ that she would be back by nine o'clock.
4 "I'm certainly not going to help." Adam ______________ to help us.
5 "I'm so sorry that I lied to you." Nate ______________ for lying.

Adverbs of Time and Manner

after a while	fluently	nowadays	patiently	secretly
eventually	gradually	occasionally	regularly	surprisingly

2 Circle the correct words.

1 They waited *secretly* / *patiently* / *gradually* for Max to arrive.
2 It was raining for hours but *eventually* / *regularly* / *nowadays* it stopped.
3 The food in the restaurant was *fluently* / *secretly* / *surprisingly* nice.
4 At first I found the lessons difficult, but *occasionally* / *after a while* / *regularly* I got better at them.
5 I went running every day and *fluently* / *patiently* / *gradually* I got fitter.

LEARN TO LEARN

Recording Words in Sentences

Writing down new words in a sentence helps you remember them.

3 Choose four words from the list above and write sentences that are true for you. Then tell your partner.

1 ______________________________
2 ______________________________
3 ______________________________
4 ______________________________

I usually drink coffee but occasionally I drink tea.

2 HISTORY

1 Look at the title and picture and discuss the questions.

1 When do you think this picture was taken?
2 Where are the people and what are they doing?

2.14 2 Read the text. Check your answer to question 2 in Exercise 1.

STARTING AGAIN

Between 1880 and 1910, 17 million Europeans made the decision to move to the United States and start a new life. Many of them never went back to their country of birth. This was part of what is known as the Great Atlantic **Migration**. It started in the 1840s and it is the largest migration in history.

For many people, it was the first time they had ever left their hometown. The two-week journey was very unpleasant, and on larger ships, up to 2,000 people were **crammed** into the lower **decks**. It was dark, there was little fresh water, and the air was **rancid**. So, why choose to go through such a difficult experience?

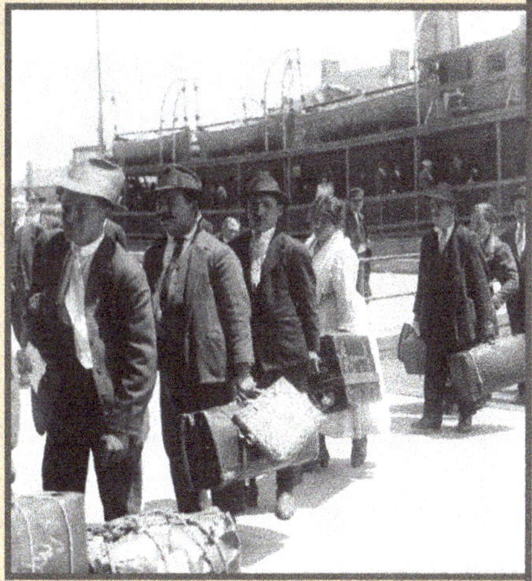

One major reason was hunger. For example, in Ireland in the 1840s, people used to depend on potatoes for food. When the potato crop failed for three years in a row, there was not enough to eat and around one million people died. After this, half of the Irish population decided to move to the United States. They were nervous about the journey, but they looked forward to a better life.

> I am exceedingly well pleased at coming to this land of plenty.
>
> *Letter from an Irish immigrant to* The Times, *London, 1850*

Immigrants from all over Europe had their own story to tell. Although they had never experienced life in the United States before, they arrived ready to **settle** in a new culture. Immigrants helped build the United States into the country it is today. Like all migrations, the Great Atlantic Migration is the story of people making difficult decisions for the chance to start again.

3 Read the text again. Write *T* (true), *F* (false), or *DS* (doesn't say).

1 Most immigrants to the United States eventually returned to their country of birth. ___
2 There wasn't much room on board the ships. ___
3 Poverty was a major reason for migration. ___
4 Irish immigrants felt hopeful about their future. ___
5 Immigrants from all over Europe moved for the same reasons as the Irish. ___
6 Immigrants made a positive contribution to American society. ___

4 Discuss other possible causes of migration throughout history and up to the present day.

5 Complete the definitions with the words in bold in the text.

1 ________ (n) the act of moving from one place to another
2 ________ (n) the floors of a ship
3 ________ (v) to make a home
4 ________ (v) to be filled with something so there is no more room
5 ________ (adj) having a very bad smell (or taste)

Explore It!

Guess the correct answer.

How many people live in a country different from the one they were born in?

a over 50 million
b over 150 million
c over 250 million

Find another interesting fact about migration. Write a question for your partner to answer.

Echolocation

Imagine you are walking with a flashlight through a forest at night. Suddenly, the light goes out and you cannot see a thing. You feel a branch brush your face and smell the leaves on the trees. You need to go home, but how can you find your way?

If you were a bat, you would use echolocation. Echolocation is a technique used by some animals to move around in the dark. It helps them identify friends and enemies and "see" where they are going. Here are two examples of how animals use it.

Bats

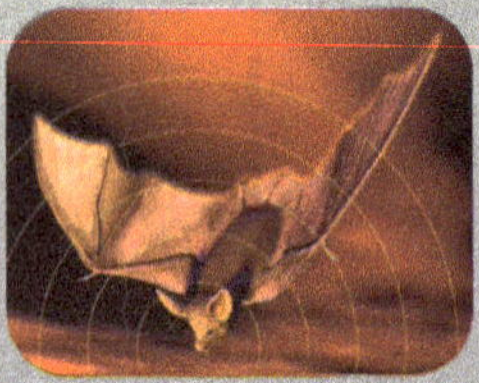

To hunt for insects in the dark, bats make a **high-pitched** call as they fly, then listen for the returning **echo**. They calculate how far away something is by how long it takes the echo to return. A bat can **detect** an insect in the dark from a distance of five meters!

Dolphins

To identify objects in deep, dark waters, dolphins produce high-frequency **clicks**. These create sound waves that **bounce back** as echoes. This information helps dolphins figure out the distance, direction of travel, speed, and size of things.

But you don't have to be a bat or a dolphin to echolocate. You might be surprised to learn that some humans can echolocate, too. One such person is Daniel Kish. Daniel is completely blind, so he gets information about what is around him by clicking his tongue and listening to the echo. This technique allows him to safely ride a bike or go hiking in the wild. He also trains other blind people to echolocate. Amazing, isn't it?

1 Discuss the questions.

1 What special skills do the animals in the pictures have?

2 What do they use these skills for?

2 Read the article. Check your answers to Exercise 1. 4.10

3 Complete the chart with information from the article.

	Sound	How It Helps
Bat		
Dolphin		
Daniel Kish		

4 Complete the text with the words in bold from the article.

Whales, like dolphins, produce [1] ________________ to figure out an object's distance, direction, speed, and size. These sounds can be low- or [2] ________________. The sounds hit an object and [3] ________________ to the whale's throat. The time it takes the [4] ________________ of these sounds to return to the whale helps the animal [5] ________________, or sense, what is around it.

Explore It!

Guess the correct answer.

Some bats have a scream as loud as a …

a jet engine 30 meters away.

b very loud opera singer.

c machine that breaks rocks.

Find another interesting fact about bats, whales, or echolocation. Write a question for your partner to answer.

6 CITIZENSHIP

1 Discuss the questions.

1 What is digital citizenship?
2 How can the way we use technology affect our relationships with people?

6.12 2 Read the article. Check your ideas in Exercise 1.

3 Read the nine themes of digital citizenship and mark (✓) the ones that apply to each case study. Some apply to both and some to neither.

Nine Themes of Digital Citizenship	CS1	CS2
1 Have equal access to technology.		
2 Buy and sell safely online.		
3 Share information safely.	✓	✓
4 Learn how to use technology appropriately.		
5 Follow an ethical code of conduct.		
6 Use technology lawfully.		
7 Act responsibly.		
8 Promote physical and psychological well-being.		
9 Protect online safety.		

4 Discuss the questions in the case studies in the article.

5 Complete the sentences with the correct form of the words in **bold** from the article.

1 That is a very ______________ photo. You look great!
2 You cannot ______________ some websites to be safe. You should check your online privacy.
3 Please don't ______________ me. Turn off your phone and listen to what I am saying.
4 I am going to ______________ how often I use social media. I want to use it less.
5 He is always very polite and ______________ when he sends messages.

Digital Citizenship: Case Studies

Today's citizens can make the most of living, learning, and working in a digital world. However, this brings responsibilities as well as opportunities, as these digital citizens need to act in a safe, legal, and ethical way. Digital citizenship is similar to traditional citizenship in that it means being kind, **respectful**, and ready to take part in activities that make the world a better place.

If teens take risks with the way they use digital devices, it could lead to problems. These case studies illustrate some common situations.

Case Study 1

Some friends are having fun at the beach. Later, one of them posts photos of the others online. She does not ask permission and some of the pictures are not very **flattering**. If you had been in possession of these photos, what would you have done?

Case Study 2

A group of friends is sitting in a café. One of them gets a call on his phone. He answers the call, **ignores** his friends, and has a loud, personal conversation in front of them. How would you feel if you were in the group?

The way these people use technology raises serious questions about **trust**, friendship, and social relationships.

Digital citizenship involves many things, from sharing information safely to acting responsibly online. If we want to get the best out of a fast-changing world, we should **monitor** our digital habits. In this way, we can meet the challenge of becoming good digital citizens.

Explore It!

Guess the correct answer.

In an average lifetime, people will spend … on social media.

a one year and two months
b three years and five months
c five years and four months

Find another interesting fact about the digital world. Write a question for your partner to answer.

8 ART AND DESIGN

1 Discuss the questions.

1 Where do you see print ads?
2 How do print ads communicate their messages?
3 What are the main elements of a print ad?

8.11 **2 Read the article. Check your ideas in Exercise 1.**

How to Design an Effective Print Advertisement

We are surrounded by print ads. When we walk down the street, there are slogans, logos, and images everywhere. Think about how many ads you have seen today. How many of them can you actually remember?

Marketing companies, which are responsible for advertising campaigns, charge a lot of money for their services. Therefore, a printed message needs to effectively communicate a brand's image. In fact, the person who creates an ad is a communicator more than a designer. So, how is an **effective** print ad designed?

The **headline** is the most important element. An ad has approximately two seconds to catch the reader's eye, so the headline needs to be clear and focus on one idea. A **subhead**, which still needs to be brief, can then give more information.

Next is the image. Sometimes an image can become the center of attention and distract from the message of a print ad. The headline and image need to work well together, and it is essential that the image is relevant to the product. Also, advertising research shows men and women respond to images differently. Many advertisers use brighter colors in ads for women and darker shapes in ads for men.

Once an ad has these features, it is time to decide on a final **layout**. The top-to-bottom layout in the picture, which is widely used, is very effective. Most ads try to influence potential buyers by putting the most important information at the top.

A good ad tells us we need things that previously we didn't even know existed. Next time you walk down a street full of print ads, think about how effective they are.

3 Complete the sentences with your own ideas.

1 Marketing companies need to effectively communicate a brand's image because …
2 A headline is the most important element of a print ad because …
3 An image should not be the main focus of a print ad because …
4 Different images are used for men and women in print ads because …

4 Choose an idea and turn it into a headline of three or four words for an ad.

1 This toothpaste will leave your mouth fresh and your teeth white.
2 You must buy these jeans because they are more comfortable and cheaper than others.

____

____

5 Complete the definitions with the words in bold in the article.

1 ______________ (n) the design of something
2 ______________ (n) the title written in big letters
3 ______________ (n) a heading that comes after the headline
4 ______________ (adj) successful

Explore It!

Guess the correct answer.

More than … a year is spent on advertising.

a $6 billion b $60 billion c $600 billion

Find another interesting fact about advertising. Write a question for your partner to answer.

PRONUNCIATION

UNIT 1

The Letters *ea*

1.08 **1 Listen and repeat.**

1 /e/ bread 2 /iː/ meat 3 /eɪ/ steak

2 Put the words in the correct column according to the pronunciation of the letters ea.

~~break~~ clean great head jeans please

/e/	/iː/	/eɪ/
		break

1.09 **3 Listen, check, and repeat.**

UNIT 2

Used To

2.04 **1 Listen and repeat.**

1 He used to go out with his friends every weekend.
2 Did you use to like cats when you were younger?

2.05 **2 Listen to the sentences. Are the words in bold pronounced the same in each sentence?**

1 She **used a** friend's phone to call her parents.
2 She **used to** have her mom's phone.

2.06 **3 Listen and write the sentences.**

1 ______________________
2 ______________________
3 ______________________
4 ______________________

4 Practice saying the sentences.

1 She used to play basketball after school.
2 My dad used to listen to classical music.
3 Did you use to live here?

2.07 **5 Listen and check.**

UNIT 3

The Letters *ch*

3.03 **1 Listen and repeat.**

1 /ʃ/ machine 2 /tʃ/ cheese 3 /k/ school

2 Put the words in the correct column according to the pronunciation of the letters *ch*.

~~chef~~ chemistry chop lunch mechanic mustache parachute stomachache such which

/ʃ/	/tʃ/	/k/
chef		

3.04 **3 Listen, check, and repeat.**

UNIT 4

Weak Form of *To*

4.06 **1 Listen and repeat.**

1 He has to work late tonight.
2 I need to buy new shoes.
3 We ought to take an umbrella.

4.07 **2 Listen and underline the stressed words.**

1 I'd like to know what time the movie starts.
2 We have to leave early tomorrow.
3 You ought to study more for your exams.
4 Do you need to make a phone call?

4.07 **3 Listen, check, and repeat.**

UNIT 5

The Letters *mb* and *bt*

5.07 **1 Listen and repeat.**

1 She's a climber. 2 I doubt he's coming.

2 Circle the silent *b* in each sentence.

1 I had a dream about a bomb.
2 I don't have any debts.
3 He hurt his thumb with a hammer.
4 I saw a sheep with two lambs.

5.08 **3 Listen, check, and repeat.**

UNIT 6

Stress in Multi-Syllable Words

6.02 **1 Listen and repeat.**

1 temperature 2 different 3 comfortable

6.03 **2 Underline the stressed syllable in each word. Listen and check.**

1 interesting 4 several 7 vegetable
2 Wednesday 5 chocolate 8 memorable
3 business 6 favorite

3 Identify the sounds in the words in Exercise 2 that are not pronounced.

1 interesting

4 Practice saying the words in Exercise 2.

UNIT 7

Initial Consonant Clusters with *s*

7.07 **1 Listen and repeat.**

1 stress 3 strength
2 strong 4 straight

7.08 **2 Listen and repeat the tongue-twisters.**

1 **Strong** winds **spread** the sparks through the **streets**.
2 Stella has **straight** hair and **stripes** on her skirt.
3 Stuart **sprayed** his phone with a **screen** cleaner.

7.09 **3 Listen, repeat, and practice the words in bold from the tongue-twisters.**

UNIT 8

The Letters *-tion*

8.04 **1 Listen and repeat.**

1 /ʃən/ celebration 2 /tʃən/ suggestion

2 Look at the *-tion* ending in the words. Write *1* (/ʃən/) or *2* (/tʃən/).

1 competition 1 5 vacation ___
2 digestion ___ 6 question ___
3 creation ___ 7 exhaustion ___
4 solution ___

8.05 **3 Listen, check, and repeat.**

4 Answer the questions.

1 What's your idea of the perfect celebration?
2 What question would you like to ask your favorite celebrity?
3 Where would you go for your ideal vacation?

UNIT 9

The Letters *cia*

9.02 **1 Listen and repeat.**

1 social 3 musician 5 commercial
2 sociable 4 special

2 Practice saying the words.

1 magician 4 politician
2 beneficial 5 mathematician
3 artificial

9.03 **3 Listen, check, and repeat.**

4 Student A reads a definition. Student B says the correct word from Exercises 1 or 2.

1 When someone likes meeting new people.
2 Someone who likes numbers.
3 Something good and useful.
4 Someone who plays an instrument.
5 Not real or natural.
6 Someone who pulls a rabbit out of a hat.

IRREGULAR VERBS

Infinitive	Simple Past	Past Participle
be	was/were	been
beat	beat	beaten
become	became	become
begin	began	begun
bite	bit	bitten
blow	blew	blown
break	broke	broken
bring	brought	brought
build	built	built
buy	bought	bought
catch	caught	caught
choose	chose	chosen
come	came	come
cost	cost	cost
cut	cut	cut
do	did	done
draw	drew	drawn
drink	drank	drunk
drive	drove	driven
eat	ate	eaten
fall	fell	fallen
feel	felt	felt
fight	fought	fought
find	found	found
fly	flew	flown
forget	forgot	forgotten
get	got	gotten
give	gave	given
go	went	gone
grow	grew	grown
hang	hung	hung
have	had	had
hear	heard	heard
hide	hid	hidden
hit	hit	hit
hold	held	held
hurt	hurt	hurt
keep	kept	kept
know	knew	known
leave	left	left
lend	lent	lent

Infinitive	Simple Past	Past Participle
let	let	let
lie	lied	lied
light	lit	lit
lose	lost	lost
make	made	made
mean	meant	meant
meet	met	met
pay	paid	paid
put	put	put
read	read	read
ride	rode	ridden
ring	rang	rung
rise	rose	risen
run	ran	run
say	said	said
see	saw	seen
sell	sold	sold
send	sent	sent
shine	shone	shone
shoot	shot	shot
show	showed	shown
shut	shut	shut
sing	sang	sung
sit	sat	sat
sleep	slept	slept
speak	spoke	spoken
spend	spent	spent
stand	stood	stood
steal	stole	stolen
swim	swam	swum
take	took	taken
teach	taught	taught
tear	tore	torn
tell	told	told
think	thought	thought
throw	threw	thrown
understand	understood	understood
wake	woke	woken
wear	wore	worn
win	won	won
write	wrote	written

ACKNOWLEDGEMENTS

The authors and publishers acknowledge the following sources of copyright material and are grateful for the permissions granted. While every effort has been made, it has not always been possible to identify the sources of all the material used, or to trace all copyright holders. If any omissions are brought to our notice, we will be happy to include the appropriate acknowledgements on reprinting & in the next update to the digital edition, as applicable.

Key: **CLIL** = Content and Language Integrated Learning; **SU** = Starter Unit; **U** = Unit, **VB** = Vocabulary Bank

Text

U1: Text about Moziah Bridge. Copyrighyt © Adriann Ranta Zurhellen. Reproduced with permission; **U4:** Text about Jordy Cernik. Copyright © Peter Cernik MA aka Jordy. Reproduced with kind permission; Text about Neil Harbisson. Copyright © Neil Harbisson. Reproduced with kind permission; Text about surfer Bethany Hamilton. Copyright © Becky Hamilton. Reproduced with kind permission.

Photography

The following photographs are sourced from Getty Images.

SU: danchooalex/E+; Dave and Les Jacobs/Blend Images; Django/E+; jhorrocks/E+; Vostok/Moment; Lennart Schreiber/EyeEm; Hill Street Studios/Blend Images; yayayoyo/iStock/Getty Images Plus; YasnaTen/iStock/Getty Images Plus; Tigatelu/iStock/Getty Images Plus; Elizabeth Parsons/EyeEm Premium; sbk_20d pictures/Moment; Yavuz Meyveci/iStock Editorial/Getty Images Plus; arabianEye arabianEye; vetdoctor/iStockphoto/Getty Images Plus; U1: Westend61; Henrik Sorensen/Stone; Ryan Smith/Corbis; jhorrocks/E+; Halfpoint/iStock/Getty Images Plus; Timur Emek/Getty Images Entertainment; by Lili Ana/Moment Open; Artur Debat/Moment Mobile; Maciej Frolow/The Image Bank; Sidekick/E+; Pascal Deloche/Godong/Corbis Documentary; Chris Ryan/OJO Images; Andy Crawford/Dorling Kindersley; khvost/iStock/Getty Images Plus; GeorgePeters/E+; Paul Simcock; jboater/iStock/Getty Images Plus; Feifei Cui-Paoluzzo/Moment; Leon Bennett/WireImage; mocoo/iStock/Getty Images Plus; ozgurdonmaz/iStock/Getty Images Plus; Jenny Jones/Lonely Planet Images/Getty Images Plus; Erik Isakson; **U2:** Jennifer Perry/EyeEm; mantaphoto/E+; Mark Daffey/Lonely Planet Images; KIKILOMBO/iStock/Getty Images Plus; alejandrophotography/iStock/Getty Images Plus; plherrera/E+; Emanuele Ravecca/EyeEm; Science Photo Library; luoman/E+; Spod/iStock/Getty Images Plus; Steve Shott/Dorling Kindersley; Gregory_DUBUS/iStock/Getty Images Plus; DNY59/E+; Oleg Golovnev/EyeEm; Westend61; Betsie Van der Meer/Stone; ajr_images/iStock/Getty Images Plus; pixdeluxe/iStock/Getty Images Plus; LisaAFischer/iStock/Getty Images Plus; H. Armstrong Roberts/ClassicStock/Archive Photos; Allan Tannenbaum/Archive Photos; Michael Ochs Archives; funky-data/E+; baona/E+; mocoo/iStock/Getty Images Plus; cjmacer/iStock Editorial/Getty Images Plus; **U3:** WIN-Initiative; tgasser/iStock/Getty Images Plus; Jamie Grill/The Image Bank; Andreas Schlegel; Capelle.r/Moment; xujun/Moment; mikroman6/Moment; EasterBunnyUK/iStock/Getty Images Plus; Valentyn Semenov/EyeEm; © 2011 Dorann Weber/Moment Open; Caliphoto/iStock/Getty Images Plus; mikroman6/Moment; Blend Images - JGI/Jamie Grill; Eskay Lim/EyeEm; Jamie Stamey/iStock/Getty Images Plus; Ian Cuming/Ikon Images; NosUA/iStock/Getty Images Plus; D-Keine/E+; Andrey Suslov/iStock/Getty Images Plus; Sirikunkrittaphuk/iStock/Getty Images Plus; Creativ Studio Heinemann; Slawomir Tomas/EyeEm; Maximilian Stock Ltd./Photographer's Choice; Hayley Harrison/The Image Bank; Dorling Kindersley; Pierre-Yves Babelon/Moment; Nickilford/E+; William Whitehurst/Corbis; Klaus Vedfelt/DigitalVision; Maskot; Maica/iStock/Getty Images Plus; Tetra Images; Diana Miller/Cultura; Peter Cade/The Image Bank; marilyna/iStock/Getty Images Plus; Tobias Titz; Hauke Dressler/LOOK-foto/LOOK; Melanitta/iStock/Getty Images Plus; Jami Tarris/Corbis Documentary; GMVozd/E+; Image Source; Rosemary Calvert/Photographer's Choice; Tanya Zouev/StockFood Creative; Neustockimages/iStock/Getty Images Plus; Tim Platt/The Image Bank; Westend61; Rasulovs/iStock/Getty Images Plus; WoodyUpstate/iStock/Getty Images Plus; Joff Lee/Photolibrary; mocoo/iStock/Getty Images Plus; petekarici/E+; Jbryson/iStock/Getty Images Plus; boonsom/iStock/Getty Images Plus; **U4:** Dmytro Ponomarenko/EyeEm; Huntstock; cnicbc/iStock/Getty Images Plus; Tetra Images; Andy Sotiriou/Photodisc; Tai/Moment; Raimund Linke/Oxford Scientific; bugphai/iStock/Getty Images Plus; Jamie Brand/EyeEm; Ian O'Leary/Dorling Kindersley; DragonImages/iStock/Getty Images Plus; bergamont/iStock/Getty Images Plus; Stephen Stickler/Photographer's Choice; Douglas Sacha/Moment; Natthakan Jommanee/EyeEm; Sam Edwards/Sam Edwards; Danita Delimont/Gallo Images; Jutta Klee/Canopy; Jacqui Hurst/Photolibrary; hphimagelibrary/Gallo Images; IAN HOOTON/Science Photo Library; Christian Adams/Photographer's Choice; Coleman515/iStock/Getty Images Plus; kiankhoon/iStock/Getty Images Plus; c11yg/iStock/Getty Images Plus; Buena Vista Images/DigitalVision; AVIcons/iStock/Getty Images Plus; Amin Yusifov/iStock/Getty Images Plus; appleuzr/DigitalVision Vectors; Bruce Mclean/EyeEm; mocoo/iStock/Getty Images Plus; Marko Stavric Photography/Moment/Getty Images Plus; Elena Pueyo/Moment; Arrow/DigitalVision; manoa/Moment; Alberto Ghizzi Panizza/Biosphoto; Davies and Starr/The Image Bank/Getty Images Plus; Mkucova/iStock/Getty Images Plus; **U5:** Andyworks/iStock/Getty Images Plus; Peter Schaefer/EyeEm; urfinguss/iStock/Getty Images Plus; Fabien_Gouby/iStock/Getty Images Plus; DiyanaDimitrova/iStock/Getty Images Plus; pskeltonphoto/Moment; chombosan/iStock/Getty Images Plus; Kitti Boonnitrod/Moment; HandmadePictures/iStock/Getty Images Plus; Ringo_Wong_hkherper/iStock/Getty Images Plus; Michele Falzone/Photographer's Choice; Stígur Már Karlsson/Heimsmyndir/E+; Stefan Cristian Cioata/Moment; Marko Stavric Photography/Moment/Getty Images Plus; Robin-Angelo Photography/Moment; Olivia ZZ/Moment; Nitish Waila/iStock/Getty Images Plus; IndiaPictures/Universal Images Group; kajornyot/iStock/Getty Images Plus; Amos Chapple/Lonely Planet Images; mocoo/iStock/Getty Images Plus; Anton Jankovoy/Moment; kdshutterman/iStock/Getty Images Plus; Shin Okamoto/Moment; Dorling Kindersley; Satyan Chawla/500px Prime; **U6:** dennisvdw/iStock/Getty Images Plus; Philip Lee Harvey/The Image Bank; egon69/E+; Noel Hendrickson/DigitalVision; Andersen Ross Photography Inc/DigitalVision; Igor Emmerich/Cultura; Scott Sansenbach - Sansenbach Marine Photo/Moment; Lawrence Lucier/FilmMagic; Blend Images - Erik Isakson; dtiberio/iStock/Getty Images Plus; SolStock/E+; Juice Images Ltd; Frank Wijn/Moment Open; mocoo/iStock/Getty Images Plus; **U7:** martin-dm/E+; bestdesigns/iStock/Getty Images Plus; BrianAJackson/iStock/Getty Images Plus; Thomas Del Brase/Photographer's Choice/Getty Images Plus; Spohn Matthieu/PhotoAlto Agency RF Collections; SasinParaksa/iStock/Getty Images Plus; KatarzynaBialasiewicz/iStock/Getty Images Plus; doble-d/iStock/Getty Images Plus; Maskot; mocoo/iStock/Getty Images Plus; Ismailciydem/iStock/Getty Images Plus; **U8:** Juanmonino/iStock/Getty Images Plus; Maskot; Hero Images; JohnnyGreig/E+; filo/DigitalVision Vectors; Milkos/iStock/Getty Images Plus; SPL IMAGES/Photographer's Choice; monkeybusinessimages/iStock/Getty Images Plus; photo/iStock/Getty Images Plus; mocoo/iStock/Getty Images Plus; Julian Kreler/EyeEm; Westend61; robertiez/iStock/Getty Images Plus; **U9:** Hero Images; XiFotos/E+; Westend61; sarah5/iStock/Getty Images Plus; photosindia; kelly bowden/Moment; Westend61; mocoo/iStock/Getty Images Plus; LazingBee/iStock/Getty Images Plus; **F1:** Anthony Lee/OJO Images; vgajic/E+; Rafael Ben-Ari/The Image Bank; Imgorthand/E+; -VICTOR-/DigitalVision Vectors; **F4:** Nenov/Moment Open; Christopher Daley/500px; MirageC/Moment; PhotoAlto/Odilon Dimier/PhotoAlto Agency RF Collections; **VBS:** Asia-Pacific Images Studio/iStock/Getty Images Plus; Watchara Panyajun/EyeEm; majaiva/E+; Caiaimage/Sam Edwards; LeoPatrizi/E+; Kentaroo Tryman/Maskot; **VB1:** domin_domin/iStock/Getty Images Plus; mawielobob/iStock/Getty Images Plus; Tarzhanova/iStock/Getty Images Plus; kitthanes/iStock/Getty Images Plus; Floortje/E+; Lalouetto/iStock/Getty Images Plus; Mehmet Hilmi Barcin/E+; FlamingPumpkin/iStock/Getty Images Plus; Rermrat Kaewpukdee/EyeEm; Ng Sok Lian/EyeEm; **VB2:** Karl Tapales/Moment; JuergenBosse/iStock/Getty Images Plus; Melanie Hobson/EyeEm; kk2s/iStock/Getty Images Plus; MartinPrescott/E+; Gado Images/Photodisc; TARIK KIZILKAYA/E+; Jorge Alberto Bohorquez Suarez/EyeEm; LeMusique/iStock/Getty Images Plus; Somsak Bumroongwong/EyeEm; **VB3:** tirc83/iStock/Getty Images Plus; Westend61; UpperCut Images; Paula ./FOAP; KucherAV/iStock/Getty Images Plus; dlewis33/E+; Lucy Lambriex/DigitalVision; Adam Radosavljevic/EyeEm; lolostock/iStock/Getty Images Plus; uuurska/iStock/Getty Images Plus; Lakshmi3/iStock/Getty Images Plus; Capelle.r/Moment; **VB4:** Dalia Rady/EyeEm; Imagevixen/RooM; DragonFly/iStock/Getty Images Plus; Pierre-Yves Babelon/Antananarivo, Antananarivo Province, Madagascar; Mike Whitby/EyeEm; malerapaso/E+; stockstudioX/E+; Stefka Pavlova/Moment; Theerapan Bhumirat/EyeEm; luknaja/iStock/Getty Images Plus; **VB5:** Mike Korostelev www.mkorostelev.com/Moment; Johannes Hulsch/EyeEm Premium; RapidEye/E+; Vicki Jauron, Babylon and Beyond Photography/Moment; sturti/E+; Marina Malikova/500px; Alex Barlow/Moment Open; MaximShebeko/iStock/Getty Images Plus; Baac3nes/Moment; apomares/E+; © Marco Bottigelli/Moment; **VB6:** Muhammad Faidz Zainal Abidin/EyeEm; Indeed; deimagine/E+; BJI/Blue Jean Images; Sam Edwards/Caiaimage; PhotoAlto/Eric Audras/PhotoAlto Agency RF Collections; digitalskillet/iStock/Getty Images Plus; Chris Whitehead/Cultura; Caiaimage/Martin Barraud; Ricardo Lim/Moment Unreleased; **VB7:** Plume Creative/DigitalVision; slavemotion/E+; Paul Bradbury/OJO Images; Tom Merton/Caiaimage; moodboard/Cultura; MediaProduction/E+; Elva Etienne/Moment; Mordolff/E+; Mint

Images - Tim Robbins; Jose Luis Pelaez Inc/DigitalVision; xavierarnau/E+; Daisy-Daisy/iStock/Getty Images Plus; Emilija Manevska/Moment; **VB8:** littleny/iStock Editorial/Getty Images Plus; LeoPatrizi/E+; **VB9:** mikroman6/Moment; Maskot; **CLIL2:** Bettmann; Thinkstock Images/Stockbyte; **CLIL4:** VICTOR HABBICK VISIONS/SCIENCE PHOTO LIBRARY; **CLIL6:** SeventyFour/iStock/Getty Images Plus; Anna_leni/iStock /Getty Images Plus; **CLIL8:** paseven/iStock/Getty Images Plus.

The following photographs are sourced from other libraries/sources:

U1—U9: Carboxylase/Shutterstock; **U4:** Copyright © Peter Cernik MA aka Jordy; Copyright © Neil Harbisson.

Cover design and illustrations: Collaborate Agency

Illustration

U2, U8, U9, EM: Claire Rollet (Illustration Web); **U2, U4:** Joanna Kerr; **SU, U5:** Sean Longcroft.

Video Stills

The following stills are sourced from Getty Images:

US: Feng Wei Photography/Moment; **U1:** Alexander Spatari/Moment; FG Trade/Creatas Video; Merlas/iStock/Getty Images Plus; **U2:** RWP UK/DigitalVision; Sirinarth Mekvorawuth/EyeEm; Getty Images/EyeEm; taavet/Creatas Video+; **U3:** Neustockimages/Creatas Video+; Besjunior/iStock/Getty Images Plus; andresr/Creatas Video; **U4:** nattanan726/Creatas Video+; gpointstudio/Creatas Video+/Getty Images Plus; yacobchuk/iStock/Getty Images Plus; **U5:** Schroptschop/Creatas Video; dottedhippo/iStock/Getty Images Plus; Marko Stavric Photography/Moment; Barry Kusuma/DigitalVision; **U6:** Westend61; Anita Bunk/EyeEm; helivideo/Creatas Video+; Westend61; Hill Street Studios/DigitalVision; © Randy Faris/Corbis/VCG; **U7:** Rost-9D/Creatas Video+; urbazon/E+; Jose Luis Pelaez Inc/DigitalVision; silverkblack/Creatas Video+; **U8:** Stusya/Creatas Video+; Kevin Dodge; LeoPatrizi/E+; **U9:** FilmColoratStudio/Vetta; Grafissimo/E+; Karl Weatherly/Corbis Documentary; Maskot; Eastfootage/Image Bank Film.

Video production: Lucentum Digital

Audio Recordings: Eastern Sky Studios

Typesetting: Aphik, S.A. de C.V.

Contributing authors: Daniel Vincent, Liz Walter, and Kate Woodford

Versioner: Suzanne Harris

American English Consultant: Multimodal Media

Freelance Editors: Mandie Drucker, Penny Nicholson, Cara Norris-Ramirez, and Rebecca Raynes

The authors and editors would like to thank all the teachers and consultants who have contributed to the development of the course, in particular:

Mexico: Ana Belem Duran; Nelly Marina Elizalde; Julio Andrés Franco Del Campo; Nimbe García Haro; Raoul Josset Paquette; Adriana Maldonado Torres; Ana Edith Ramos Ramírez

Brazil: Beatriz Affonso; Alessandra Bautista; Ana Carolina De Luca; Esdras Fattobene; Maria Claudia Ferreira; Itana Lins; Maria Helena Meyer; Valéria Moraes Novoa; Odinéia Morandi; Regina Pedroso De Araujo; Andrea Perina; Simone Rodrigues; Jacqueline Saback; Clice Sales; Silvia Teles

Turkey: Belgün Akçelik; Peggy Alptekin; Hayri Arslan; Ayşe Aylin Kündüroğlu; Nihan Çalışkan; Selin Dinçkal Erkenci; Bengü Özbek; Saliha Şimşek

SHAPE IT! 4 COMBO

WORKBOOK

Eoin Higgins and Philip Wood

CAMBRIDGE
UNIVERSITY PRESS

CONTENTS

STARTER

WELCOME!

VOCABULARY AND READING

Travel

1 ☆ **Match the words with the definitions.**

accommodation backpacking resort sightseeing tourist attractions ~~trip~~

1 a journey where you visit a place for a short time and then come back again _trip_
2 visiting places that are interesting because they are historical, famous, etc. ______
3 traveling or walking, carrying your things in a bag on your back ______
4 monuments or places that people on vacation like to visit ______
5 a town or place where people go on vacation, very often next to the ocean ______
6 a place where you live or stay ______

2 ☆ **Complete the sentences with information that is true for you. (See the *Learn to Learn* tip in the Student's Book, p4.)**

1 ______ is a famous tourist attraction in my country.
2 For our accommodation on our last vacation, we stayed in ______.
3 ______ is a popular resort in my country.
4 The last trip I went on was to ______.
5 In my opinion, going backpacking is a ______ way to spend your vacation.
6 I would like to go sightseeing in ______.

Music and Theater

3 ☆☆ **Complete the text. The first letter of each word is given.**

I was very surprised when Ms. Bayliss gave me the biggest [1]_part_ in the school musical. It wasn't easy to learn all my [2]l______, but after several [3]r______, I knew them perfectly. I was nervous on the day of the [4]s______ because my whole family was in the [5]a______. But everything went well, and after the final [6]s______, everyone stood up and clapped!

An Interview

4 ☆ **Read the interview. What did Jed do on vacation? Choose the correct photo.**

a

b

MIA So, where did you go on vacation, Jed?
JED Italy – it was a fantastic trip!
MIA Did you stay at a resort?
JED No, it was a hotel. We did a lot of sightseeing. We went to some famous tourist attractions, like the Colosseum in Rome. It was amazing!
MIA So, what was the best part of your trip?
JED Oh, that was when we saw an opera: *The Barber of Seville* in the Teatro Argentina – it's almost 300 years old! It's an amazing place – so beautiful!
MIA But wasn't the opera in Italian?
JED Yes, it was, and most of the audience was Italian, but there were subtitles.

5 ☆☆ **Read the interview again and answer the questions.**

1 Where did Jed stay?
______
2 What did Jed think of the Colosseum?
______
3 What else did Jed do in Rome?
______
4 Why could Jed understand the opera?
______

GRAMMAR IN ACTION AND VOCABULARY

Past and Present, Simple and Continuous

1 ★★ **Write the sentences in the past.**

1 Dan is reading the paper.

Dan was reading the paper.

2 They aren't listening to music.

3 Am I making a lot of noise?

4 Beth usually plays soccer on Saturdays.

5 They don't live in an apartment.

6 Does Michael like school?

2 ★★ **Complete the conversation with the verbs in the box in the correct tense.**

~~be~~ do enjoy have help visit

A How [1] *was* your trip to Paris?

B Great, thanks! I [2] ______ it a lot!

A What [3] ______ you ______ there?

B We [4] ______ a lot of tourist attractions!

A You're so lucky! While you [5] ______ a great time in Paris, I [6] ______ my dad paint the house!

3 ★★★ **Answer the questions with information that is true for you.**

1 What did you do last weekend?

2 What were you doing at nine o'clock last night?

3 What does your dad do?

4 What's your mom probably doing at the moment?

Ways of Communicating

4 ★ **Circle eight more communication verbs in the word snake.**

(post)shoutwhisperdescribesmiletranslateshakehandsgreetwave

5 ★★ **Complete the chart with the verbs from Exercise 4. Some verbs go in both columns.**

You Can Use Your Hands to Do This	You Can Use Your Mouth to Do This
1 *post*	6
2	7
3	8
4	9
5	10
	11

6 ★★ **Complete the sentences with the verbs from Exercise 4.**

1 Do you know anyone who can *translate* from English into Chinese?

2 Did you ______ a comment on my blog?

3 Please don't ______! I can hear you!

4 How would you ______ your personality?

5 When you ______, you feel happier.

6 If you don't know the answer when the teacher asks you, I'll ______ it to you very quietly.

7 When movie stars arrive at the Oscars, they often ______ to the crowd.

8 When I have my interview tomorrow, how should I ______ the person who is interviewing me? Should I ______ with them?

LISTENING AND GRAMMAR IN ACTION

A Conversation

a

b

c
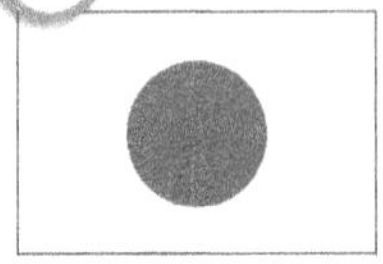

1 ☆☆ **Match the flags a–c with the countries 1–3.**

1 Spain ____ 2 Japan ____ 3 the U.S.A. ____

2 S.01 ☆ **Listen to the conversation. Which of the countries from Exercise 1 does the girl's dad sometimes go to?**

____

3 S.01 ☆☆ **Listen again. Put the pictures a–f in the order that they are mentioned.**

a

b

c

d

e

f

1

4 ☆☆☆ **Answer the questions.**

1 Which country would you like to visit? Why?

____

2 Would you like to travel a lot for your job? Why?

____

3 Do you think people smile a lot in your country? Give a reason for your answer.

____

Present Perfect and Simple Past

5 ☆ **Complete the sentences with the words in the box. There are two extra words.**

at ever for from ~~have~~ never 's since

1 *Have* you finished the book?
2 We've been here ______ four o'clock.
3 Have you ______ been to Japan?
4 John's studied French ______ three years.
5 I've ______ seen snow before.
6 Beth ______ sent me a message.

6 ☆☆ **Circle the correct options.**

1 Last year, I *went* / *'ve been* to London.
2 *Did you ever climb* / *Have you ever climbed* a mountain?
3 My sister *liked* / *'s liked* chocolate since she was a baby.
4 I *didn't do* / *haven't done* my homework. I'm going to start now!
5 I *called* / *'ve called* you just a minute ago!
6 We *were* / *'ve been* at the mall for three hours now!

7 ☆☆ **Complete the text with the simple past or present perfect form of the verb in parentheses.**

TO: Aidan
FROM: Paola

Hi Aidan,

I [1] *'ve been* (be) in Rome for almost a week now. I [2] ______ (arrive) last Friday. My Italian [3] ______ (not get) much better, which isn't very surprising, really. I need more time. I [4] ______ (do) a lot of sightseeing! Yesterday I [5] ______ (go) to the Vatican. The museum is incredible! I [6] ______ (eat) some very good food because the woman I'm staying with is a great cook. Last night she [7] ______ (make) *cannelloni al ragù*. Tomorrow, I start at the language school. I [8] ______ (not feel) so happy or excited for a long time!

Love, Paola

WRITING

An Informal Email

1 **Read Jack's email to his friend Ethan. Which two of the activities in the pictures a–c did he do?**

a 

b 

c 

TO: Ethan@postit.com
FROM: Jack@comunica.com
SUBJECT: News!

[1]Hi Ethan,

1 [2]How are things? Are you enjoying life in Mexico? [3]I just wanted to get in contact because I haven't sent you an email for a long time. Sorry about that!

2 I've been really busy lately. I'm in the school play, and we've had a lot of rehearsals after school. I have a big part, so it hasn't been easy to learn all my lines! But I think I've finally managed to do it. I hope so because the play's next week! Have you ever done any acting? Perhaps you can give me some advice!

3 Last Saturday was my dad's 50th birthday, so he took us all out for a meal in a really nice restaurant in the country. All his brothers and sisters came, and everyone gave him a present. I gave him a D.C. United soccer scarf because he's a big fan. I think he liked it!

4 So, that's my news. When are you coming back to visit?

[4]Bye for now!

[5]Take care,

Jack

2 **Read the email again. Match the paragraphs (1–4) with the information (A–D).**

A say goodbye ☐
B things Jack has done recently ☐
C things Jack did at a particular time ☐
D say hello and why you're writing ☐

3 **Look at paragraphs 2 and 3 again. What tenses does Jack use to describe his actions? Why?**

____

____

____

4 **Match the underlined phrases in the email 1–5 with the phrases a–e.**

a Love, ☐
b I'm writing to ☐
c Hello ☐
d See you soon! ☐
e How are you? ☐

PLAN

5 **Write an email to a friend in the U.S.A., telling them what you've done recently. Make two lists.**

1 Things I've done when the exact time is not important or that are not finished (present perfect):

____

____

____

____

2 Things I did at a particular time (simple past):

____

____

____

____

WRITE

6 **Write your email. Remember to include four paragraphs, your ideas from Exercise 5, vocabulary from this unit, and phrases from the *Useful Language* box (see Student's Book, p9).**

CHECK

7 **Do you ...**

- start and end the email correctly?
- give the reason why you are writing?
- use verbs in the correct tense?

1 What is fashion?

VOCABULARY

Describing Clothes and Shoes

1 ☆ Circle the correct adjectives to describe the clothes.

1 

a *cotton* / *denim* skirt (denim circled)

2 

a *tight* / *baggy* sweater

3 

a *plain* / *checkered* shirt

4 

baggy / *high-heeled* boots

5 

a *striped* / *flowery* T-shirt

6 

a *long-sleeved* / *polka-dot* dress

2 ☆☆ Complete the conversations with the words in the box. There are two extra words.

cotton	checkered	denim	flowery
high-heeled	leather	long-sleeved	~~tight~~

1 A Are those shorts OK?
  B No, I need a bigger size. They're very *tight*!

2 A Do you want a plain or a checkered T-shirt?
  B No, I want something really different! That ______ one is nice!

3 A What do you usually wear in the summer?
  B Cool clothes made of ______!

4 A Do you like my new black and white ______ shirt?
  B Not really! It looks like a chess board!

5 A Are you going to pack some jeans for your trip to Córdoba?
  B Are you joking? It's 40°C there at the moment! I don't want to wear anything made of ______!

6 A How often do you wear ______ shoes?
  B Not often. Only when I go to a party or formal dinner.

3 ☆ Match the adjectives 1–5 with the categories a–c. (See the *Learn to Learn* tip in the Student's Book, p11.)

1 baggy, tight — c
2 checkered, striped
3 denim, cotton
4 high-heeled, long-sleeved
5 plain, polka-dot

a material
b pattern
c shape

4 ☆☆ Put the words in the correct order.

1 a / checkered / red and green / shirt
a red and green checkered shirt

2 a / skirt / denim / plain

3 jeans / cotton / tight / white

4 jacket / denim / red / baggy / a

5 striped / brown and blue / T-shirt / a / tight / cotton

6 brown and white / shoes / leather / polka-dot / high-heeled

5 ☆☆☆ Write four sentences about clothes that you like and don't like to wear. Use adjectives from Exercise 1.

Explore It!

Guess the correct answer.

In what decade did miniskirts become popular?

a the 1950s b the 1960s c the 1970s

Find another interesting fact about popular fashion in a past decade. Write a question and send it to a classmate in an email, or ask them in the next class.

READING

A Blog Entry

1 ☆ **Look at the text quickly and circle the correct answers.**

1 The text is a *an advertisement* / *a personal opinion*.

2 It's about *how often to wash jeans* / *what jeans to buy*.

2 ☆☆ **Read the blog entry. Check the meaning of the words in the box in a dictionary. Then complete the sentences.**

brand	claim	~~eliminate~~	harm	research	turn out

1 Cheese gives me a headache. I need to *eliminate* it from my diet.

2 Don't wash that shirt in very hot water. It will definitely ______ the material!

3 I'm going to do some ______ before I buy a new phone.

4 I like these jeans, but I don't know this ______. Is it any good?

5 Some people ______ that shopping online is 100 percent safe, but I'm not so sure.

6 I'm making a dress, but I have a feeling that it's not going to ______ well.

3 ☆☆ **Are the sentences *T* (true) or *F* (false)? Correct the false sentences.**

1 In the writer's opinion, the question of how often to wash jeans is very important.
F It's not the most important topic in the world.

2 The writer agrees with her friend about how often to wash jeans.
______

3 In the writer's opinion, an important person in the clothing industry has a strange idea.
______

4 Freezing jeans is a good way to clean them.
______

5 It's best not to wash your jeans too often.
______

6 The experts make a good recommendation.
______

4 ☆☆☆ **Do you think the information in the blog entry is useful and interesting? Why / Why not?**

______

______

NEW YORK CALLING! | **BLOG** | ABOUT ME | CONTACT ME

TO WASH OR NOT TO WASH JEANS? THAT IS THE QUESTION!

I haven't written an entry recently because I've been taking exams all week! Did you miss me? Today, I want to talk about a very important subject: how often to wash denim jeans! OK, maybe it's not the most important topic in the world, but people have very different ideas about it. One of my friends even thinks that you should never wash jeans because it harms them. I don't know about that! Imagine wearing a pair of tight jeans that you haven't washed for over a year! So, anyway, I decided to do some research online about how often you should actually wash jeans. One thing I read really surprised me: the head of a company that makes a very well-known brand of jeans says that he hardly ever washes his. He just puts them in the freezer. He claims that this keeps them clean! Speaking personally, I wouldn't want to put my jeans next to a bag of frozen peas! And it turns out that the "freezer theory" isn't correct. After you wear your jeans just once, they're covered in bacteria, skin cells, and the natural oils from your body. And freezing them won't eliminate these things. According to the experts, there is one good reason for not washing your jeans very often: they get a little baggier every time you wash them. And most of us don't want to wear baggy jeans! Experts actually say there's no specific recommended frequency for washing jeans – but you should definitely wash them when they start to smell! That sounds like good advice to me!

GRAMMAR IN ACTION

Present Perfect Simple and Present Perfect Continuous

1 ☆☆☆ **Match the beginnings of the sentences 1–6 with the ends a–f.**

1 I've done [b]
2 Jack's been playing soccer [ ]
3 Have they had [ ]
4 You've been wearing [ ]
5 Bethany hasn't been going [ ]
6 Has your dad finished cleaning [ ]

a that shirt all week!
b all my homework.
c the bathroom?
d for three hours!
e lunch yet?
f to the gym recently.

2 ☆☆☆ **Complete the sentences with the verbs in parentheses. Use the present perfect simple (PPS) or present perfect continuous (PPC).**

1 We *haven't made* (not make) lunch yet. (PPS)
2 I ______ (do) a lot of clothes shopping recently. (PPC)
3 Ana ______ (visit) her family. (PPC)
4 ______ (they / finish) the game? (PPS)
5 My tablet ______ (not work) all day. (PPC)
6 My aunt ______ (have) a lot of different jobs. (PPS)

3 ☆☆☆ **Circle the correct options.**

1 I've *felt* / *been feeling* very tired recently.
2 John hasn't *answered* / *been answering* my last email.
3 Rachel isn't here. Has she *gone* / *been going* shopping?
4 Our neighbors have *made* / *been making* a lot of noise.
5 Why have *you bought* / *you been buying* three baggy sweaters?
6 *Did you study* / *Have you been studying* for your exams all week?

4 ☆☆☆ **Write sentences in the present perfect simple or continuous.**

1 what / you / do / recently?
What have you been doing recently?
2 I / finish / finally / my school project!
______
3 Nick / wear / the same clothes / all week.
______
4 you / ever / be / to Los Angeles?
______
5 I / try / to contact you / all day!
______
6 Jan / not decide / what to do
______

5 ☆☆☆ **Complete the messages with the correct form of the verbs in the box.**

find	go shopping	~~look for~~	not buy	try on	wait

You [1] *'ve been looking for* a dress for the party for a long time! [2] ______ you ______ anything yet? Maxine

No! And I [3] ______ for hours! I [4] ______ six different dresses, but I [5] ______ anything yet! Sarah

Well, I [6] ______ for you in the café for too long! I'm leaving! Maxine

6 ☆☆☆ **Write a sentence about something that you have or haven't done before and a sentence about something that you have or haven't been doing recently.**

I've never been to Seattle.
I've been playing a lot of video games recently.
______
______
______
______

VOCABULARY AND LISTENING

Verbs Related to Clothes and Shoes

1 ☆ **Circle the correct options.**

1 These pants are very tight. They don't *fit* / *look good on* me.

2 Can you please *hang* / *fit* up the pants over there?

3 Could you help me *unzip* / *fold* my dress. I want to take it off.

4 People will still wear jeans in 100 years. They will never *wear out* / *go out of style*.

5 Do these shoes *go with* / *wear out* this dress?

6 You look great with those earrings. They really *match* / *look good on* you!

2 ☆☆ **Complete the text with words and phrases from Exercise 1.**

HOW TO LOOK GOOD!

- Some clothes [1] *go out of style* quickly! So, don't wear something that was popular last year!
- Your clothes must [2] ______ you perfectly! Don't buy something that you really like if it isn't the right size!
- Buy clothes with "easy" colors that [3] ______ a lot of other colors.
- Know what kinds of clothes [4] ______ you! Some people look great in stripes – but do you?
- Don't [5] ______ your clothes and put them in drawers. It's much better if you [6] ______ them ______.

3 ☆☆☆ **Write sentences that are true for you. (See the *Learn to Learn* tip in the Student's Book, p14.)**

1 How quickly do you wear out your clothes?

______

2 Do all your clothes fit you well? Give details.

______

3 What colors look good on you? Why?

______

4 Do you ever wear clothes that have gone out of style? Why / Why not?

______

An Interview

1.01 **4** ☆ **Listen to Caitlin talking about her job as a salesperson. Put the things she talks about in the correct order.**

a ☐ the bad points of the job

b ☐ the good points of the job

c ☐ why she wanted to work as a salesperson

1.01 **5** ☆☆ **Listen again and circle the correct options.**

1 Why did Caitlin decide to work as a salesperson in a clothing store?

a She wants to work as a fashion designer.

b She's very interested in clothes.

c She likes helping people.

2 What are Caitlin's coworkers like?

a They're nice.

b Some are nice; some aren't.

c She really likes her boss.

3 What happens every one or two months?

a She buys clothes at a discount.

b She helps with window displays.

c New clothes arrive at the store.

4 How much of a discount does Caitlin get?

a 15 percent

b 50 percent

c It depends on the clothes.

5 What are two negative aspects of the job?

a Some of the jobs are a bit boring, and the pay isn't very good.

b Some of the customers can be rude, and you're standing up all the time.

c Some customers aren't polite, and not all the jobs are interesting.

GRAMMAR IN ACTION

Modifiers

1 ☆ **Read the phrases and (circle) the options that have the same meaning.**

1 absolutely wrong
   (a) totally wrong   b a bit wrong
2 fairly nice
   a extremely nice   b pretty nice
3 a lot more difficult
   a a bit more difficult   b far more difficult
4 a bit bigger
   a a little bigger   b far bigger
5 extremely tired
   a pretty tired   b really tired
6 pretty far
   a fairly far   b extremely far

2 ☆☆ **Look at the information from a price comparison website. Are the sentences *T* (true) or *F* (false)?**

1 Exclu jeans are extremely expensive. T
2 Exclu jeans are far more expensive than Basic Co jeans. ______
3 Basic Co jeans aren't really cheap. ______
4 Wright Brothers jeans are a bit less expensive than Exclu jeans. ______
5 Basic Co jeans are pretty expensive. ______

3 ☆☆ **(Circle) the correct options.**

1 These pants aren't "a little" baggy. They're *pretty* / (*extremely*) baggy!
2 Your watch was a bit more expensive than mine, but it's *a little* / *far* better! It's fantastic!
3 I'm *pretty* / *really* hungry, but I'm not very hungry.
4 The weather was *a bit* / *far* hotter than we imagined. It was a big surprise.
5 Mike's *fairly* / *really* generous. I think he's the most generous person I know.
6 I'm *fairly* / *totally* sure that the store's closed today, but maybe I'm wrong.

4 ☆☆ **Complete the conversation with the missing words. (Circle) the correct options.**

A How was your vacation in San Sebastian?
B Only [1] ______ good, I'm afraid.
A So, not [2] ______ fantastic?
B No. The weather was [3] ______ terrible. It rained all the time!
A Oh, no! What about the food? I've heard it's fantastic there – [4] ______ better than the food in the U.S.A.!
B Yes, it was [5] ______ delicious! I think it was [6] ______ more expensive than the U.S.A., but my dad said the prices weren't too bad.

1	a totally	(b) fairly	c far
2	a a lot	b fairly	c absolutely
3	a really	b a bit	c a little
4	a pretty	b far	c a little
5	a absolutely	b pretty	c a lot
6	a far	b really	c a bit

5 ☆☆☆ **Complete the sentences so they are true for you. Use modifiers from this page.**

1 Living in my hometown is ______.
2 My family is ______.
3 For me, buying clothes is ______.
4 When I compare English and math, I think English is ______.
5 In my opinion, soccer is ______.
6 When I compare drinking water or soda, I think ______.

WRITING

A Blog Comment

FIVE WAYS TO SPEND LESS MONEY ON CLOTHES

- Go to secondhand stores!
- Buy your clothes online!
- Swap clothes with friends!
- Only buy clothes on sale!
- Buy clothes with neutral colors (black, gray, or white). They'll go well with all your other clothes!

Great post! Thanks for sharing! TBH, I've always thought that buying clothes online was a bit dangerous. I mean, what happens if you get something and it doesn't fit you? That's a problem! But since reading your post, I've looked at some online clothing sites, and they really help you find the right size. What's more, some of the clothes are extremely inexpensive, especially if you buy from China or Hong Kong! I've just bought a flowery dress online, and it fits me perfectly! It's absolutely amazing! Sonya

Your post really got me thinking about how to save money on clothes! I've been spending too much recently, so it's become a BIG problem! IMO, going to secondhand stores is a really good idea. I had no idea that they had such great stuff! I thought they only had clothes that were out of style! I've already bought a great denim shirt and a cool polka-dot T-shirt. And I've decided to get all my clothes from secondhand stores in the future! They're far cheaper! Aidan

1 **Read the blog entry and the comments and answer the questions.**

1 What is the blog entry about?

2 Which ideas from the blog have Sonya and Aidan used?

2 **Read the comments again and answer the questions in your notebook.**

1 What do *TBH* and *IMO* mean?

2 Why does Sonya use an exclamation point in: *It's absolutely amazing!* ?

3 Why does Aidan use capital letters in: *It's become a BIG problem!* ?

3 **Complete the *Useful Language* phrases. Look at the underlined phrases in the blog for help.**

1 You really *got* me thinking about how much I spend.

2 I've been thinking and I've ______ to go shopping far less often.

3 Great ______ ! Thanks for ______ !

4 I had ______ that buying online was so easy!

5 ______ reading your post, I've really started to think about how I shop.

PLAN

4 **Write your own blog comment. Choose one of the five ideas from the blog entry and take notes about these things.**

Do you like the idea? Why / Why not? ______

Other ideas you would like to try in the future: ______

WRITE

5 **Write your comment. Remember to include the present perfect simple and continuous, modifiers, vocabulary from this unit, phrases from the *Useful Language* box (see Student's Book, p.17), and the features from Exercise 2.**

CHECK

6 **Do you ...**

- explain why an idea might or might not work well?
- explain what you would like to try in the future?

1 REVIEW

VOCABULARY

1 Complete the crossword. Use the clues.

ACROSS →

2 ________ pants
3 ________ shirt
6 ________ scarf
7 ________ - ________ dress
9 ________ sweater
10 ________ jeans
11 ________ skirt

2
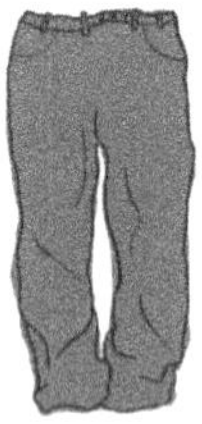

3

6

7

9

10

11

DOWN ↓

1 ________ - ________ shoes
4 ________ - ________ top
5 ________ skirt
6 ________ T-shirt
8 ________ shoes

1

4

5

6

8

2 Complete the sentences with the words in the box.

fit fold go out of style go with hang up look good on match unzip wear out zip up

1 I don't think these shoes will ________ soon. Sneakers are always popular.
2 You need to ________ your coat. It's very cold!
3 These shorts don't ________ me now, but they weren't too small last year!
4 Do you think these earrings ________ the color of my eyes?
5 I never wear brown. It doesn't ________ me.
6 I only ________ shirts when I pack a bag. I always ________ them ________ at home.
7 That shirt doesn't ________ those pants. They look terrible together!
8 You can ________ the zipper on the tent. It isn't raining anymore.
9 Those are nice shoes, so please don't play soccer in them. You'll ________ them ________ very quickly!

GRAMMAR IN ACTION

3 Complete the sentences with the present perfect simple or continuous form of the verbs in parentheses.

1 I ________________ (not see) that movie. Is it good?

2 Claudia ________________ (try) to buy tickets all afternoon!

3 Oh, no! I ________________ (lose) my earring!

4 Dan ________________ (never / play) chess.

5 I ________________ (finish)! I'm sorry you ________________ (wait) so long.

6 ________________ (we / buy) everything we need?

4 Read the conversations and circle the correct options.

1 **A** How was the party?
  B It was *really* / *pretty* good, but not amazing.

2 **A** Did you enjoy the movie!
  B Yes, it was *fairly* / *absolutely* amazing!

3 **A** How are you feeling?
  B Only *a little* / *a lot* better.

4 **A** Did you do well on your exams?
  B My results were *extremely* / *pretty* good, but they weren't fantastic.

5 **A** This school project is hard!
  B Yes, it is! It's *fairly* / *far* harder than Ms. Taylor said!

6 **A** I'm the best player on the team!
  B I'm sorry, but you're *fairly* / *totally* wrong about that!

CUMULATIVE LANGUAGE

5 Complete the email with the missing words. Circle the correct options.

TO: Amy | FROM: Zoe

Hi Amy,

How are you? I'm sorry that I [1] ______ for a while. I have a lot of news! I [2] ______ a course in fashion design, and it [3] ______ really well! I [4] ______ on a dress with a flowery design all week. I [5] ______ it because it's [6] ______ hard work. But I love it!

I [7] ______ that I want to work as a fashion designer in the future. I think it would be a [8] ______ awesome job – and [9] ______ more interesting than working in an office! How about you? [10] ______ life in Chile? Your Spanish must be [11] ______ fantastic now because it was [12] ______ good before!

Anyway, talk to you soon!

Zoe

	a	b	c
1	haven't written	haven't been writing	don't write
2	've been starting	start	've started
3	's gone	goes	's been going
4	work	've been working	've worked
5	haven't finished	don't finish	haven't been finishing
6	far	a little	really
7	decide	've decided	've been deciding
8	fairly	far	totally
9	far	pretty	a bit
10	Do you enjoy	Have you been enjoying	Have you enjoyed
11	a bit	a lot	absolutely
12	pretty	well	a lot

2 What can you change?

VOCABULARY

Phrasal Verbs: Changes

1 ☆☆ **Circle the correct options.**

1 Max has settled *down* / *up* well at his new school.

2 I'm really *looking* / *seeing* forward to next weekend.

3 I'm going to sign *up* / *down* for yoga classes.

4 Let's *try* / *do* out the new skate park.

5 I'm *having* / *going* through a hard time at the moment.

6 Are you going to turn *up* / *down* Juan's invitation?

2 ☆☆ **Complete the sentences with the phrasal verbs in the box.**

do without	end up	go back
move out	~~sign up~~	turn out

1 Did you ___sign up___ for the school trip to San Diego?

2 The party didn't ______ very well in the end. Not many people came.

3 My sister wants to ______ and be more independent.

4 If you don't work hard at school, you probably won't ______ with a good job.

5 I don't think I could ______ chocolate! I love it!

6 I probably won't ______ to my hometown when I finish college.

3 ☆☆☆ **Complete the personality quiz with the correct form of the verbs in the box and the correct prepositions.**

do   go   look forward   ~~move~~   move   sign   try   turn

Are You a Positive Person?

1 Would you like to ___move out___ of your family's home before you're 25?

2 In your life, do things usually ______ well?

3 When you are ______ a hard time, do you look for solutions?

4 Do you ______ for a lot of optional activities at school?

5 Do you like to ______ new ways of doing things?

6 When you get up, do you always ______ everything you will do in the day?

7 Would you like to ______ a new country?

8 Could you ______ the Internet for a week?

4 ☆ **Answer *Yes* or *No* to the questions from Exercise 3. How positive are you?**

7–8 *yes* answers: very positive!

5–6 *yes* answers: fairly positive!

Less than 5 *yes* answers: not very positive!

5 ☆☆☆ **Write four sentences with phrasal verbs about what kind of person you are. (See the *Learn to Learn* tip in the Student's Book, p23.)**

______

______

______

______

Explore It!

Guess the correct answer.

What is the minimum age when you can start working in the U.S.A. without your parents' permission?

a 14   b 16   c 18

Find an interesting fact about when you can legally do something for the first time in your country. Write a question and send it to a classmate in an email, or ask them in the next class.

READING

A Blog Entry

1 ☆ **Look at the blog entry quickly. Why is Chloe's life new? Mark (✓) the correct answer.**

a She's just gotten married. ☐
b She's in college now. ☐
c She's just finished college. ☐

2 ☆☆ **Read the blog entry and check the meaning of the words in the box in a dictionary. Then complete the sentences.**

~~disappointed~~ into law lecture plenty of surrounded

1 I did badly on my exams. I'm really *disappointed* !
2 I'm really ______ comic books. They're my favorite thing to read.
3 The campsite was ______ by trees, so it was very beautiful.
4 My cousin's studying ______. He says it's a lot of work.
5 I know ______ people, but do I have any real friends?
6 I've just been to a really interesting ______.

3 ☆☆ **Read the first paragraph of the blog entry and answer the questions. Write "no information" if there is no answer in the text.**

1 Which college does Chloe go to?

2 What does Chloe mean when she says that you "have to start from zero"?

3 Why are things turning out well?

4 ☆☆ **Read the second paragraph of the blog entry and complete the chart.**

	Studying in High School	Studying in College
1	*classes in small groups*	
2		
3		

5 ☆☆☆ **Do you think it's a good idea to study away from home? Write three or four sentences.**

CHLOE'S CORNER BLOG ABOUT FAQS

A NEW LIFE!

Have you ever had a really special time in your life? Well, I'm having one now because I've just started college! I was really looking forward to it, and so far, I haven't been disappointed! My biggest worry before coming was: would it be easy to make new friends? It's a good question because when you go to college, you have to start from zero. The old friends you used to see at home aren't there anymore, so you need to create a completely new social life. Well, I'm glad to say that things are turning out really well. I'm living in a dorm, which is a special building just for students. It's the ideal place to be during your first year because you're surrounded by new faces! And everyone's into making new friends.

Studying in college feels very different from how things used to be in high school. Although there were a lot of students in my high school, there are over 100 students in my lectures now! In high school, we would have the chance to ask questions and discuss things with our teachers. Now you just sit down and take notes! Another big difference is that I only have 12 hours of lectures per week (I'm studying law). The rest of the time I spend studying alone. That can be pretty difficult because you need a lot of discipline! And there are plenty of other, more interesting things to do!

I've settled down really well into college life. There's just one "small" problem: I need to study more!

GRAMMAR IN ACTION

Used To, *Would*, and Simple Past

1 ☆☆ Complete the sentences with the correct form of *used to* and the verbs in parentheses.

1 I used to hate (hate) going to the dentist.
2 My dad ______ (have) more hair.
3 I ______ (not like) carrots.
4 My mom ______ (not go) to the gym.
5 ______ (you / play) the violin?
6 ______ (Matt / be) your best friend?

2 ☆☆ Rewrite the sentences with *used to* when it is possible.

1 I went to bed at ten o'clock last night.
not possible
2 In the past, did your grandpa ride a bike to work?
______
3 People went to the movies more often before the Internet.
______
4 Clothes didn't wear out so quickly before.
______
5 Oh, no! Did you leave the keys at home?
______
6 Was there a castle in this town before?
______

3 ☆☆☆ Write four sentences about what people *used to* and *didn't use to* do. Use the photos for ideas.

1
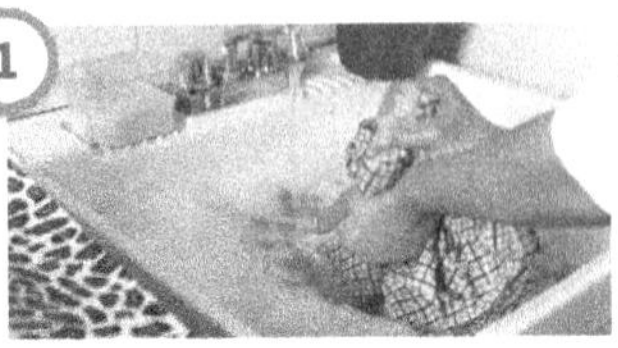
2

3

4

1 ______
2 ______
3 ______
4 ______

4 ☆ (Circle) the correct options.

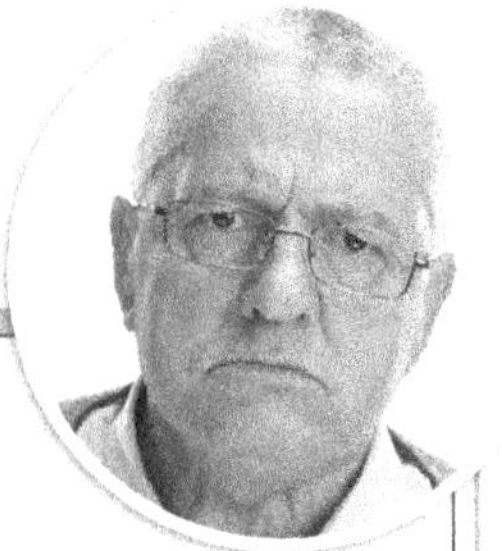

Things Were Different When I Was Young!

Children [1](would)/ *wouldn't* listen to their parents and teachers. Now they don't listen!
People [2]*would* / *wouldn't* run everywhere. They had more time.
We [3]*would* / *wouldn't* play in the street. It wasn't dangerous then.
People [4]*would* / *wouldn't* think about money all the time. They had better values.
Families [5]*would* / *wouldn't* go to another country on vacation. And some families didn't go anywhere!
We [6]*would* / *wouldn't* listen to the radio more because not everyone had a TV.

5 ☆☆ Rewrite the underlined part of the sentences with *would*. If it isn't possible, rewrite the sentences with *used to*.

1 <u>We lived</u> in the country before.
We used to live in the country.
2 <u>I often arrived</u> late to school when I was younger.
______
3 <u>Did you wear</u> glasses before?
______
4 <u>My grandma always went</u> for a walk after breakfast.
______
5 <u>My dad often swam</u> in the ocean when he lived in Salvador.
______
6 <u>My mom was</u> a nurse before.
______

6 ☆☆ (Circle) the correct option OR options.

A [1]*Did you take* / *Did you use to take* tennis lessons?
B Yes, I did.
A So, why [2]*did* / *would* you stop?
B My teacher [3]*would* / *used to* criticize me all the time. So one day I [4]*decided* / *used to decide*, "No more tennis lessons!"
A Really? I [5]*didn't* / *didn't use to* know anything about that! Who [6]*did you* / *did you use to* take lessons with?
B My dad!

VOCABULARY AND LISTENING

Parts of Objects

1 ☆ **Find nine more parts of objects in the word search.**

B	O	L	S	L	E	N	S
H	B	U	T	T	O	N	D
A	C	O	R	D	O	W	P
N	R	C	A	B	O	E	L
D	I	M	P	Z	A	Y	U
L	L	C	O	V	E	R	G
E	I	H	K	E	Y	O	U
T	D	I	S	P	L	A	Y

2 ☆☆ **Complete the sentences with words from Exercise 1.**

1 Oh, no! A *strap* on my backpack has broken.

2 There's a problem with the ______ on my phone. It's very dark.

3 These photos have turned out badly because the ______ on my camera was dirty.

4 Let's carry this bag together. You take one ______ and I'll take the other.

5 Where's the ______ for the saucepan?

6 Is this the ______ for charging your phone?

7 This ______ on my laptop is for changing the audio volume.

8 The ______ of this book looks really great, but the book wasn't very interesting!

9 You need to attach this ______ to the printer.

3 ☆☆☆ **Write a description of a "mystery object." Use at least four of the words from Exercise 1. Send your description in an email to a classmate, or ask them to guess the object in the next class.**

It has a display and it has one or two buttons, but it doesn't have a plug. It doesn't have a handle, but it has a strap. What is it?

A Conversation

2.01 **4** ☆ **Listen to a conversation about the past between Katie and her grandma. Mark (✓) the things they mention.**

1 a plug ✓

2 a calculator ☐

3 a video cassette ☐

4 a TV ☐

5 a camera ☐

6 a PowerPoint presentation ☐

5 ☆ **Underline the key words in the sentences. (See the *Learn to Learn* tip in the Student's Book, p26.)**

1 Katie is going to work on a history project. *F*

2 Her grandma thinks that young people spend too much time using "technological things." ______

3 Katie's grandma didn't use a calculator in school. ______

4 There weren't many shows on TV before. ______

5 Katie thinks that life before sounds fun. ______

6 When her grandma was in school, each student had a small blackboard to write on. ______

2.01 **6** ☆☆ **Listen again. Are the sentences in Exercise 5 *T* (true) or *F* (false)?**

7 ☆☆☆ **What three modern inventions could you not do without?**

GRAMMAR IN ACTION

Past Perfect with *Never, Ever, Already, By (Then), By the Time*

1 ☆ **Read the sentences and underline the action that happened first.**

1 I <u>had already had lunch</u> when my sister arrived.
2 My sister had already gotten married by the time she was 20.
3 Dan wasn't happy because I had turned down his invitation.
4 By the time the game ended, we had scored five goals!
5 We had walked a very long way by the time we found the river.

2 ☆☆ **Match the beginnings of the sentences (1–5) with the ends (a–e).**

1 I had never seen snow [c]
2 We had only been at the hotel a few minutes when [ ]
3 Had you ever run more than 5 km [ ]
4 By the time my grandpa settled in the U.S.A., [ ]
5 We had already been to six different stores [ ]

a by the time Clara decided to buy something.
b before today?
c before I went to Sierra Nevada.
d he'd lived in six different countries.
e the storm started.

3 ☆☆ **Put the words in the correct order to make sentences.**

1 car / seen / had / the / already / .
I had already seen the car.
2 had / then / back / by / come / .
Jack ______
3 called / woken up / you / I / when / already / ?
Had ______
______
4 Europe / never / year / had / last / been / I / to / .
Before ______
5 then / a snake / ever / you / before / seen / ?
Had ______
______

4 ☆☆ **Complete the sentences with the simple past or the past perfect form of the verbs in parentheses.**

1 Pablo had never taken (never / take) guitar lessons before he gave (give) his first concert.
2 ______ (Sean / ever make) lasagna before yesterday?
3 School ______ (already / start) when I ______ (arrive).
4 By the time Sara ______ (leave) England, she ______ (learn) to speak English very well.
5 I ______ (never / feel) real terror until I ______ (see) that movie!
6 ______ (everyone / already / go) to bed by the time the fire ______ (start)?

5 ☆☆☆ **Complete the text with the simple past or the past perfect form of the verbs in parentheses.**

Emma [1] moved (move) to a new school last year. By the time she [2] ______ (be) there a couple of weeks, she [3] ______ (already / settle) down very well. And now things are going even better! Last week, she [4] ______ (become) the captain of the school soccer team.

She [5] ______ (be) very happy about this because she [6] ______ (always / want) to be the team captain. And yesterday she [7] ______ (receive) her exam results. More good news! She [8] ______ (never / get) such good grades before!

6 ☆☆☆ **Complete the sentences with your own ideas. Use the past perfect.**

1 Before this year, I ______
2 We didn't win the game because we ______
______
3 I signed up for karate lessons because ______
______
4 By the time Ella finished college, ______
______
5 Alan was going through a hard time because ______
______

WRITING

An Opinion Essay

1 ☆ **Look at the essay quickly. Does the writer think that life used to be better in the past?**

____

2 ☆☆ **Read the essay and answer the questions. Mark (✓) and circle the correct answers.**

1 In which TWO paragraphs does the writer give ideas to support their opinion?

A ☐ B ☐ C ☐ D ☐

2 In paragraph A, the writer …
- a asks the reader a question.
- b gives their opinion.

3 In paragraph D, the writer …
- a repeats their opinion.
- b asks the reader a question.

3 ☆☆ **Complete the essay with the *Useful Language* phrases in the box.**

~~first~~	in addition	in conclusion	second	therefore	this means that

4 ☆☆ **What different words or phrases does the writer use to avoid repeating items 1–4 below?**

1 in the past (paragraph B)

____

2 better (paragraph B)

____

3 situation (paragraph B)

____

4 look at (paragraph D)

____

5 ☆☆ **Complete the sentence.**

In paragraphs B and C, to describe life in the past, the writer uses the simple past, ______________, and ______________.

Did Life Use To Be Better?

A Older people often say that, in the past, life used to be better. However, in my opinion, this is simply not true.

B [1] ___First___, let's look at the situation of women. In the old days, many men (and some women) used to think that a woman's role in life was to be a mother and to do the housework and the cooking. Fortunately, attitudes have changed a lot since then! [2] ______________ women today are in a much more favorable position.

C [3] ______________, the number of very poor people around the world has decreased significantly in the last 20 or 30 years. [4] ______________, healthcare has improved in poor countries. In the past, many children would die when they were still very young in those places. This happens far less often now. [5] ______________, we can talk about huge change in two very important areas.

D [6] ______________, the world today is a much better place. If we examine the facts, no one would want to go back to "the golden past." This past only exists in some people's imaginations. It never existed in reality.

PLAN

6 ☆☆ **Write an opinion essay. Look at the statement. Write down three reasons why you agree or disagree with it.**

> It's more important to speak English today than in the past.

____

____

____

WRITE

7 ☆☆☆ **Write your opinion essay. Remember to include four paragraphs and examples of *used to*, *would*, the simple past, the past perfect, and the *Useful Language* phrases from Exercise 3.**

CHECK

8 **Do you …**
- give your opinion?
- give reasons for your opinion?
- summarize your opinion?

2 REVIEW

VOCABULARY

1 Rewrite the second sentence so that it has a similar meaning to the first. Use the phrasal verbs in the box and any other words you need.

do without	go back	go through	look forward to	move to	settle down	try out	turn down

1 Let's return to the bus station.
Let's ______ the bus station.

2 I'm very excited about the concert on Saturday.
I'm ______ the concert on Saturday.

3 I have to take a shower every morning.
I can't ______
every morning.

4 I'm sorry, but I can't accept your invitation.
I'm sorry, but I have to ______.

5 Mike's adapting well to life in Milan.
Mike's ______ in Milan.

6 Beth isn't enjoying life at all right now.
Beth is ______ a hard time right now.

7 Jose used to live in California, but he went to live in New York.
Jose ______ New York.

8 Let's see what this new video game is like!
Let's ______ video game!

2 Complete the crossword. Use the picture clues.

Down ↓

1

2
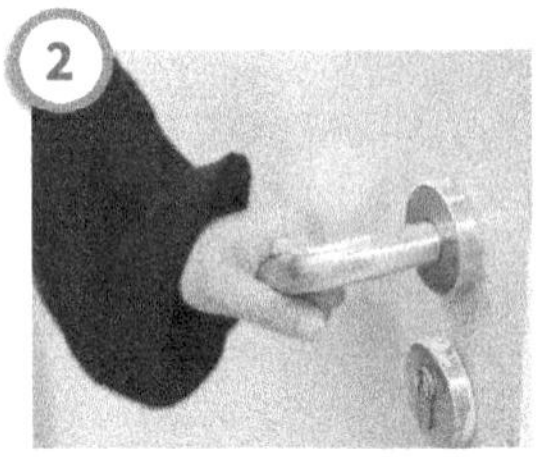

3

6

7
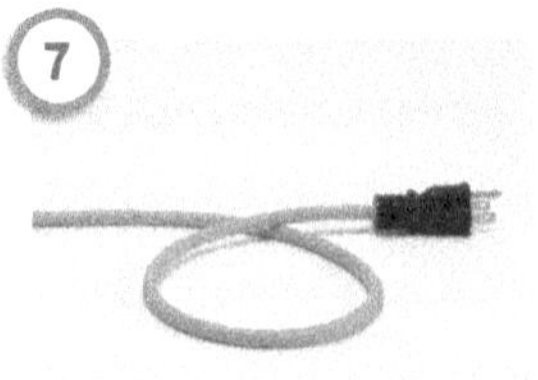

8
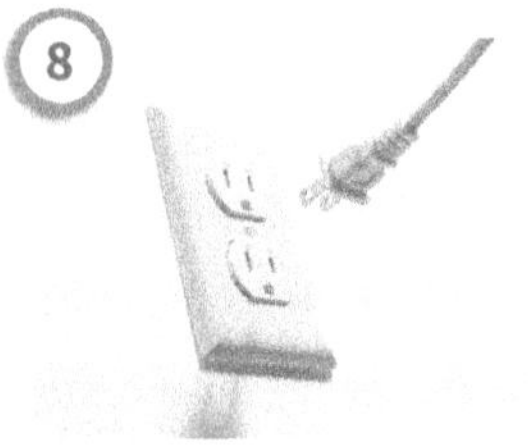

Across →

4

5

7

9

GRAMMAR IN ACTION

3 **Circle the correct answer.**

When my mom was ten, she [1]*got / would get* a cat for her birthday. She [2]*would love / loved* the cat, and it used to follow her everywhere. The cat [3]*did explore / would explore* other people's yards, and it [4]*didn't fight / used to fight* with other cats from time to time. Then one day, the cat [5]*didn't come / used to come* home. Mom [6]*used to be / was* so sad – she [7]*put up / would put up* posters to try and find it. Finally, it came home five days later. Mom was very happy!

4 **Circle the sentence (a or b) that has a similar meaning to the first.**

1 The train had already left when we got to the station.
  a When we got to the station, the train left.
  b We arrived at the station late, so we missed the train.

2 Before we went to Brazil last year, I'd never been there.
  a Last year was the first time I was in Brazil.
  b I didn't visit Brazil last year.

3 By the time I learned to drive, I'd spent a lot of money on driving lessons.
  a I spent a lot of money before I could drive.
  b I learned to drive before I spent a lot of money.

4 Amy hadn't finished her homework when Aidan came.
  a Aidan arrived and Amy finished her homework.
  b When Aidan came, Amy was still doing her homework.

5 Ryan had never seen a lion before he went to the zoo last week.
  a Ryan didn't see a lion at the zoo.
  b Before his trip to the zoo last week, Ryan hadn't seen a lion.

6 We had taken a lot of photos by the time our vacation was over.
  a We took a lot of photos on vacation.
  b When our vacation ended, we took a lot of photos.

CUMULATIVE GRAMMAR

5 **Complete the text with the missing words. Circle the correct options.**

Joe said, "I [1] ______ to this new school a month ago, but I [2] ______ down to life here very well."
"[3] ______ through a hard time?" I asked him.
"Yes, I [4] ______," he said. "It's been [5] ______ difficult. At my old school I [6] ______ a lot of friends.
And I [7] ______ them very often after school. Before I came here, I [8] ______ that it would be so hard to make new friends.
It's been [9] ______ harder than I thought."
"[10] ______ up for any school clubs?" I asked.
"Yes, I [11] ______ to two or three different ones," Joe replied. "You know, I [12] ______ really popular at my old school," he continued. "Nothing like this [13] ______ to me before."

1 a moved
  b had moved
  c used to move

2 a didn't settle
  b haven't settled
  c hadn't settled

3 a Did you go
  b Had you gone
  c Have you been going

4 a did
  b have
  c been

5 a far
  b absolutely
  c really

6 a would have
  b used to have
  c have had

7 a had seen
  b have been seeing
  c would see

8 a hadn't expected
  b haven't expected
  c wouldn't expect

9 a pretty
  b totally
  c far

10 a Did you sign
  b Have you signed
  c Had you signed

11 a 've been going
  b had gone
  c would go

12 a used to be
  b would be
  c 've been

13 a had happened
  b has happened
  c has been happening

3 What's usually on your plate?

VOCABULARY

Cooking Verbs

1 ☆ **Find 11 more verbs for cooking in the word search.**

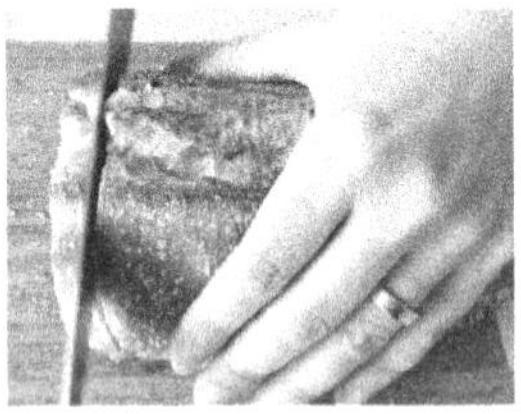

C	H	O	P	O	(P	E	E	L)
R	O	V	G	R	I	L	L	D
I	S	E	A	S	O	N	S	I
S	P	R	E	A	D	O	L	B
H	O	C	R	A	M	F	I	O
A	R	O	A	S	T	F	C	I
R	E	O	V	E	R	R	E	L
B	A	K	E	M	Y	Y	O	T
O	M	U	G	R	A	T	E	E

2 ☆ **(Circle) the verb that goes with the food.**

1 (*grate*) / *peel* cheese
2 *bake* / *boil* water
3 *peel* / *season* an apple
4 *grate* / *roast* a chicken
5 *spread* / *roast* butter
6 *chop* / *slice* bread
7 *grate* / *fry* eggs
8 *peel* / *overcook* fish

3 ☆☆ **Complete the sentences with the words in the box.**

bake chop grill ~~overcook~~ season spread

1 Please don't *overcook* the meat. One or two minutes is enough.
2 ________ the onions into small pieces.
3 Do you often ________ bread in the oven?
4 When you barbecue, you ________ meat over a fire.
5 ________ the dish with salt and pepper.
6 Do you have a knife to ________ the jam?

4 ☆☆ **Complete the recipe with the words in the box.**

fry grate overcook
season ~~slice~~ spread

A Fantastic Snack

[1] *Slice* some bread and toast it. Take some refried beans and [2] ________ them on the bread. [3] ________ some cheese and put it on the refried beans. In a pan, heat up some oil. Then put an egg in the pan and [4] ________ it for only one or two minutes. Don't [5] ________ it! Put the egg on the bread. [6] ________ with black pepper. It's ready to eat!

5 ☆☆☆ **Write how to make something simple (e.g., an omelet, a milkshake, your favorite sandwich).**

____

____

____

____

6 ☆☆ **Write the adjective form of the verbs from Exercise 1. (See the *Learn to Learn* tip in the Student's Book, p35.)**

Add -*ed*	Add -*d*	Irregular
peeled		

Explore It!

Guess the correct answer.

What is the main ingredient of this dish called Bombay Duck?

a duck b horse meat c fish

Find another interesting fact about food or a special dish. Write a question and send it to a classmate in an email, or ask them in the next class.

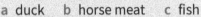

READING

An Online Forum

1 ☆ **Match the photos 1–4 with the four comments on the online forum A–D.**

2 ☆☆ **Complete the article with the missing sentence parts a–f.**

a The food was OK

b and they read some poems

c because it's so incredibly beautiful

d My sister doesn't eat meat

e ~~The highlight of the trip was when we went to an underwater restaurant~~

f in the summer

3 ☆☆ **Read the text and check the meaning of the words in the box in a dictionary. Then complete the sentences.**

~~costume~~	freezing	highlight
hiking	melt	practical

1 What *costume* are you going to wear in the school play?

2 Riding your bike at night without lights is not ________ at all.

3 Eat your ice cream quickly or it'll ________ !

4 My friend Mia goes ________ even in the middle of winter!

5 It's ________ outside, so put on a warm coat.

6 The ________ of the meal was when they brought out my birthday cake.

4 ☆☆☆ **Which of the four places would you most like to eat at? Why? Write three or four sentences.**

____

____

____

____

____

____

ASK IT!

HOME ANSWER NOTIFICATIONS SEARCH

Where's the most memorable place you've ever eaten?

A My dad won $100,000 in the lottery, and he decided to do something very practical with it: he took all of us on vacation to the Maldive Islands! (They're about 640 kilometers southwest of India.) [1] *e* . Beautiful tropical fish swam past as we ate! It was an experience that I'll never forget! [2] ________ but nothing special.

Sam, Toronto

B In northern Finland, there's a fantastic snow hotel with a restaurant made of ice! It's only open in the winter. Perhaps it melts [3] ________ ! You need to wear warm clothes or you're going to be freezing because you sit on ice chairs all the time! We had grilled salmon (very good!), but the roasted meat for the main course was a bit overcooked. Oh, well, nowhere's perfect!

Oona, Helsinki

C When we were on vacation in Ireland, we went for a medieval dinner at Bunratty Castle. It was a lot of fun! They had actors in traditional costumes, [4] ________ . There was also Irish music. The food was good, but we didn't eat with our hands like in medieval times! They had vegetarian food, too. [5] ________ and she loved the baked carrots with grated cheese.

Charlotte, Denver

D The most memorable place I've eaten was Pulpit Rock in Norway. The meal wasn't exactly spectacular – a sandwich, an energy bar, and an apple! But the view *was* spectacular! You could see for miles! And the food didn't taste bad after hiking for a couple of hours! It's not easy to get to Pulpit Rock from Ireland. But I might go back a second time [6] ________ !

Conor, Dublin

GRAMMAR IN ACTION

Future Forms

1 ☆ Match the verbs in sentences 1–6 with the uses a–c.

1 We're meeting at six o'clock. [c]
2 The bus leaves at 10 a.m. [ ]
3 I'm going to study more this year. [ ]
4 Are you and Luis playing tennis tonight? [ ]
5 The restaurant opens at 7 p.m. [ ]
6 Zoe's going to try to make lasagna. [ ]

a to talk about future plans and intentions
b to talk about scheduled or timetabled events
c to talk about fixed arrangements in the future

2 ☆☆ (Circle) the correct options.

1 What *do you do* / (*are you doing*) tonight?
2 The game *starts* / *is starting* in five minutes!
3 My sister *learns* / *is going to learn* to drive next year.
4 We *meet* / *'re meeting* in the park at six o'clock.
5 I *make* / *'m going to make* dinner in a few minutes.
6 Joel *has* / *is going to have* a piano lesson in a few minutes.
7 I*'m getting* / *'m going to get* my green belt in judo this year. It's my big goal for the year.
8 We *go* / *'re going* skateboarding this weekend.

3 ☆☆☆ Write about two fixed future arrangements that you have or haven't made and two future intentions that you have or don't have.

____
____
____
____

4 ☆ Match the underlined verbs in sentences 1–3 with the uses a–c.

1 Those cookies smell amazing. And I'm sure they're going to taste delicious! [ ]
2 More people will become vegetarians in the future. [ ]
3 I might want some more pizza. Let me finish this first! [ ]

a a future prediction that we don't feel sure about
b a future prediction based on evidence in the present
c a future prediction that we feel sure about

5 ☆☆ Complete the predictions with *be going to*, *will*, or *may/might*, and the verbs in the box.

come	have	love	~~miss~~	not cost	not finish

1 Oh, no! It's 5:59! We *'re going to miss* the six o'clock train!
2 John _______________ to the party. Let's wait and see!
3 I'm sure Deborah _______________ the present you chose for her. You have great taste.
4 This meal _______________ a lot! Prices are cheap!
5 Some experts say that one day everyone in the world _______________ enough food to eat.
6 I _______________ this book tonight, but I'm going to try.

6 ☆☆☆ Complete the conversation with the correct form of the verbs in parentheses. Use the simple present, present continuous, *be going to*, *will*, or *may/might*.

A I [1] *'m never going to cook* (never / cook) a big meal again!
B Why? It wasn't so bad. And I'm sure your cooking [2] _______________ (get) better in the future.
A Hmm … I suppose I [3] _______________ (make) some progress.
B Don't be so negative! Anyway, what [4] _______________ (you / do) after lunch?
A I [5] _______________ (go) to the movies with Will. The movie [6] _______________ (start) at 5 p.m.

7 ☆☆☆ Complete the sentences with your own ideas.

1 In ten years, I might _______________
_______________.
2 In 100 years, everyone will _______________
_______________.
3 I might _______________
_______________.

VOCABULARY AND LISTENING

Quantities

1 ☆ **Circle the correct quantity to describe each photo.**

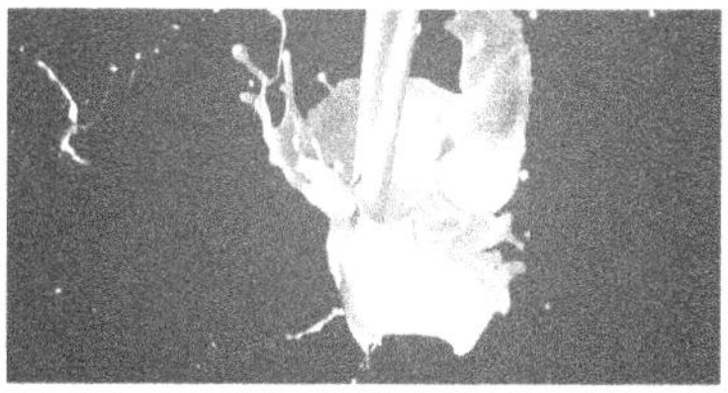

1 *a splash* / *cup* of milk

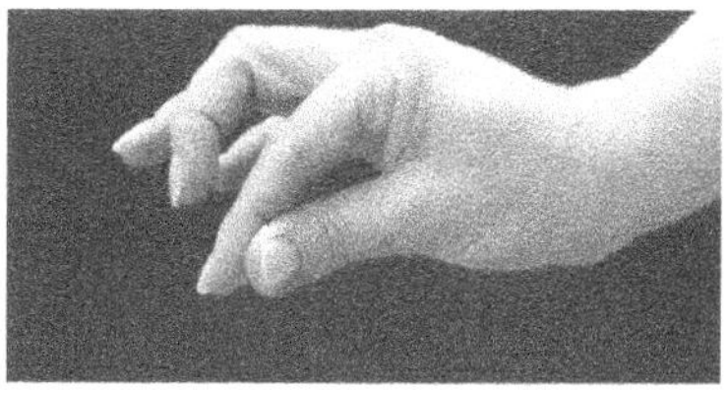

2 a *bag* / *pinch* of salt

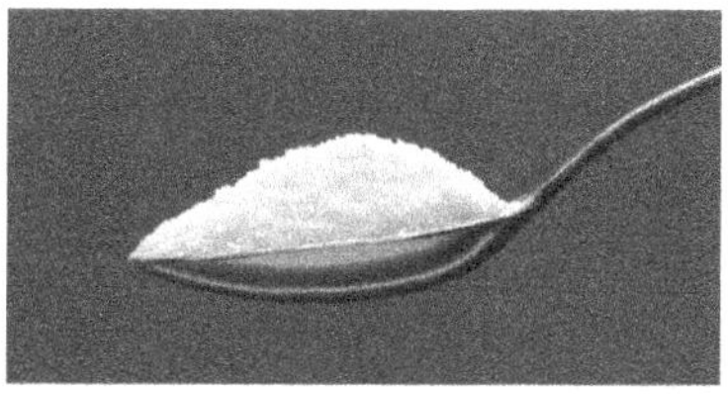

3 a *spoonful* / *bag* of sugar

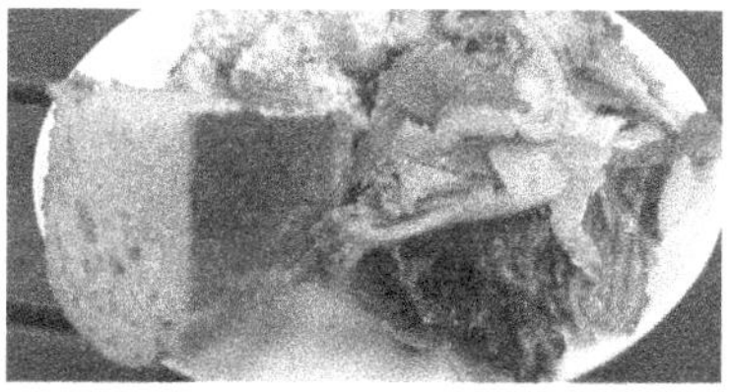

4 a *slice* / *piece* of bread

5 a *sprinkle* / *handful* of sugar

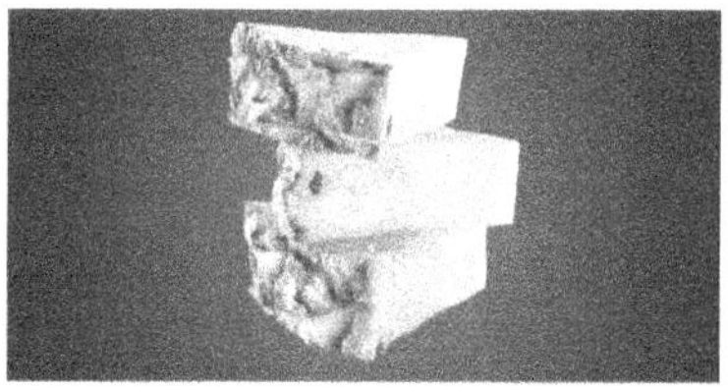

6 *cups* / *chunks* of pineapple

2 ☆☆ **Complete the chart with the quantities in the box. (See the *Learn to Learn* tip in the Student's Book, p38.)**

a bag of · a cup of · a handful of · a piece of · a pinch of · a slice of · a splash of · a spoonful of · a sprinkle of · ~~chunks of~~

Sugar	Milk	Cheese
		chunks of

3 ☆☆☆ **Write about three things you like to eat or drink. Use the quantities from Exercise 2.**

I love two slices of toast and jam for breakfast.

An Interview

3.01 **4** ☆ **Listen to a man talking about his job. Are the sentences *T* (true) or *F* (false)?**

1 James has his own food store. ____
2 James works a lot. ____
3 His job has several good points. ____
4 He never has time to eat the food that he cooks. ____

3.01 **5** ☆☆☆ **Listen again and complete the sentences with ONE word from the interview.**

1 James works in the city of *Chicago* .
2 In the restaurant, there can be ____ people eating at the same time.
3 The food needs to arrive at customers' tables quickly and the dishes need to be of ____ quality.
4 James doesn't ____ down very often while he's working.
5 It's a profession for people who are ____ .
6 It's very different from an ____ job.
7 The opinion of the ____ is important to James.
8 It's important to ____ the food.

6 ☆☆☆ **Would you like to do James' job? Why / Why not? Write three or four sentences.**

GRAMMAR IN ACTION

Future Continuous and Future Perfect

1 ★ Complete the sentences with the verbs in parentheses in the future continuous.

1 I *'ll be reading* (read) this book all evening.

2 He ________ (listen) to the podcast later.

3 I ________ (not lie) on the sofa all afternoon!

4 My parents ________ (not work) this time tomorrow.

5 ________ (we / eat) at two o'clock?

6 ________ (Ryan / cook) for a long time?

2 ★★ Look at Carmen's diary. Complete the sentences with the correct future continuous form of the verbs in parentheses and short or long answers.

Monday	Tuesday	Wednesday
tennis (5 p.m.)	homework (morning)	dance class (6 p.m.)

1 She *'ll be playing* (play) tennis at 5 p.m. on Monday.

2 She ________ (not do) homework on Tuesday afternoon.

3 She ________ (start) her dance class at 6 p.m. on Wednesday.

4 **A** ________ (Carmen / play tennis) on Monday?

B ________

5 **A** What day ________ (she / take) her dance class?

B ________

3 ★ (Circle) the correct options.

1 I'm going to bed very late tonight. I *'ll* / *(won't)* have gone to bed by 11 p.m.

2 I hope that I *'ll* / *won't* have learned to drive in a few years. I think it would be fantastic!

3 My mom works in another country. By tomorrow, I *'ll* / *won't* have seen her for two months.

4 My dad often cooks for the family. He *'ll* / *won't* have cooked several meals for us by the end of this week.

5 **A** Will you have become a doctor by the time you're 20?

B That's impossible! *Yes, I will.* / *No, I won't.*

4 ★★ Complete the conversation with the verbs in the box in the future perfect and short answers.

arrive   grill   ~~make~~   not fry   not have   slice

A [1] *Will* you *have made* lunch by one o'clock?

B No, [2] ________. Why?

A The guests [3] ________ by then!

B Oh, no! I [4] ________ the potatoes to make the fries, but I [5] ________ them.

A And [6] ________ you ________ all the meat?

B No, [7] ________. I [8] ________ time!

5 ★★ (Circle) the correct time expression.

1 I'll be sleeping *(in two hours)* / *since next week*.

2 Will you be sitting by the pool *this time tomorrow* / *since the time you were 18*?

3 We'll have finished all our exams *by the end of this month* / *for three hours*!

4 *Next Tuesday* / *By the end of this year*, we'll have visited five different countries!

5 We'll be eating that roasted chicken *in five minutes* / *by the time it's cooked*.

6 ★★★ Use the future continuous or future perfect to write about things that you will do or hope that you will do.

1 By the end of this year, ________.

2 At nine o'clock tonight, ________.

3 Next weekend, ________.

4 By the time I'm 30, ________.

WRITING
A Listicle

1 ☆ **Look at the listicle quickly. What is it about?**

2 ☆☆ **Read the listicle. Are the sentences *T* (true) or *F* (false)?**

1 Tight clothes will be popular. F
2 We will need to buy new clothes more often.
3 We will wear very different shoes from today.
4 We'll have less choice when we buy clothes.
5 Clothes will become intelligent.

3 ☆☆☆ **Rewrite the sentences with the underlined *Useful Language* phrases in the listicle.**

1 More information here soon!
Watch this space!

2 Smart clothes will be the usual thing we wear.

3 I can't imagine anything more exciting than being a fashion designer.

4 T-shirts will always be popular. *(three expressions)*

FIVE FUTURE FASHION TRENDS!

1 Baggy clothes will be everywhere!

Comfortable baggy clothes will be the norm as the planet gets hotter. Tight denim jeans will have gone completely out of style by 2030, and clothes made of cool cotton will be in all the stores.

2 Clothes will wear out more quickly!

Fast fashion will mean that most clothes will only last five or six months. Clothes will become cheaper as a result.

3 Sneakers are here to stay!

People of all ages wear sneakers nowadays, and that isn't going to change. If you ask me, sneakers will be around forever. I love sneakers, so what could be better news than that?

4 Clothes to match eyes and hair color!

Very soon, we won't just be buying clothes by size. You'll be able to buy clothes to match your eyes or hair color. Everything will be personalized. Watch this space!

5 High-tech clothes!

We already have smartphones, and they aren't going anywhere. But soon we'll have smart clothes, too! They'll adapt to our body temperature and even to our size! The future's going to be exciting!

PLAN

4 ☆☆ **Write your own listicle. Take notes in your notebook on the theme "Five ways my life will be different in 20 years." Use the spidergram to generate ideas.**

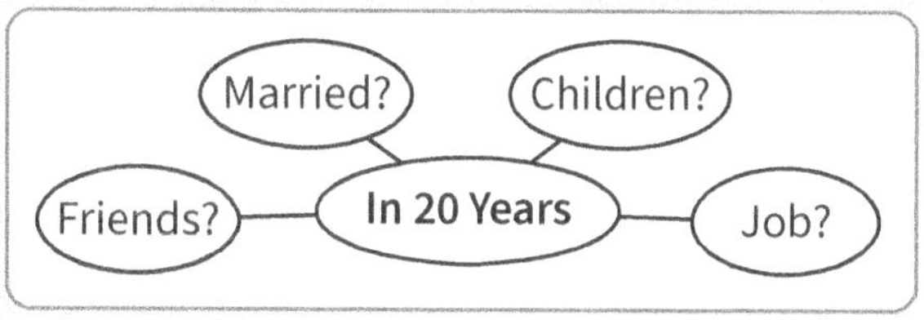

WRITE

5 ☆☆☆ **Write your listicle. Remember to include future forms, vocabulary from this unit, and phrases from the *Useful Language* box (see Student's Book, p41).**

CHECK

6 Do you …

- explain what you will or might be doing in the future?
- explain what will be normal in the future?
- make any other predictions?

3 REVIEW

VOCABULARY

1 Complete the crossword. Use the clues.

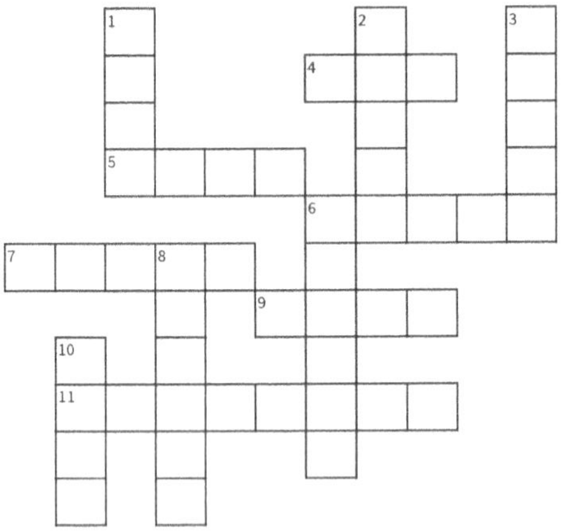

ACROSS →

4 ________ an egg
5 ________ an apple
6 ________ bread
7 ________ chicken
9 ________ a cake
11 ________ sausages

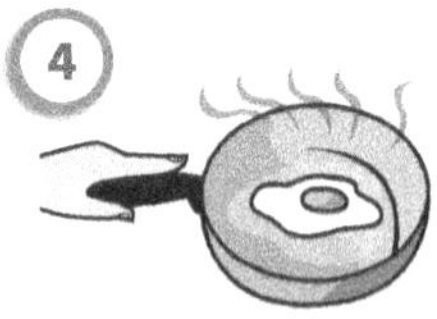

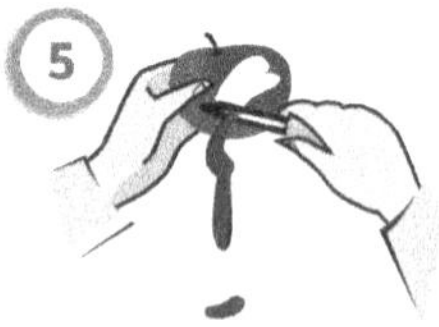

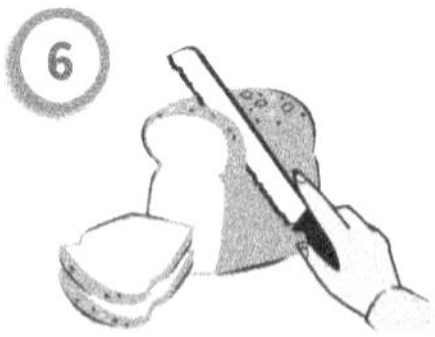

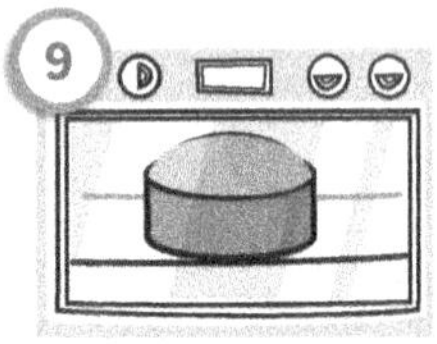

DOWN ↓

1 ________ onions
2 ________ a veggie burger
3 ________ cheese
6 ________ meat
8 ________ butter
10 ________ water

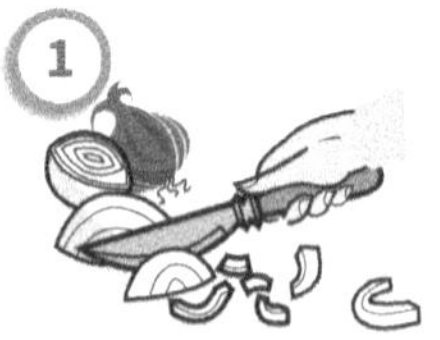

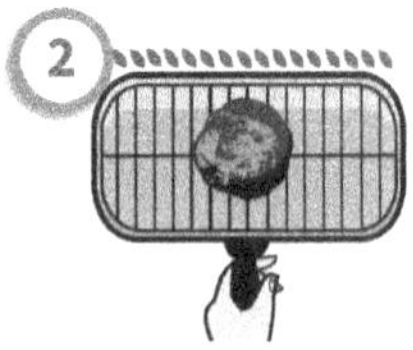

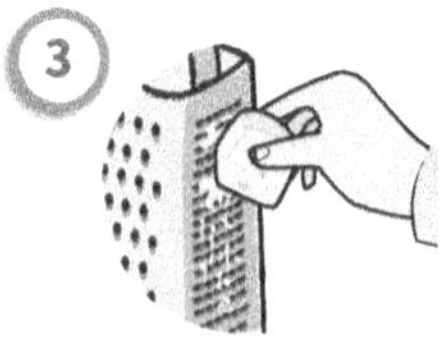

2 Circle the correct options.

1 a cup of *sugar / fish*
2 a piece of *salt / chocolate*
3 a slice of *cake / milk*
4 some chunks of *yogurt / cheese*
5 a handful of *nuts / milk*
6 a bag of *water / chips*
7 a pinch of *pepper / chicken*
8 a sprinkle of *potatoes / grated cheese*
9 a spoonful of *apples / olive oil*
10 a splash of *vinegar / salt*

GRAMMAR IN ACTION

3 Circle the correct options.

1 What time *does / will* the movie start?
2 I *will / 'm going to* make pizza for the first time next weekend.
3 *Do you go / Are you going* to the market with Sean this weekend?
4 Dad *might / will* be late for dinner tonight. It depends on when he finishes work.
5 I think that in the future people *will eat / are eating* less meat.
6 My cousin *will stay / is staying* at my house tonight.

4 Complete the predictions with the future perfect or future continuous form of the verbs in parentheses.

Space Predictions

- In 20 years, scientists [1] ________________ (discover) a new planet in our solar system.
- People [2] ________________ (live) on Mars by the end of this century.
- A big asteroid [3] ________________ (not hit) the Earth by the end of this millennium.
- People [4] ________________ (go) to the moon for their vacations in 50 years.
- We [5] ________________ (not find) intelligent life in the rest of the universe by the end of this century.
- Scientists [6] ________________ (plan) journeys outside the solar system very soon.

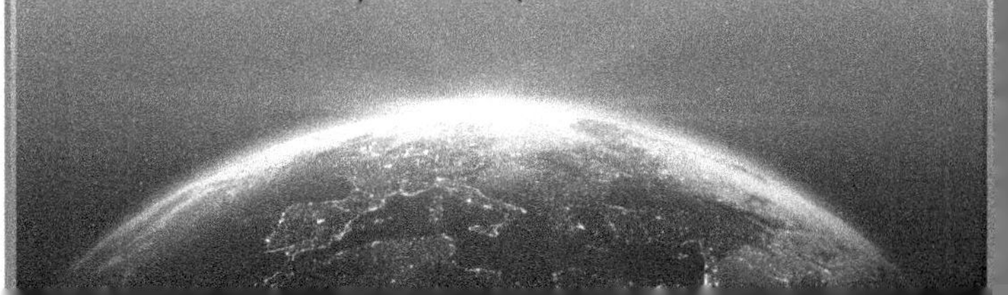

CUMULATIVE GRAMMAR

5 **Complete the text with the missing words. Circle the correct options.**

Teen Fashion: Past, Present, and Future

Teenagers [1] ______ clothes especially designed for them for long. Before the 1950s, they [2] ______ their own fashion, and clothing companies [3] ______ about making special clothes for them. In the past, young teenagers [4] ______ children's clothes, and teenagers that were [5] ______ older wore adults' clothes. Clothes for teenagers [6] ______ a lot since then! It's [7] ______ hard to predict what kind of clothes teenagers [8] ______ in the future because fashion changes very quickly. They [9] ______ wear high-tech clothes, or perhaps they [10] ______ 1960s hippie-style clothes soon. Who knows? Two things are [11] ______ clear, though – fashion designers [12] ______ very good at inventing new teen styles in the past, and they [13] ______ to continue doing this in the future, too.

1 a weren't wearing	b haven't been wearing	c haven't worn
2 a didn't use to have	b wouldn't have	c weren't having
3 a have never thought	b would never think	c had never thought
4 a have been wearing	b would wear	c were wearing
5 a a bit	b really	c a far
6 a had changed	b have changed	c have been changing
7 a extremely	b a lot	c absolutely
8 a are wearing	b will have worn	c will be wearing
9 a will	b might	c 're going to
10 a wear	b 're wearing	c 'll be wearing
11 a pretty	b a lot	c far
12 a are	b have been	c had been
13 a are trying	b will have tried	c are going to try

4 How do you use your senses?

VOCABULARY

The Five Senses

a

b

c

d
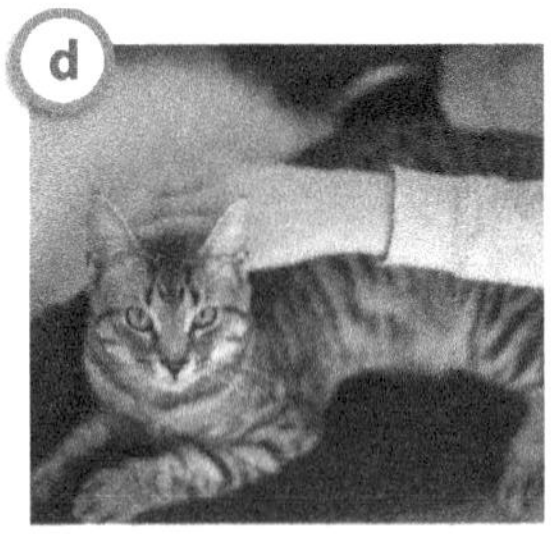
e

1 Match the sentences 1–5 with the pictures a–e.

1 It sounds good. [e]
2 It looks amazing! [ ]
3 It smells good. [ ]
4 It feels nice. [ ]
5 It tastes great. [ ]

2 Complete the sentences with the correct form of *feel*, *look*, *smell*, *sound*, or *taste*, and *like* if necessary.

1 That song ___sounds___ good. Who is it?
2 I love this ice cream. It ________ fantastic!
3 You ________ a movie star in those sunglasses!
4 Can you give me a massage? Oh, that ________ so good!
5 Please open the window. It doesn't ________ good in here!
6 Do I ________ an American when I speak English?
7 This bread ________ cardboard! It's very dry!
8 The sky ________ dark. I think it's going to rain.

3 Complete the chart with your own ideas. Write three things for each column. (See the *Learn to Learn* tip in the Student's Book, p47.)

It Feels Good	It Looks Good	It Smells Good	It Sounds Good	It Tastes Good
a cat's fur				

4 Write four sentences about what you experienced with your senses yesterday. Use *feel*, *look*, *smell*, *sound*, or *taste*, and *like* if necessary.

My new shoes looked good.

____

____

____

Explore It!

Guess the correct answer.

How far away can elephants smell water?

a 5 km b 12 km c 19 km

Find another interesting fact about animal senses. Write a question and send it to a classmate in an email, or ask them in the next class.

THE BEST JOB IN THE WORLD?

HOME | **STORIES** | PHOTOS

For most of us, eating chocolate is a pleasure. But for Alice Schaffer, it's much more than that – it's a full-time job! Alice, you see, works for an important food company, and she eats their chocolate to see how it tastes. Before she worked there, she didn't have a **background** in food science. She was, in fact, working as a salesperson. Then one day, a neighbor told her that her company was looking for people to work as taste-testers. Alice immediately thought, "That sounds like a great job! And I might be good at it because I love chocolate!" So she applied and ... they gave her the job! Of course, it isn't enough to like chocolate if you want to get a job tasting chocolate. You need to be able to identify and **accurately** describe different **flavors** and textures. And that's something you can't learn – you're either born with it or you aren't.

When Alice tells people what she **does for a living**, they often look surprised because they imagine that she must spend all day eating chocolate. But her job isn't really like that at all. When she tastes the chocolate from a bar, she just eats a little piece. You don't need to eat the whole bar to know what it tastes like! The hardest part of the job is when she tastes something that isn't 100 percent right. The **challenge** is to describe exactly what's wrong with the taste. The food technicians need this precise information so they can investigate the problem.

Alice is extremely **proud** of her job, and it's easy to see why: there can't be many people in the world whose job helps give so much pleasure to others!

READING

A Magazine Article

1 ☆ **Read the magazine article quickly. What is Alice Schaffer's job?**

a She makes chocolate.

b She checks the taste of chocolate.

c She sells chocolate.

2 ☆☆ **Match the words in bold in the article with the definitions.**

1 feeling pleasure because you've done something well

proud

2 particular tastes

3 someone's past situation

4 correctly, without making any mistakes

5 does to earn money

6 something that needs effort or might be hard to do

3 ☆☆ **Read the text again. For each question, (circle) the correct option.**

1 What is the writer trying to do in this article?

a explain how to get a job as a chocolate taster

b write a biography of Alice Schaffer

c describe what a chocolate taster does

(d) tell the reader about the professional life of Alice Schaffer

2 What kind of useful experience had Alice had before?

a She had worked as a salesperson.

b She had studied food science.

c She hadn't really had any experience.

d Her neighbor had taught her about the job.

3 What is the principal quality you need to be a chocolate taster?

a dedication b natural talent c to love chocolate d to write very well

4 What is the most difficult part of the job?

a giving precise information when the quality isn't good

b not eating the chocolate

c people not thinking it's a serious job

d working with the food technicians

5 What might Alice say to a friend about her job?

a It's an easy job.

b I love my job!

c There's often a lot of stress in my job.

d The chocolate is bad for me.

4 ☆☆☆ **Would you like to do Alice Schaffer's job? Why / Why not?**

GRAMMAR IN ACTION

Modals of Deduction and Possibility

1 ☆ **Match the sentences 1–3 with their meanings a–c.**

1 I'm sure it's nice to work as a chocolate taster. ☐
2 Perhaps it's nice to work as a chocolate taster. ☐
3 I'm sure it isn't nice to work as a chocolate taster. ☐

a It can't be nice to work as a chocolate taster.
b It must be nice to work as a chocolate taster.
c It might be nice to work as a chocolate taster.

2 ☆☆ **Look at the sentence *It might be nice to work as a chocolate taster.* Which two modal verbs can we use in place of *might*, without changing the meaning?**

____

3 ☆ **Circle the correct options to describe the pictures.**

1 

He *can't* / *must* (circled) be tired.

2 

He *can't* / *must* feel relaxed.

3 

That car *can't* / *must* be expensive!

4 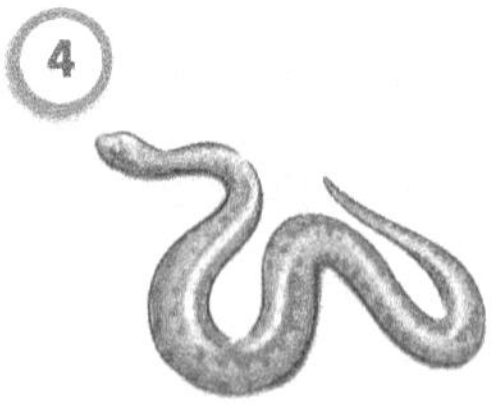

Careful! It *might* / *must* be dangerous.

5 

It *can't* / *must* be raining.

6 

They *may* / *can't* still have some good bargains.

4 ☆☆ **Complete the conversation about the photo with *must*, *might*, or *can't*.**

A Look at this photo! What is it?
B It [1] might be a house!
A No, it [2] ________ be! How would you get in?
B It [3] ________ be a fake photo. You never know …
A No, the photo's real. I think it [4] ________ be art or something. There [5] ________ be another explanation. I'm sure the artist is famous.
B Perhaps … you [6] ________ be right. The person who designed it [7] ________ be very creative!

5 ☆☆☆ **Rewrite the sentences so that they have the same meaning. Use *must*, *might*, *may*, *could*, or *can't*.**

1 Perhaps Nathan's still at school.
Nathan might/may/could still be at school.
2 I'm sure that isn't the right answer.
____
3 I'm sure you need good exam results to study medicine in college.
____
4 This is possibly the worst movie I've seen!
____
5 I'm sure it doesn't take a long time to make that dish.
____

6 ☆☆☆ **Write deductions about these situations. Use *must*, *might*, *could*, or *can't*.**

1 Edison is a professional soccer player.
He must be very fit.
2 All the stores are closed.
____
3 Your phone isn't working.
____
4 Everyone is looking at the sky.
____

VOCABULARY AND LISTENING

Describing Texture, Sound, Taste, Etc.

1 Complete the adjectives.

1 spic y
2 rou ____
3 shin ____
4 fain ____
5 color ____
6 sou ____
7 smoo ____
8 shar ____
9 smell ____
10 transpar ____

2 Write an appropriate adjective from Exercise 1 before the nouns.

1 spicy curry
2 dirty, ________ socks
3 nice, ________ skin
4 ________ cream
5 ________, new scissors
6 ________ flowers

3 Complete the sentences with adjectives from Exercise 1.

1 A crocodile has very sharp teeth.
2 This sauce is too ________ for me. My mouth's burning!
3 Can you pass the sugar? This yogurt is very ________.
4 Does this cake have bananas in it? I can detect a ________ taste of them, but it's not very strong.
5 This lotion is great! My hands feel so ________!
6 This metal box looks very ________ when it's in the sun.
7 Tom's chin felt ________ because he hadn't shaved.

4 Write short descriptions of the items in the box. Use at least one adjective from Exercise 1 in each description. You can use affirmative or negative verbs.

apple	cats	my favorite food	snakes

1 ________
2 ________
3 ________
4 ________

An Interview

5 4.01 Listen to an interview about the senses. According to Simon Redding, which of our senses is the most important?

a hearing ☐
b sight ☐
c smell ☐
d touch ☐

6 4.01 Listen again. For each question, circle the correct option.

1 Simon says that some people ...
(a) can't smell very much.
b use sight and smell well.
c feel cold all the time.

2 What does Simon say about dreams?
a Some people open their eyes when they dream.
b It's good to have colorful images.
c Taste and smell are not usually part of dreams.

3 When we are communicating, we ...
a shouldn't only be listening.
b need to smile.
c shouldn't be negative.

4 What has the biggest impact on us in a conversation?
a how well the other person listens
b how the other person moves and looks at us
c the language that the other person uses

5 What would Simon Redding like people to do?
a depend on their eyes to understand better
b remember to use all of their senses
c close their eyes and feel objects

7 Think about what you have done today. When have you used each of the five senses?

GRAMMAR IN ACTION

Obligation, Prohibition, Necessity, and Advice

1 ☆☆ **(Circle) the correct options.**

How to Use Music to Relax

- You [1](should) / *don't need to* listen to calm music.
- You [2]*don't have to* / *must not* listen to heavy metal. It's not relaxing!
- You [3]*ought to* / *shouldn't* sit in a comfortable position.
- You [4]*need to* / *must not* concentrate on the music.
- To help you concentrate, you [5]*don't need to* / *should* close your eyes.
- You [6]*shouldn't* / *don't need to* be with other people when you listen to the music. It's far better if you are alone.
- You [7]*must not* / *don't need to* wear headphones, but it's better if you have them.

2 ☆☆ **Complete the the interview with a perfume maker with the missing words. (Circle) the correct options.**

A [1] ______ study a lot before you became a perfume maker?

B Yes, I [2] ______ . I [3] ______ study chemistry for four years.

A And I suppose that a perfume maker [4] ______ to have a good sense of smell!

B Yes, of course. You [5] ______ consider becoming a perfume maker without that! And you [6] ______ to be very patient because it takes a long time to create the right smell. And you [7] ______ copy other people. That's bad! You [8] ______ to be original!

1	a Must you	b Should you	(c) Did you have to
2	a must	b have	c did
3	a had to	b need to	c ought to
4	a must	b should	c needs
5	a should	b shouldn't	c don't have to
6	a must	b need	c don't have
7	a must not	b don't need to	c should
8	a must	b have	c should

3 ☆☆☆ **Rewrite the sentences with *must*, *should*, *need*, or *have to*.**

1 I recommend that you see a doctor.
You should see a doctor.

2 It's not permitted to walk on the grass.

3 There's no obligation for us to watch the game.

4 Antonio didn't have an obligation to give me a present.

5 It's necessary for us to contact him.

6 Being in the sun without a hat is not recommended.

Past Obligation

4 ☆☆☆ **Put the words in the correct order.**

1 had / exams / yesterday / two / to / I / take / .
I had to take two exams yesterday.

2 didn't / have / She / year / walk / last / to / school / to / .

3 party / had / Miguel / to / so / study, / didn't / the / go / he / to / .

4 have / people / to / tickets / Did / buy / ?

WRITING

An Encyclopedia Entry

Marlee Matlin, August 24, 1965

1 Marlee Matlin is an actress. She is the only deaf actress who has won an Oscar.

2 Marlee was born in 1965 and grew up in a small town near Chicago. At the age of 18 months, she lost almost all her hearing. She acted for the first time at the age of seven in a production of *The Wizard of Oz* with actors who were all deaf. In 1986, she won the Oscar for best actress at the age of only 21. In the movie, she didn't have to speak. She played the role of a deaf woman who refuses to speak because the rest of the world refuses to learn sign language.

3 Marlee has appeared in many movies and TV shows, including *Sesame Street*. She isn't just famous as an actress; she is also known as an enthusiastic worker for many charities.

4 Marlee can speak quite well, and she doesn't always need to use an interpreter because she can read people's lips. According to her autobiography, she never planned to become an actress. She thought there wouldn't be any opportunities for deaf people.

1 **Read the encyclopedia entry. What is Marlee's occupation?**

____

2 **Complete the sentences with information from the encyclopedia entry.**

1 She was born in 1965.
2 When she was seven, __________.
3 In the movie where she won an Oscar, her character was __________.
4 She is also famous as __________.
5 She can read people's lips, so __________.
6 When she was young, she used to think that __________.

3 **Complete the sentences with the underlined *Useful Language* in the encyclopedia entry.**

Javier Bardem, March 1, 1969

Javier Bardem [1] grew up in Madrid, but he [2] __________ in Las Palmas in the Canary Islands. In his career, he has acted in many movies, [3] __________ *Skyfall*, a James Bond movie. He actually appeared in his first movie [4] __________ only six. [5] __________ Bardem, he originally wanted to be a painter, but he didn't have enough talent. Outside of movies, Bardem is [6] __________ a firm defender of ecological causes.

PLAN

4 **Write an encyclopedia entry. First, take notes in your notebook about your favorite actor, fictional character, or athlete.**

- Name and date of birth
- A short general description
- Information about their life
- An interesting fact

WRITE

5 **Write your entry. Remember to include four paragraphs, vocabulary from this unit, and phrases from the *Useful Language* box (see Student's Book, p53).**

CHECK

6 **Do you ...**

- include the person's name and date of birth?
- include information about the person's life?
- include information about the person's work?

4 REVIEW

VOCABULARY

1 Complete the sentences with the correct form of *feel* (*like*), *look* (*like*), *smell* (*like*), *sound* (*like*), or *taste* (*like*).

1 It doesn't __________ very good in here. Please open the windows.
2 When you sing, you don't really __________ an angel!
3 Wow! That photo __________ a painting! It's so artistic!
4 **A** Do you want to go skateboarding?
B Yes, that __________ a good idea!
5 This perfume __________ roses and oranges. It's great!
6 It __________ an oven in here! Please turn the air conditioning on!
7 This strawberry ice cream __________ great! Did you make it yourself?
8 These tomatoes __________ really green, and they __________ really hard. So, I don't think they're going to __________ very good!

2 Complete the crossword. Use the clues.

Down ↓

1 There's a __________ taste of lemon in this cake, but it isn't very strong.
2 That sweater is __________. You need to wash it.
3 I like the feel of this leather. It's very __________.
5 Be careful – it's very __________! Don't cut yourself!

Across →

2 If you have a stomachache, you shouldn't eat __________ food.
3 I love Chinese food, especially sweet and __________ chicken.
4 That bird is very __________. It looks beautiful.
5 The metal buttons on your coat look very __________ under these lights.
6 A rhinoceros has hard, __________ skin.

GRAMMAR IN ACTION

3 Complete the conversation with *might*, *must*, or *can't*.

A Is the new *Mission Impossible* movie good?
B I haven't seen it yet, but it [1] __________ be pretty good. It has four stars in the newspaper.
A You never know, it [2] __________ be awful.
B You [3] __________ be serious! They spend a lot of money to make those movies. So, it [4] __________ be fantastic!
A Hmm, you [5] __________ be right. But it [6] __________ be as good as the last one. That's the best movie I've ever seen.
B You [7] __________ be surprised. David's seen it and he couldn't stop talking about it!
A Really? Then it [8] __________ be great! David and I always agree about movies!

4 Complete the sentences with the correct form of *must* (*not*), (*not*) *need to*, *should*, or (*not*) *have to*.

1 You ______ touch the paintings. It's not allowed!

2 We ______ get up early this morning because the train left at seven o'clock.

3 I don't think you ______ wear green with purple, but it's your decision.

4 I ______ borrow your bike, but thanks for the offer.

5 ______ you ______ wear a uniform at your old school?

6 I ______ clean up my bedroom tonight, but I'm not going to do it.

7 You ______ help me, but it'd be great if you could.

8 ______ we ______ get a visa to travel to Argentina?

CUMULATIVE GRAMMAR

5 Complete the conversation with the missing words. Circle the correct options.

CHRIS What [1] ______ this weekend?

TOM I [2] ______ any plans yet.

CHRIS What about this new Sensorium exhibition? It [3] ______ be good. You never know.

TOM I [4] ______ to it! It was so interesting that I [5] ______ about it all the time. It [6] ______ be the best exhibition I've ever been to. I'm [7] ______ sure about that. I [8] ______ that going to museums to look at paintings was boring. But this exhibition is different because you listen to music and smell things while you're looking at each painting. I [9] ______ that an exhibition could be like that! You [10] ______ go, Chris! You [11] ______ disappointed!

CHRIS Thanks! I [12] ______ miss it! By next Monday, both of us [13] ______ it!

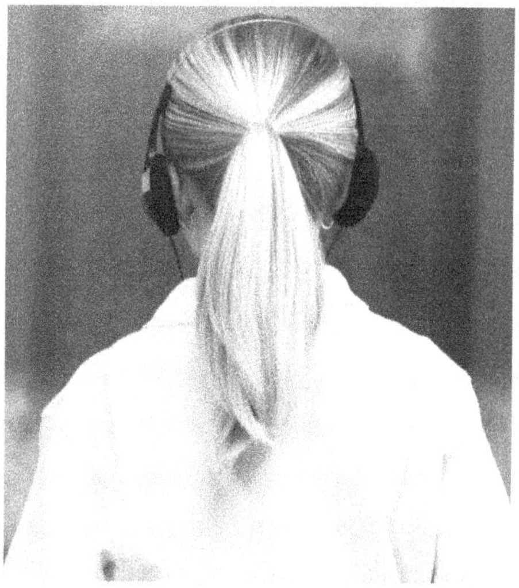

1	a do you do	b will you do	c are you doing
2	a don't make	b haven't made	c haven't been making
3	a might	b must	c will
4	a 'd already been	b may have been	c 've already been
5	a 've been thinking	b 've thought	c think
6	a can	b needs to	c must
7	a pretty	b absolutely	c far
8	a would think	b used to think	c 've been thinking
9	a 've never imagined	b might never imagine	c 'd never imagined
10	a should	b don't have to	c 'll
11	a can't be	b won't be	c haven't been
12	a won't	b don't need to	c aren't going to
13	a will see	b will have seen	c will be seeing

5 What amazes you?

VOCABULARY

Processes

1 ☆ **Find 11 more verbs in the word search. Write them below. You have the first letter of each verb.**

C	O	P	R	O	D	U	C	E	P	Z	C
M	E	A	S	U	R	E	G	V	C	Q	O
E	S	C	S	U	P	P	L	Y	R	M	M
B	R	T	I	D	E	L	I	V	E	R	M
Z	A	R	O	E	Y	U	I	D	A	C	U
N	S	I	C	V	C	O	L	E	T	O	N
C	O	N	N	E	C	T	O	P	E	L	I
H	L	O	T	L	O	I	L	L	O	L	C
T	V	P	G	O	L	B	N	Z	G	E	A
E	E	X	V	P	A	T	T	R	A	C	T
W	Y	G	I	U	V	K	W	A	S	T	E

1 p*roduce* 5 c ______ 9 c ______
2 m ______ 6 a ______ 10 d ______
3 s ______ 7 w ______ 11 c ______
4 d ______ 8 c ______ 12 s ______

2 ☆☆ **Circle the correct options. (See the *Learn to Learn* tip in the Student's Book, p59.)**

1 The school supplied us ______ books and other materials for the project.
   a with b for c on
2 Flowers attract bees and other insects ______ bright colors and nice smells.
   a about b with c at
3 We measured the distance ______ the door to the window.
   a between b with c from

3 ☆☆ **Complete the amazing facts with verbs from Exercise 1.**

1 The albatross, a type of seabird, has wings that *measure* almost 3.5 meters.
2 Some scientists say that trees in forests ______ with each other.
3 One cow can ______ around 12 liters of milk every day.
4 Europeans ______ an average of around 180 kilograms of food every year.

5 The man who ______ pizza to the 2014 Oscars ceremony got a tip of $1,000 from the actors.
6 The UK tea company Twinings has been ______ the British Royal family with tea since 1837.

4 ☆☆☆ **Find out some other amazing facts and write sentences about them. Use verbs from Exercise 1.**

The tallest building in the world is the Burj Khalifa in Dubai. It measures 828 meters.

Explore It!

True or false?
Cats always land on their feet.

Find another interesting fact about an animal and write a true or false sentence about it. Send it to a classmate in an email, or ask them in the next class.

READING

A Webzine Article

1 **Read the article quickly. What color is the aurora borealis normally? In what color has it been seen in southern Europe?**

2 **Match the underlined words in the article with the definitions 1–6.**

1 when the sun appears in the sky sunrise

2 used physical force to win against someone

3 spirits of dead people

4 problems or difficulties

5 parts of a war, fights between two armies

6 the person who makes something

3 **Read the article again. Are the sentences *T* (true) or *F* (false)? Correct the false sentences.**

1 Aurora, Helios, and Selene were all sisters.
F, Helios was the brother of Aurora and Selene.

2 It is unusual to find a story about the aurora borealis in a culture.

3 The French Revolution happened after red lights were seen in the sky over England and Scotland.

4 The Cree people in Canada believed the lights were a bad sign.

5 The Vikings believed the lights helped lead dead soldiers to their resting place.

6 Electrical energy from the sun produces the aurora borealis.

4 **Write your answer to the question at the end of the article.**

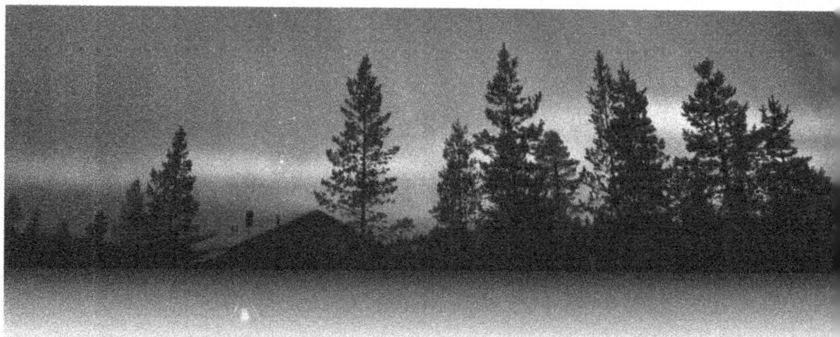

Aurora Borealis: A Wonder of Nature

Origin of the Name

The aurora borealis is an amazing natural light show around the Arctic Circle – a wonder of nature. The name comes from ancient Greek – *aurora* means "sunrise" and *boreas* means "wind." The ancient Greeks believed that Aurora was the sister of Helios (the sun god) and Selene (the moon goddess). As the sun rose in the morning, Aurora flew across the sky to remind her brother and sister that a new day had arrived. Strange stories connected to the lights are found in many cultures.

Europe: Bad Signs

It was strange that the lights, normally green in color, were seen in Greece. Scientists believe that the lights appeared red so far south. In 1789, red lights were seen by the inhabitants of England and Scotland. Shortly after this the French Revolution started, and many believed that the lights had been a sign of the trouble to come.

North America: Other Meanings

The Algonquin people in Canada believed the lights came from a fire that was built by Nanahbozah, their creator. This fire was a sign that Nanahbozah was watching over everyone. Their neighbors, the Cree, on the other hand, thought that the lights were like ghosts who were trying to communicate with the living.

Viking Women

Another ancient civilization – the Vikings – thought the lights were made by the Valkyrie, women who fought in their battles. This light delivered dead soldiers safely to Valhalla, where they could finally rest.

The Scientific Explanation

Now we know that the lights are created by the sun. Sometimes, scientists say, the sun sends huge amounts of electrical energy into space. When this energy reaches Earth, it produces these strange lights in the sky. But which explanation do you prefer?

GRAMMAR IN ACTION

The Passive

1 ☆ **Circle the correct options.**

1 This coffee (is) / *are* produced in Kenya – try it.
2 The problem with my computer *was* / *were* solved by turning it off and then on again.
3 In the future, a lot of diseases *are* / *will be* cured with technology.
4 We're going to recycle all the plastic bags so nothing will be *waste* / *wasted*.
5 Some people thought the aurora borealis *is* / *was* created by gods.
6 Was there a loud bang when all the cords *was* / *were* connected?

2 ☆☆ **Complete the sentences with the correct form of the verbs in the box.**

attract	build	collect	~~deliver~~	measure	use

1 These books *will be delivered* tomorrow morning to your house.
2 The church ________ in the 15th century, but now it's a library.
3 Huge rocks ________ to build Stonehenge in England.
4 The ingredients ________ carefully, but the cake still tasted strange.
5 Old clothes ________ at the school, and we'll give them all away to charity.
6 The picnic is terrible! These flies ________ to the food. They're everywhere!

3 ☆☆ **Complete the conversation with the correct form of the verbs in parentheses.**

CHRIS Hey, Alison! Let's see if you can answer these questions.
ALISON A quiz? Sure.
CHRIS OK, first question. How many languages [1] *are spoken* (speak) in India?
ALISON Umm … it's a lot; I know that. Two hundred?
CHRIS No, four hundred! Next one: When [2] ________ the first phone app ________ (create)?
ALISON I think it was 1998.
CHRIS Very good! What [3] ________ (measure) in megabits per second?
ALISON That's easy! Your internet connection speed.
CHRIS And … where [4] ________ 5.6 million cars ________ (produce) in 2017?
ALISON Umm … France?
CHRIS No, it was in Germany. So, after all your hard work, would you like some lunch?
ALISON Great idea. But first, answer this question. What [5] ________ (deliver) by drones in the future?
CHRIS That's obvious … pizza!

4 ☆☆☆ **Write five passive sentences about smartphones. Use these ideas.**

1 What are they made of?
2 Where are they produced?
3 What year was an important model produced?
4 How are apps downloaded?
5 How will they be used in the future?

____
____
____
____
____

VOCABULARY AND LISTENING

Extreme Adjectives

1 ☆ **(Circle) the correct options.**

We visited New York in January. It's a [1]*(stunning)* / *terrifying* city, with its long straight avenues and [2]*boiling* / *marvelous* buildings. The weather in the city can be extreme: the heat in the summer can be [3]*deafening* / *awful*, and there can be very low temperatures in the winter. It snowed while we were there, so Central Park was [4]*deafening* / *gorgeous*, all covered in snow, but I had to buy a new hat and gloves because it was [5]*freezing* / *boiling*! We took the subway to Wall Street – the noise of the trains was [6]*deafening* / *enormous*, but it was [7]*stunning* / *fascinating* to see so many people from all around the world living together in this [8]*enormous* / *awful* city.

2 ☆☆ **Complete the sentences with adjectives from Exercise 1.**

1 Can I borrow your gloves? My hands are *freezing*.
2 Turn down that music! It's ______.
3 I couldn't watch the end of that horror movie. It was ______.
4 Ms. Griffin's a very interesting teacher, and her history classes are ______.
5 I didn't realize the London Eye was really this big! It's ______!
6 When we were in Oaxaca in July, it was ______ : 39°C!
7 Paul had a ______ vacation – he went to Sweden and Norway, and he had a great time.
8 Ana's brother is a fashion model – he's totally ______!
9 The view from the top of the mountain was absolutely ______.

3 ☆☆☆ **Complete the sentences so they are true for you.**

1 When it's boiling in the summer, I ______.
2 When it's freezing in the winter, I ______.
3 The most terrifying experience I've ever had was when I ______.
4 You can get a stunning view of my town/city if you go to ______.
5 A fascinating fact that I know is ______.

A Virtual Reality Tour

5.01 **4** ☆ **Listen to a virtual tour of the Eiffel Tower. Match the numbers 1–5 with what they refer to a–e. (See the *Learn to Learn* tip in the Student's Book, p62.)**

1 1889	c	a	pieces
2 1887		b	visitors
3 300		c	year of the World Fair
4 18,000		d	height in meters
5 7 million		e	year building was begun

5.01 **5** ☆☆ **Listen again. Answer the questions with two to four words.**

1 What is the first image in the tour?
the original drawing
2 How long after the French Revolution did they build the Eiffel Tower?
______
3 What were the professions of the men who helped Gustave Eiffel?
______
4 Where were the pieces of the tower produced? ______
5 When it was finished, what did the Parisians call the Eiffel Tower?
______

6 ☆☆☆ **Look up some facts about the Eiffel Tower. Write three things you found out about it.**

______

GRAMMAR IN ACTION

Question Tags

1 ☆ **Match the sentences 1–8 with the question tags a–h.**

1 It's freezing, [d]
2 You stayed at a hotel in London, [ ]
3 She won't waste any money, [ ]
4 Mark has red hair, [ ]
5 You can't solve this math problem, [ ]
6 This museum doesn't attract a lot of people, [ ]
7 You are coming to dinner, [ ]
8 I don't have to clean my room, [ ]

a do I?
b can you?
c didn't you?
d isn't it?
e does it?
f doesn't he?
g aren't you?
h will she?

2 ☆☆ **Complete the sentences with the correct question tags.**

1 We don't have to go to school tomorrow, *do we* ?
2 Pat and Tim have tickets for us, too, ______ ?
3 Sofia listens to a lot of music, ______ ?
4 You'll send me a message when you get there, ______ ?
5 Laura can speak Spanish, ______ ?
6 Andre has never been to Chicago before, ______ ?
7 It's going to be cold outside, ______ ?
8 Alex won't make that mistake again, ______ ?

3 ☆☆ **Complete the questions with the correct words.**

1 *You're* not scared, are you?
2 He can't be serious, ______ he?
3 The food ______ be collected later, won't it?
4 You aren't looking for her, ______ you?
5 Ian clearly doesn't like Fiona, ______ he?
6 The pictures were beautiful, ______ they?

4 ☆☆☆ **Use the prompts to write questions with question tags.**

1 **A** Hi, Tomás.
I / can call / you / Tom / ?
I can call you Tom, can't I?
B Yes, of course. Everyone calls me Tom.

2 **A** I'm nervous about the English exam.
B you / study / every night / ?
______

3 **A** That's a gorgeous bag.
it / make of / wool / ?
______
B Yes, it is. It's a traditional Peruvian bag. I bought it last year.

4 **A** We're going out for pizza after class.
you / will come with us / ?
______
B Yes, of course. See you later.

5 ☆☆☆ **Write four sentences with question tags you could use to start a conversation with a person you've just met for the first time.**

______
______
______
______

WRITING

A Competition Entry

1 **Read the competition entry. Which of these topics is not mentioned?**

a origins of the city
b population
c famous places to visit
d the food

THE BEST CITY I'VE EVER VISITED

HOME | **STORIES** | PHOTOS

London attracts millions of visitors, and on my last visit I understood why. It's a fascinating city, and it has many marvelous places to visit.

The first town was built there by the Romans around 2,000 years ago on the River Thames. The city grew and now has a population of almost nine million! London is enormous – this is the fact that impressed me most, and you are reminded of it when you fly into one of its airports.

There are a lot of places to visit in the city, but the highlight of any visit to London is the London Eye. This huge Ferris wheel was opened in 2000 and is located next to the Thames, near Westminster Bridge. It moves around very slowly, but when you finally get to the top, you are 135 meters high, and the views from there are stunning.

I'm absolutely certain that London deserves to win because it has so many incredible places to visit! Without a doubt, London is the best city in the world to visit!

2 **Read the entry again and answer the questions.**

1 How old is London? *over 2,000 years old*
2 What most impressed the writer about the city?
3 Where is the London Eye?
4 How tall is it?
5 Why does London deserve to win the competition?

3 **How does the writer express these ideas? Find the *Useful Language* phrases in the text.**

1 what was most amazing
this is the fact that impressed me the most
2 the best part of a visit
3 I'm sure
4 it should win
5 it is certain

PLAN

4 **Write a competition entry. Think of the best city you have ever visited. Take notes in your notebook about these things.**

- A short introduction to the city
- General facts about the place
- A detailed description of what impressed you
- Why the place should win

WRITE

5 **Write your competition entry. Remember to include four paragraphs, the passive, extreme adjectives, and phrases from the *Useful Language* box (see Student's Book, p65.)**

CHECK

6 **Do you ...**

- give an introduction?
- describe its highlights?
- explain why you think the place should win?

5 REVIEW

VOCABULARY

1 Match the words in the box with the definitions 1–8. There are two words you don't need.

awful boiling create deafening enormous freezing gorgeous measure solve waste

1 very cold ______
2 make something new ______
3 to use too much of something ______
4 very loud ______
5 find the answer to ______
6 find out the size of something ______
7 very bad ______
8 very beautiful ______

2 Circle the correct options.

1 My phone is *connected* / *communicated* to Wi-Fi, but the video isn't playing.
2 Vero thought the movie was *fascinating* / *boiling*, but I fell asleep after 20 minutes.
3 Some of the scenes in the horror movie were *gorgeous* / *terrifying* – I couldn't watch.
4 What time will my new computer be *solved* / *delivered* tomorrow?
5 Olives are *collected* / *supplied* by shaking the tree really hard so that they all fall on the ground.
6 The wedding was *deafening* / *marvelous*, and the bride's dress was *stunning* / *terrifying*.
7 A lot of insects were *developed* / *attracted* by the smell of the food.
8 Several *enormous* / *freezing* rocks fell from the side of the mountain.

GRAMMAR IN ACTION

3 Complete the text with correct passive form of the verbs in parentheses.

Help Us Fix the Castle

Originally, to build the old castle, enormous rocks 1 ______ (collect) from the mountains near here, and they 2 ______ (deliver) by teams of hundreds of people pulling them. The thick walls 3 ______ all ______ (create) by hand, and the rocks 4 ______ (measure) very carefully because they had to go together perfectly.

Now all the rocks are lying on the ground, so each rock 5 ______ (pull) up and then it 6 ______ (drop) into the right place. We're making good progress.

Next year, we will start on the roof. The roof 7 ______ (make) of wood. Trees from the local forest 8 ______ (cut) down, and then they 9 ______ (bring) here.

4 Complete the sentences with question tags.

1 It's a gorgeous day, ______?
2 We can't connect the printer, ______?
3 Emily hasn't figured out the answers, ______?
4 Dennis didn't return the book, ______?
5 These problems will be solved, ______?
6 Rosanna doesn't waste any time, ______?
7 All the pieces of the table have been measured, ______?
8 Bees produce honey, ______?

CUMULATIVE GRAMMAR

5 Complete the conversation with the missing words. Circle the correct options.

EMILIA What [1] ______ to do for the physics presentation next week?

GEORGE I'm not sure. I [2] ______ do something about the tallest buildings in the world.

EMILIA That's … umm … different. I mean … doing something about the stars and planets is easier, [3] ______?

GEORGE Well, I [4] ______ this documentary about the Jeddah Tower yesterday – it's in Saudi Arabia. When it's finished, it's going to be the tallest building they'll [5] ______.

EMILIA How tall is the one in Dubai?

GEORGE The Burj Khalifa? That's only 828 meters tall. This one will be [6] ______ bigger! They [7] ______ to make it a mile high – that's 1.6 kilometers – but there were too many problems with that. They think it'll be over one kilometer.

EMILIA Seriously? That's [8] ______ enormous. But what do you mean "they think"?

GEORGE Well, it could be [9] ______ taller than one kilometer. They're not sure yet.

EMILIA I [10] ______ believe they actually don't know. Someone [11] ______ know.

GEORGE Well, of course, but it's a secret, I think.

EMILIA So, when are they going to finish it?

GEORGE Well, [12] ______ on it since 2013, and they [13] ______ it for around eight years.

EMILIA That's amazing, isn't it?

GEORGE Yeah … and to think the tallest thing in the world [14] ______ the Eiffel Tower.

EMILIA Anyway, so what does all this have to do with the physics presentation?

	a	b	c	d
1	do you do	you will do	are you going	may you do
2	must	should	must not	might
3	it is	doesn't it	isn't it	won't it
4	had watched	used to watch	watched	have watched
5	have never built	ever build	have ever built	already have built
6	a little	far	really	fairly
7	have planned	had planned	have been planning	will have planned
8	really	extremely	a lot	a little
9	pretty	absolutely	really	a bit
10	must not	don't have to	shouldn't	can't
11	doesn't	must	can't	may
12	they've been working	they're working	they work	they'll be working
13	'll build	're going to build	'll be building	build
14	would be	is	used to be	had been

6 When do you push the limits?

VOCABULARY

Verb Collocations with *To Get*, *To Take*, and *To Have*

1 ★ Complete the chart with the words and phrases in the box.

~~advantage of~~ a lot out of
an interest in bored doubts fun
lost on my nerves pleasure in risks
the chance to know

To Get	To Have	To Take
		advantage of

2 ★★ Match the beginnings of the sentences 1–6 with the endings a–f.

1 Oscar has really been getting [a]
2 Sergio actually takes [ ]
3 How did you get [ ]
4 Victor really got [ ]
5 I had never taken [ ]
6 Chefs shouldn't take [ ]

a on my nerves lately.
b lost on your way to school?
c risks when they're chopping food – they might cut themselves!
d an interest in doing anything dangerous before.
e pleasure in eating really spicy food.
f a lot out of his time in San Francisco – his English is a lot better.

3 ★★ Complete the conversation with one word in each blank.

MIA What's the matter?
ROSE It's Laura again. She's really [1] *getting* on my nerves.
MIA What did she do?
ROSE Well, I'd just like her to take an interest [2] ________ the things I like doing. She just says she [3] ________ bored when she's with my friends.
MIA That's not fair. She should try getting to [4] ________ them. She [5] ________ the chance to join our group at the party on Friday, and she didn't take advantage [6] ________ it. She just stood in the corner on her own!
ROSE Exactly! When we go out with her friends, I always try to [7] ________ fun. I'm having [8] ________ about our friendship!

4 ★★★ Complete the sentences so they are true for you. (See the *Learn to Learn* tip in the Student's Book, p71.)

1 When I get lost, I ________________.
2 It really gets on my nerves when ________________.
3 I always have fun when I ________________.
4 I once had the chance to ________________, but I didn't do it!

Explore It!

Guess the correct answer.

What is the most dangerous job in the world?

a a lumberjack (a person who cuts down trees)

b a firefighter

c an astronaut

Find another interesting fact about dangerous jobs. Write a question and send it to a classmate in an email, or ask them in the next class.

READING

An Article

1 ☆ **Read the text. Which two places have Mari and Patricio lived in?** ________________

2 ☆☆ **Look at the words in bold in the text. Use them to complete the sentences.**

1 A long time ago, humans used to ___hunt___ for all their meat.

2 When we visited the village, we stayed in a ________.

3 I find that very hard to believe. It sounds ________.

4 In the desert, we met a ________ who lived in tents.

5 Eliza ________ that she made a mistake.

6 There are a lot of interesting animals and plants in the ________.

3 ☆☆ **Read the text again and circle the correct options.**

1 In this text, the writer is trying to …

a encourage people to visit Ecuador.

b give her opinion of Patricio and Mari's relationship.

c show how difficult it is to live in England.

d explain why Mari decided to go and live in Ecuador.

2 What does the writer think of Mari's actions?

a She agrees that they are ridiculous.

b She admires Mari because she wasn't afraid.

c She finds it hard to believe.

d She's amazed by the story of how Mari met Patricio.

3 Patricio went back to Ecuador because he …

a found a job building houses.

b wanted to spend more time with his daughter.

c didn't like living so far from his community.

d couldn't find work in Essex.

4 What does Mari think about her new life?

a It isn't easy for her because everything is different.

b She misses the life she had in Essex.

c It's difficult because she can't catch fish.

d She would like to go back to her family and business.

Moving to the Jungle

If you had the chance to give up everything to go and live in the Amazon jungle, would you do it? You would certainly have to be very brave, but 52-year-old Mari Muench took the risk.

Her story, which even she describes as "completely **ridiculous**," started in 2010 when she was on vacation in Ecuador. There she met Patricio, who is a shaman in his **tribe**. Patricio asked Mari to dance, and as they got to know each other, he told her an amazing story. He said that when he was just 15 years old, he had a dream in which he saw her. Mari also felt a very strong connection to the place. "Unless I come to live here with Patricio," she thought, "I'll never be happy."

A few months after this first meeting, Mari and Patricio got married! Then they decided to move to Essex, near London, where their daughter Samai was born. But Patricio had many doubts about living so far from his community.

So Patricio moved back to Ecuador and took advantage of the time there to begin making preparations for Mari and Samai's arrival. With help from his tribe, over a period of four months, he cleared a small piece of land in the **rainforest** and built a traditional **hut** using only materials from the forest, his hands, and a lot of hard work.

In 2018, Mari left her Essex home, her family, and her successful go-karting business, as well as the advantages of modern life, for the Ecuadorian jungle. After a two-day journey, Mari and Samai reached Patricio's community. Mari is learning how to **hunt** and fish, eat insects, and share her life with her new family. "It's the hardest thing I've ever done," she **admits**, but she says she's very happy.

4 ☆☆☆ **What do you think life will be like for Mari, Patricio, and Samai? Write four sentences.**

____

____

____

____

GRAMMAR IN ACTION

First and Second Conditional

1 ★ **Match the beginnings of the sentences 1–5 with the ends a–e.**

1 If you had the chance, [d]
2 We'll almost certainly get lost [ ]
3 Unless he pays attention, [ ]
4 Mateo would work harder [ ]
5 If you had a blog, [ ]

a he won't get a lot out of Mr. Smith's classes.
b I would read it.
c unless we stop and ask someone.
d would you fly in a helicopter?
e if you encouraged him more.

2 ★★ **Complete the second sentence so that it means the same as the first. Use no more than three words.**

1 In case of any doubts, you can call me.
If you *have* any doubts, you can call me.

2 Without taking risks, you'd get really bored.
You'd get really bored if you ______ ______ any risks.

3 You don't like Rafael because you don't really know him.
You'd really like Rafael if you ______ ______ to know him.

4 I'll put the cat out in the yard if he annoys you.
I'll put the cat out in the yard ______ ______ on your nerves.

5 You can get a lot out of playing team sports.
______ team sports, you can get a lot of them.

3 ★★ **Complete the conversation with the correct form of the verbs in parentheses.**

GRETA What are you doing, James?
JAMES I'm making pizza. If you [1] *'re* (be) nice to me, I [2] ______ (give) you a slice.
GRETA Great. But if you [3] ______ (put) pineapple on it, I [4] ______ (not eat) it.
JAMES Well, if you [5] ______ (not like) pineapple, I think I [6] ______ (put) some extra chunks on it!
GRETA Come on, James. If I [7] ______ (make) pizza, I [8] ______ (not use) any ingredients you didn't like.
JAMES That's true – but you don't cook! If you ever want to learn, I [9] ______ (help) you.
GRETA Oh, please. You only know how to make pizza! If I [10] ______ (take) an interest in cooking, I [11] ______ (ask) Mom or Dad to help me.
JAMES OK, that's it! Extra chunks of pineapple!

4 ★★ **Underline and correct one mistake in each sentence.**

1 If I <u>have</u> a drone, I would fly it really fast. *had*
2 If you folded your clothes properly, your room won't be such a mess. ______
3 Will we get lost if we won't follow the map? ______
4 If I listen to classical music, it might be inspire me. ______
5 Unless you don't try it, you'll never know what it's like. ______
6 What you would do if you had doubts about your future? ______

5 ★★★ **Complete the sentences with your own ideas.**

1 If I knew how to cook well, ______.
2 If I had a blog, ______.
3 I would take more risks if ______.
4 Unless I fail all my exams, ______.
5 If I get a really good job, ______.
6 If I get bored later, ______.

VOCABULARY AND LISTENING

Inspiration and Challenge

1 ☆ **Find nine more words connected with challenges in the word search.**

E	N	C	O	U	R	A	G	E	I	D	G
N	F	A	P	T	X	C	N	I	R	E	D
I	N	S	P	I	R	E	T	A	S	T	C
B	E	R	O	B	S	T	A	C	L	E	H
X	O	B	R	A	V	E	R	Y	B	R	A
Q	V	T	T	O	R	Z	T	T	O	M	L
P	E	F	U	U	T	Y	B	G	O	I	L
U	R	C	N	R	G	U	D	V	Y	N	E
A	C	H	I	E	V	E	W	O	R	A	N
L	O	T	T	P	V	I	S	A	E	T	G
V	M	W	I	P	L	D	A	Q	W	I	E
B	E	X	E	R	W	A	U	X	D	O	K
R	U	S	S	U	P	P	O	R	T	N	E

2 ☆☆ **Match the words from Exercise 1 with the definitions.**

1 You'll need this in a dangerous situation. *bravery*

2 My parents do this so that I read more books. ______

3 You'll have to go around or over it. ______

4 Your family and friends will always do this. ______

5 An extraordinary person does this to other people. ______

6 You'll need to work hard when you have one. ______

7 When you keep trying and never give up, you have this. ______

8 You do this if you deal with something successfully. ______

9 If you're lucky, you have these. ______

10 When you reach your goal, you do this. ______

3 ☆☆☆ **Write a paragraph about someone who acted with bravery. You can write a true story or invent one.**

______

______

______

A Radio Show

6.01 **4** ☆ **Listen to the radio show about what people think is "risky behavior." Put the pictures in the order you hear about them.**

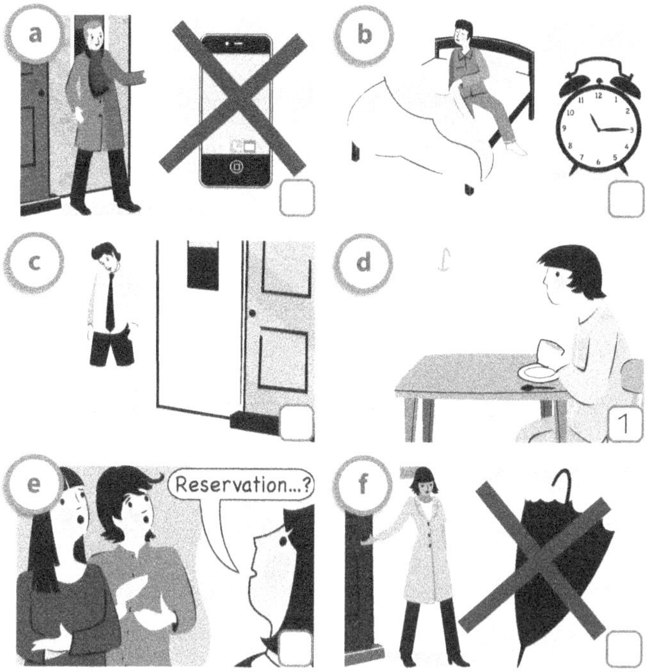

6.01 **5** ☆☆ **Listen again and circle the correct options. (See the *Learn to Learn* tip in the Student's Book, p74.)**

1 How many people took part in the survey?
   (a) 2,000   b over 2,000   c 40

2 People think it's risky to drink coffee or tea before ....
   a going out   b having breakfast   c going to bed

3 What do people think is risky when they go to a restaurant?
   a ordering foreign food
   b going without making a reservation
   c reserving a table after 11 p.m.

4 What shouldn't you do with your smartphone?
   a leave it charging for too long
   b take it everywhere you go
   c leave it at home

5 People also think it's risky to leave the house ....
   a with different shoes or socks
   b with wet hair
   c in their pajamas

GRAMMAR IN ACTION

Third Conditional

1 Match the sentences 1–4 with the pictures a–d.

1 If Charlie had missed the bus, he wouldn't have met Hannah. d

2 If Charlie hadn't missed the bus, he wouldn't have arrived late. ☐

3 If I hadn't gone to the party, I wouldn't have had so much fun. ☐

4 I would have gone to the party if I hadn't agreed to watch a movie with Suzy. ☐

a

b

c

d

2 Complete the sentences with the correct form of the verbs in parentheses.

TO: Aisha

FROM: Amy

Hi Aisha,

I'm never going to have a party in my house again! First of all, if I [1] hadn't invited (not invite) so many people, there [2] ______ (be) more food for everyone. Then, Caro and Elsa [3] ______ (not get) lost if I [4] ______ (send) them a map. I don't think inviting Tomás was a good idea, either. If he [5] ______ (not jump) on the sofa, he [6] ______ (not break) the mirror in the living room.

There was one good thing. If Mira [7] ______ (not come), she [8] ______ (not bring) her friend Beatriz. She's from Brazil, and she invited me to stay with her when I go traveling this summer!

Amy

3 Complete the second sentence so that it means the same as the first. Use no more than three words.

1 Holly didn't have the same opportunities as everyone else, so she didn't go to college.
If Holly had had the same opportunities as everyone else, she would have gone to college.

2 George didn't take any interest, so he failed the exam.
If George had taken an interest, he ______ failed the exam.

3 The fish didn't taste very good because of the sauce.
The fish ______ better if it hadn't had that sauce.

4 My friend Mike went to the hospital last week because he broke his leg playing soccer.
Mike wouldn't have gone to the hospital if he ______ his leg playing soccer.

5 The party turned out really well because the music was amazing.
The party wouldn't ______ out so well if the music hadn't been so amazing.

4 Answer the questions with your own ideas.

1 What would you have done if you hadn't come to school today?

______

2 If you'd been born 50 years ago, what would your childhood have been like?

______

WRITING

A For and Against Essay

1 ☆ **Read the essay. Is the writer in favor of or against taking risks?** ____

A Life Without Risks Is Boring

1 It's difficult to imagine a life without risk. 1 ____For____ example, we take risks every day when we leave the house. In fact, doctors say your home is the most dangerous place in the world!

2 2 ____ the one hand, some people take pleasure in dangerous situations. For 3 ____, they think that if they don't do something dangerous, 4 ____ as climbing mountains, they'll get bored. Some people argue that they are overcoming obstacles with determination.

3 On the 5 ____ hand, many people would rather live a quiet life. They don't need to challenge themselves every day. 6 ____, they say that you can get a lot out of life by having fun without taking risks.

4 7 ____ conclusion, it seems to me that if you live your life worrying about the dangers around you, you'll never be happy. However, I personally 8 ____ you shouldn't take too many risks. You only live once, they say. That could mean take risks because you only have one life, but it can also mean that you should stay alive if you can.

2 ☆☆ **Complete the *Useful Language* phrases in the essay with the words in the box.**

believe	~~for~~	furthermore	in	instance	on	other	such

3 ☆☆ **Read the essay again. Complete the sentences.**

1 Doctors say our homes are ____.
2 Some people get bored if they don't ____.
3 Many people would prefer ____.
4 "You only live once" can mean ____ or ____.

4 **Read the essay again. Which paragraph (1–4) ...**

a explains the reasons against the argument? ____
b summarizes the writer's general opinion? ____
c introduces the argument ____
d explains the reasons for the argument? ____

PLAN

5 ☆☆ **Look at the essay title and take notes on your arguments in favor of and against the statement.**

Life Is Just About Having Fun

In favor: ____

Against: ____

6 ☆☆ **Decide what information to include in each paragraph. Use the information from Exercise 4 to help you.**

WRITE

7 ☆☆☆ **Write your essay. Remember to include four paragraphs, conditional sentences, vocabulary from this unit, and phrases from the *Useful Language* box (see Student's Book, p77).**

CHECK

8 **Do you ...**

- include an introduction?
- talk about negatives?
- talk about positives?
- have a conclusion?

6 REVIEW

VOCABULARY

1 Complete the expressions with *get*, *have*, or *take*.

1 ________ on my nerves
2 ________ advantage of
3 ________ fun
4 ________ risks
5 ________ bored
6 ________ doubts
7 ________ an interest in
8 ________ a lot out of
9 ________ pleasure in
10 ________ to know
11 ________ lost
12 ________ the chance

2 Complete the sentences with the words in the box.

achieve	bravery	challenge	determination	encouraged	inspired	obstacles	opportunities	overcome	support

1 We went to the stadium on Saturday to ________ our soccer team.
2 When Paola moved to Moscow, the biggest ________ was learning to speak Russian.
3 If you fail this test, they won't give you any more ________.
4 My parents ________ me to learn how to play the piano, and now I'm a professional musician.
5 Rescuing that dog from the river took a lot of ________.
6 We were losing 3–0, but our ________ helped us to come back and win 4–3.
7 Liz was ________ to write this song by things that happened when she was young.
8 Everyone has to ________ many ________ throughout their lives – that's life.
9 Gonzalo had to work very hard to ________ his dream of becoming a dancer.

GRAMMAR IN ACTION

3 Put the words in the correct order to make first and second conditional sentences.

1 I / the teacher / the answer / I'd ask / If / didn't know / .
____
2 have to / If / you / Peter / have / ask / you'll / any / doubts / .
____
3 message / send / you / If / I / bored / get / I'll / a / .
____
4 you / dreams / you'll / Unless / achieve / your / never / try harder / .
____
5 risky / I / do / it / wouldn't / was / I / thought / it / If / .
____
6 anything / this obstacle / You'll / you / never / overcome / unless / achieve / .
____

4 Complete the third conditional sentences with the correct form of the verbs in parentheses.

1 If I ________ (get) lost, I ________ (not arrive) on time.
2 He ________ (do) better in the race if you ________ (encourage) him more.
3 Steve ________ (not say) anything if you ________ (not get) on his nerves.
4 I ________ (not be) able to buy a new phone if I ________ (not save) all my allowance for months!
5 If you ________ (not sit) in the back, you ________ (hear) everything the teacher said.

CUMULATIVE GRAMMAR

5 **Complete the interview with the missing words. Circle the correct options.**

INTERVIEWER So why did you decide to become a soccer player?

JULIA I suppose it's like everyone. I [1] _____ love playing when I was a child. I always had fun playing soccer. But if I [2] _____ the support of my family, I would never [3] _____ a professional.

INTERVIEWER [4] _____ hard for you?

JULIA Yes, sometimes. When I was younger, I had doubts about my ability. But then my coach [5] _____ an interest in me, and I [6] _____ to improve and to get [7] _____ better than I was. I knew I [8] _____ improve my skills if I wanted to achieve my dreams.

INTERVIEWER You don't get bored with soccer, [9] _____ ?

JULIA No, I don't. [10] _____ pleasure in training, and my teammates really inspire me. I wouldn't be happy [11] _____ I wasn't training and playing soccer, and there are thousands of people there to support me every week. How [12] _____ I get bored?

1 a would	b used to	c could	d had to
2 a hadn't had	b hadn't	c haven't had	d haven't
3 a become	b became	c have become	d to become
4 a Is it	b Was it	c Has it been	d Had it been
5 a take	b took	c had taken	d might take
6 a was encouraged	b encouraged	c am encouraged	d encourages
7 a bit	b fairly	c totally	d far
8 a must	b will have to	c would have needed	d would have to
9 a do you	b don't you	c are you	d were you
10 a I'm always taking	b I was always taking	c I've always taken	d I could always take
11 a if	b unless	c when	d after
12 a must	b could	c should	d may

7 Why are emotions important?

VOCABULARY

Feelings

1 Complete the adjectives with the correct vowels. Then complete the chart with the adjectives.

1 r i d i c u l o u s
2 gr _ t _ f _ l
3 h _ rt
4 d _ wn
5 gl _ d
6 p _ _ c _ f _ l
7 _ ns _ c _ r _
8 _ m _ s _ d
9 _ _ g _ r
10 _ nn _ y _ d
11 h _ p _ f _ l
12 thr _ ll _ d
13 s _ t _ sf _ _ d

Positive ☺	Negative ☹

2 Circle the correct options.

1 Please don't post that photo. I look *peaceful* / *ridiculous*!
2 What did you do? Why is Emily so *annoyed* / *grateful* with you?
3 Marcos needs your help. He's feeling *glad* / *insecure* about his class project.
4 If they knew it was raining, they wouldn't be so *amused* / *eager* to go out.
5 My math teacher isn't *satisfied* / *hopeful* with my work. She thinks I can do better.
6 Kathy's *thrilled* / *down* because she's getting a new phone.

3 Complete the sentences with correct adjectives from Exercise 1.

1 Lucas is ___hurt___ because you didn't invite him to the party. You should say you're sorry.
2 I'm so ________ you called because I wanted to ask you something.
3 I like studying in the backyard because it's so ________ – all you can hear are the birds singing.
4 Liam's feeling ________ because his best friend has just moved to Germany.
5 The teacher wasn't very ________ with my joke, so she gave me extra homework.
6 We're taking a big risk, but we're all ________ that everything will turn out well.

4 Write a sentence describing how you would feel if these things happened to you. Explain why. (See the *Learn to Learn* tip in the Student's Book, p83.)

How would you feel if …

1 you had to make dinner for your family?
____
2 one of your relatives gave you some money?
____
3 a friend of yours told you she was moving to another city?
____
4 your teacher told you that you had an exam tomorrow?
____
5 you remembered it was a holiday while waiting for the school bus?
____

Explore It!

Guess the correct answers (choose two options).

Dogs can recognize whether a human is angry or happy by … .

a their facial expression
b the words they use
c the tone of their voice

Find another interesting fact about an animal that can recognize human emotions. Write a question and send it to a classmate in an email, or ask them in the next class.

READING

A Magazine Interview

1 ☆ **Read the interview. Is this sentence true or false?**

Mindfulness doesn't help students with their exams.

2 ☆☆ **Look at the underlined words in the interview. Use them to complete the sentences.**

1 I can't *concentrate* if you keep talking. You're getting on my nerves.

2 Humans have five ______ : hearing, sight, taste, smell, and touch.

3 Santiago improved his ______ in tennis with practice.

4 Dr. Morgan has done many ______ about stress.

5 That car has a very ______ engine. It's the fastest car in the world.

6 The doctor told my dad that if he ______ his weight, he'll be healthier.

3 ☆☆☆ **Read the interview again and circle the correct options.**

1 Jeremy Parker says that *concentration* / *mindfulness* can stop people from having negative feelings.

2 Mindfulness teaches us to pay more attention to *the present* / *difficult situations*.

3 Meditation is used to *control our feelings* / *make us happy*.

4 When we're depressed, *we sometimes make ourselves* / *other people sometimes make us* feel even worse.

5 Cognitive therapy *studies how mindfulness works* / *can teach people to understand their feelings*.

6 Safari Walk is *not difficult to learn* / *especially good for children*.

4 ☆☆☆☆ **Answer the questions so they are true for you.**

1 What do you do when you feel down or insecure?

______

2 Would you like to learn more about mindfulness? Why / Why not?

______

Mindfulness for Students

Sometimes you're worried and insecure about everything, and you can't concentrate. These feelings affect your personal life and your schoolwork and can sometimes get worse. The psychologist Jeremy Parker (and many other experts) suggests using mindfulness.

What is mindfulness?

Mindfulness is a very powerful tool or technique that helps people concentrate more on the here and now. It helps you stay calm in difficult situations, which you often create for yourself. The technique teaches you to practice breathing and uses meditation to calm you down and understand your feelings and thoughts.

How does mindfulness help?

Everyone has times when they feel down or they feel hurt for some reason. Your mind is full of negative feelings, and there's a voice inside you telling you that you're a failure or that you're useless. Through meditation, you learn not to listen to that voice and after a time … the voice stops. So you stop worrying about things so much, and you avoid thinking those negative thoughts.

What is the science behind mindfulness?

There's an area of psychology called "cognitive therapy" that helps people understand how they are thinking and change it. Mindfulness is based on this, and many studies show that it works. One study, for example, showed that meditating before an exam helps you get better grades. Another study shows that it reduces stress and worry.

Can you give an example of a mindfulness activity?

There's a simple activity called "Safari Walk." It works for children, adolescents, and adults, and it's very simple: you walk somewhere, and while you're walking, you notice everything. You listen to the sounds of birds singing, you look at the colors of things – you use all your senses to be in the moment. And you feel peaceful and happy.

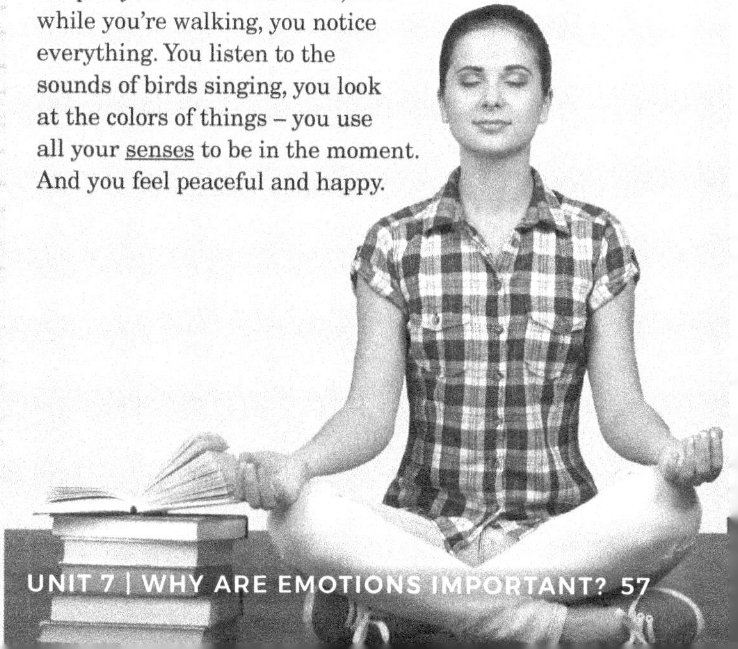

GRAMMAR IN ACTION

Gerunds and Infinitives (with *to*)

1 ☆ Circle the correct options.

1 *Getting* / *To get* lost on the way to school is not normal.

2 It's important *taking* / *to take* advantage of the opportunities you are given.

3 George says he enjoys *cooking* / *to cook*, but he doesn't have time.

4 I tasted the sauce *checking* / *to check* if it was too spicy.

5 She decided not *to wear* / *wearing* her new boots to the party.

6 I'm annoyed about *to lose* / *losing* the game.

2 ☆☆ Complete the conversation with the correct form of the verbs in parentheses.

MAE [1] *Going* (go) to that mindfulness class was a great idea.

ISA Yes, it was. I'm eager [2] ______ (try) it. I'd like [3] ______ (learn) a few more of Dr. Fraser's techniques.

MAE Well, first he told us to practice [4] ______ (breathe) … like this.

ISA Don't forget [5] ______ (hold) it for a few seconds.

MAE I feel a bit ridiculous, but after [6] ______ (do) it a few times, I know I'll feel better.

ISA [7] ______ (learn) something new is always a little strange at the beginning.

MAE I suppose it is. He suggested [8] ______ (try) it at home on our own before the next meeting.

ISA OK, I'm going home [9] ______ (practice). I'll send a message later [10] ______ (tell) you how it's going.

3 ☆☆ Complete the sentences with the correct form of the verbs in the box.

bring	hear	look	~~take~~	win	write

1 After an hour of studying, I stopped *to take* a short break.

2 I'll never forget ______ the championship last year – I was so thrilled.

3 I remember ______ a strange noise, and then all the lights went out.

4 John didn't do his homework because he forgot ______ it down yesterday.

5 Rania stopped ______ at her phone to listen to the news.

6 Did you remember ______ a sandwich to school today? We have an extra class.

4 ☆☆ Match the sentences with the correct meanings.

1 I stopped to talk to Matt. — a

2 I stopped talking to Matt.

3 I forgot to call Lisa.

4 I forgot I called Lisa.

a I stopped what I was doing to talk to Matt.

b I don't talk to Matt anymore.

c I don't remember calling Lisa.

d I didn't call Lisa.

5 ☆☆☆ Answer the questions so they are true for you. Write full sentences.

1 Do you enjoy swimming in the ocean in the summer? Why / Why not?

______

2 What did you forget to do last week?

______

3 Which sport would you be interested in learning to play?

______

4 What do you hope to do when you finish school?

______

5 What things have you stopped doing since you were a child?

______

VOCABULARY AND LISTENING

Expressions with *Heart* and *Mind*

1 ☆ What word goes on the back of these flashcards? Write *heart* or *mind*. (See the *Learn to Learn* tip in the Student's Book, p86.)

1 put his ______ into it — *heart*

2 learn something by ______

3 have something on your ______

4 break someone's ______

5 it crossed my ______

2 ☆☆ Complete the text with one word in each blank.

Making decisions is the hardest thing in the world. I just can't [1] *make* up my mind whether I want this or that. And then, when I've made a choice, I often have doubts. I'll have the decision [2] ______ my mind for days. Suddenly, it [3] ______ my mind that the other choice might be better, and I think maybe I should [4] ______ my mind. And when it's something that involves other people, I have to [5] ______ in mind what other people think. Maybe you should choose for me!

3 ☆☆☆ Answer the questions.

1 What was the last thing you had to learn by heart?

______

2 What do you do when you can't make up your mind about something?

______

3 Who do you talk to when you have something on your mind?

______

A Conversation

4 ☆ Listen to the conversation between Jack, Amy, and Valerie. What does Jack decide to do? (7.01)

______

5 ☆☆ Listen again and answer the questions. (7.01)

1 What will Jack have to do soon?

He'll have to take exams.

2 What does Valerie do after school?

______

3 Why does she do it?

______

4 What does Amy do?

______

5 How did she feel at the beginning?

______

6 Why don't Valerie and Amy support Jack's decision?

______

6 ☆☆☆ Write about something you do after school. What do you do? Why did you decide to do it? What do you like about it?

______

______

______

GRAMMAR IN ACTION

Subject and Object Questions

1 ☆ Complete the subject questions with *Who* or *What*.

1 A *Who* decided to buy this ridiculous present for Alejandro?
B It was Flavia.

2 A ________ changed your mind about the T-shirt?
B The price.

3 A ________ made such a deafening noise?
B It was thunder.

4 A ________ wants to learn all those names by heart?
B Nobody.

5 A ________ enjoyed the concert the most?
B Emilio did.

2 ☆☆ Put the words in the correct order to make questions.

1 you / exams / do / about / feeling / How / avoid / nervous / ?
How do you avoid feeling nervous about exams?

2 the / crossed / when / mind / your / drone / you / What / saw / ?
____

3 decide / to / shopping / did / with / you / go / Who / ?
____

4 get / is / soccer / to / game / going / at / Who / bored / a / ?
____

5 you / annoyed / about / did / get / What / so / ?
____

3 ☆ Match the answers a–e with the questions from Exercise 2.

a My sister. She hates going to the stadium. ☐
b I thought it was a bird! ☐
c The computer – it stopped working! ☐
d Leandro came with me. I bought these jeans. ☐
e Mindfulness helps me avoid feeling nervous. 1

4 ☆☆☆ Complete the interview. Write questions with *Who* or *What* and the words given.

A discover / your amazing ability?
[1]*Who discovered your amazing ability?*

B My coach, Alison. She saw me playing one day and told me she'd like to be my coach.

A You used to play soccer, but now you play tennis. make / you / change / your mind / ?
[2] ________

B I enjoyed them both, but I had to make up my mind, and I just loved playing tennis.

A It hasn't been easy for you. support / you in the difficult times / ? [3] ________

B My family – they're amazing.

A inspire / you / ? [4] ________

B I really admire Rafael Nadal.

A Now you're number one in your country. it / feel / like / ? [5] ________

B It's amazing. I'm thrilled.

A You always seem very calm. get / on / nerves / ?
[6] ________

B A lot of things, actually. I don't like doing interviews!

5 ☆☆☆ Answer the questions so they are true for you. Write full sentences.

1 What do you often get annoyed about?
____

2 Who calls or sends you messages every day?
____

3 Among your friends, who plays a musical instrument?
____

4 Who made dinner at home last night?
____

WRITING

An Email Reply

1 ☆ **Read the emails. Which piece of advice does Daniel not give?**

1 Find a good teacher. ☐
2 Buy an expensive guitar. ☐
3 Borrow a guitar. ☐
4 Watch videos. ☐

TO: Daniel
FROM: Monica

Hi Daniel,

Josue told me that you took up the guitar this year. I'm hoping to learn how to play, too, but I'm not sure. Is it very difficult? Any advice?

All the best,

Monica

TO: Monica
FROM: Daniel

Hi Monica,

I'm so glad you wrote to me. Playing the guitar is fun, so [1] *I would recommend* learning it. It's difficult at the beginning, so [2] ________ find a teacher. My teacher was really patient, and he never got annoyed with me when I did something silly.

Also, [3] ________ to borrow someone else's guitar for the first few weeks until you're sure you enjoy it. [4] ________, don't go out and buy an expensive guitar and then change your mind. Who wants to waste money like that?

You're probably eager to start learning songs, but first try to learn basic things like where to put your fingers. When you find a teacher, [5] ________ taking classes more often at the beginning? I took three classes a week to get a good start.

Online videos were really helpful, and I'm grateful to my teacher for suggesting that I watch them.

Anyway, good luck!

All the best,

Daniel

2 ☆☆ **Complete the email with the *Useful Language*.**

a Whatever you do
b it would definitely help to
c why don't you suggest
d ~~I would recommend~~
e it might be better

PLAN

3 ☆☆ **Write an email reply. Look at Laurie's email and think of pieces of advice.**

Hi,

I'm really insecure about my exam, and I'm feeling very nervous. Do you have any advice?

Laurie

Take notes on what you think she should and shouldn't do.

Do: ________

____

Don't: ________

____

WRITE

4 ☆☆☆ **Write your email reply. Remember to include your advice from Exercise 3, *Useful Language* phrases for recommending and suggesting (see Student's Book, p89), and reasons for your suggestions.**

CHECK

5 **Do you ...**

- say what Laurie should do?
- say what Laurie should not do?
- think the advice is useful?

7 REVIEW

VOCABULARY

1 Find 12 more feelings adjectives in the word search.

R	B	(E	A	G	E	R)	F	O	L	P	S
I	V	S	N	L	C	V	U	H	U	R	T
D	G	A	N	A	Y	A	I	N	H	V	H
I	R	T	O	D	O	W	N	N	O	P	R
C	A	I	Y	F	R	B	S	J	P	K	I
U	T	S	E	D	T	V	E	U	E	Q	L
L	E	F	D	P	E	A	C	E	F	U	L
O	F	I	A	F	Y	E	U	W	U	K	E
U	U	E	S	C	H	F	R	R	L	J	D
S	L	D	A	M	U	S	E	D	F	U	P

2 Complete the expressions.

1 b__________ my heart
2 c__________ my mind
3 s__________ my mind
4 c__________ to my heart
5 m__________ up my mind
6 l__________ by heart
7 p__________ my heart i__________ it
8 h__________ something on my mind
9 b__________ in mind
10 c__________ my mind

GRAMMAR IN ACTION

3 Circle the correct options: gerund (*G*) or infinitive (*I*).

1 after verbs like *decide*, *refuse*, *hope* G I
2 after prepositions G I
3 to explain purpose G I
4 after verbs like *avoid*, *enjoy*, *suggest* G I
5 as the subject of a sentence G I
6 after adjectives G I

4 Complete the sentences with the correct form of the verbs in the box.

feel go help learn see waste

1 I enjoy __________ things by heart sometimes.
2 Edward is eager __________ with the preparations for the party.
3 Mindfulness can help you avoid __________ nervous.
4 I don't remember __________ to the hospital after the accident.
5 __________ time is very easy when you have a phone in your hand.
6 I connected these two cords __________ what would happen.

5 Complete the questions for the interview.

INTERVIEWER [1]When / you / start playing basketball / ?
____
MATT When I was about seven years old.
INTERVIEWER [2]Who / teach / you how to play / ?
____
MATT My dad. He loves basketball.
INTERVIEWER [3]Who / give / you your first basketball / ?
____
MATT My coach, actually. Until then, I'd always played with my dad's ball.
INTERVIEWER [4]Who / be / your favorite player / ?
____
MATT LeBron James, of course.
INTERVIEWER [5]What / make / you feel insecure / ?
____
MATT Doing interviews. I never know what to say.
INTERVIEWER [6]Where / you / practice / ?
____
MATT At school. We have a very good gym.

CUMULATIVE GRAMMAR

6 Complete the text with the missing words. Circle the correct options.

Birds Come to Town

A small community called Broken Hill in New South Wales, Australia, has a problem. A group of emus – large Australian birds that can't fly – have decided [1] ______ in the town. It [2] ______ in the region for many months, and vets believe the birds [3] ______ be looking for food and water. [4] ______ along the main street of the town is [5] ______ strange. You can see the emus stopping to eat in yards. The vets in the area believe the birds [6] ______ food and water by local people, and now, of course, the emus aren't very eager to leave town. Bruce Wilson, a police officer in Broken Hill, says, "If it [7] ______, they wouldn't have come. But if people didn't give them food, they [8] ______. This isn't a natural place for them." Local people are afraid some of the birds [9] ______ by dogs. "What [10] ______ if an emu is killed by a car?" asked another neighbor.

1 a living	b live	c lives	d to live
2 a doesn't rain	b hasn't rained	c hasn't been raining	d isn't raining
3 a might	b can	c should	d had to
4 a To walk	b Walk	c Walking	d Walks
5 a too	b a lot	c extremely	d absolutely
6 a have been giving	b have been given	c have given	d are giving
7 a rained	b has rained	c will rain	d had rained
8 a wouldn't stay	b won't stay	c don't stay	d hadn't stayed
9 a are attacked	b will be attacked	c might attack	d attacked
10 a will happen	b had happened	c happened	d does happen

8 What influences you?

VOCABULARY
Advertising

1 ☆ **Complete the crossword. Use the clues.**

Across →

3 the name of a type of product
6 tell people about your product (on TV or online)
9 a person who is selling something
10 you write this to give your opinion about a product
11 a symbol that represents the product

Down ↓

1 change how someone thinks about something
2 a program that stops ads on your computer
4 the object or service a company sells
5 this type of company makes ads
7 a word or short phrase linked to a brand
8 a person who buys something

2 ☆☆ **Complete the sentences with the correct form of the verbs in the box.**

advertise block ~~buy~~ market not influence produce review sell

1 I don't want *to buy* a new phone. This one's perfectly good.
2 A lot of the people who ______ the book online said they didn't like it.
3 I saw those drones ______ on TV – they look amazing.
4 Some products are very difficult ______ in other countries because of their names.
5 Do you know anyone who ______ a bike? I need a new one.
6 Most technological devices like phones and tablets ______ in Asian countries.
7 A lot of people say that advertising ______ them – but actually it does.
8 There are so many ads on the Internet that sometimes I'd really like ______ them all.

3 ☆☆ **Look at the verbs in Exercise 2 again. What is their noun form? (See the *Learn to Learn* tip in the Student's Book, p95.)**

1 *buyer*
2 ______
3 ______
4 ______
5 ______
6 ______
7 ______
8 ______

Explore It!

Guess the correct answer.

It's not true that we don't like watching ads. An ad for Samsung in India has had over ______ million views.

a 100 b 150 c 200

Find another interesting fact about an ad. Write a question and sent it to a classmate in an email, or ask them in the next class.

READING

A Report

1 Read the report. In what ways can companies find out about our habits?

____

2 Match the underlined words in the report with the definitions.

1 open a webpage ___access___
2 looking through ______
3 collect ______
4 give someone the most recent information ______
5 information, especially facts and numbers ______
6 suppling something for free ______

3 Are the sentences *T* (true) or *F* (false)? Correct the false sentences.

1 We only provide marketing companies with information when we want to.
F. We also provide them with information without realizing it.
2 GPS is used with social media to record where we are.
______
3 A lot of data is gathered to give users recommendations.
______
4 Data could help public transportation users in the future.
______
5 We don't generate much more data than we did over 20 years ago.
______
6 Most of the figures in the last section show our internet activity in one minute.
______

4 Answer the questions in your own words.

1 Do you think companies always use our data to provide us with better services and products?
______
2 Do you think companies know too much about us?
______

HOW DO COMPANIES COLLECT DATA?

As Internet and social media users, we give out a lot of personal information about ourselves, which we often *want* to provide. But there's a lot of information that we don't even realize we're giving away, and that marketing companies gather in different ways. When we click on an ad, companies know. They also know about things that we type into a search engine the people who we follow, and whose photos we are looking at on social media. Through GPS, the companies also know where we are all the time. Every time you access your social media, your location is registered.

How Do Companies Use Our Data?

Every time you watch a video on YouTube, that information is used to recommend another video that you might like. The same thing happens with the songs that we listen to on Spotify and the products that we buy online. Companies use data to match buyers to products through advertising. But it's not just about selling things: in cities, data can update us when the next bus or train is coming, or where there's a traffic jam. Nowadays, a lot of people use technology to provide information about their health, which they can use to make important decisions about diet or visits to the doctor.

How Much Data Do We Generate?

Three billion people use the Internet, and we produce 50,000 GB of data every second! In 1992, that figure was 100 GB of data every day. We spend almost $900,000 on Amazon and download 375,000 apps.

In one minute, people …

- watch 4.3 million videos on YouTube.
- send 187 million emails.
- send 38 million messages on WhatsApp.
- post 481,000 Tweets.

In one minute, there are …

- 3.7 million searches on Google.
- 174,000 people browsing photos and videos on Instagram.

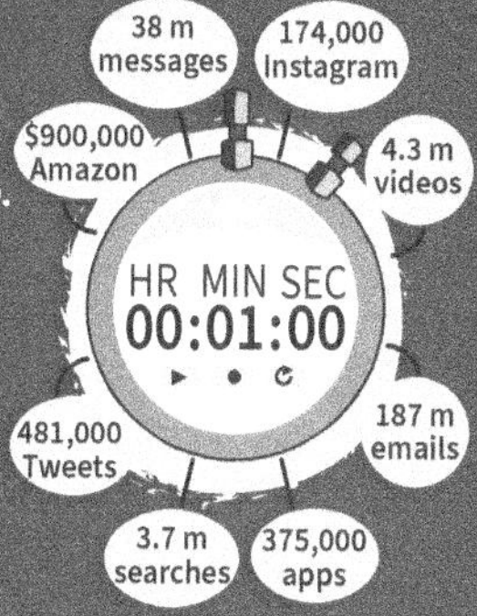

GRAMMAR IN ACTION

Defining Relative Clauses

1 ☆ **Circle the correct options.**

1 The band *that* / *what* I listen to the most is Green Day.

2 The logo *that* / *who* the company designed looked like a bird.

3 Tom and George became friends in a school *where* / *when* they are both learning Spanish.

4 They work for a company *whose* / *who* products are sold all around the world.

5 A lot of people buy products *when* / *that* they see the ad.

2 ☆☆ **Complete the text with the correct relative pronouns.**

Ad-blockers are software programs [1] that ______ stop ads from appearing on your screen. Many people [2] ______ use the Internet get annoyed with ads [3] ______ pop up on the screen, but I don't mind them. I like seeing ads from companies [4] ______ products I like. The Internet is a place [5] ______ marketing companies try to promote their brands. I don't remember a time [6] ______ there were no ads on the Internet. Do you?

Non-Defining Relative Clauses

3 ☆☆ **Complete sentences 1–5 with the correct non-defining relative clauses a–e.**

1 Sophie, __c__, is going to college next year.

2 These products, ______, are sold on beaches in the summer.

3 Freddie used to live at 30 Wilson Road, ______.

4 Our local soccer team, ______, has just won the championship.

5 The advertising campaign, ______, will display the new logo.

a whose shirts are sponsored by my dad's company

b where a famous TV star lives now

c who lives next door to us

d which come all the way from China

e which will run from September to December

4 ☆☆ **Rewrite the sentences using non-defining relative clauses.**

1 This is a very popular product. This product is sold in around 50 different countries.

This product, which is sold in 50 different countries, is very popular.

2 This ad is very funny. I've seen it about five times.

______

3 Mr. Cooper is very satisfied with our work. This means we'll pass the course.

______

4 That girl over there speaks French very well. Her sister lives in Paris.

______

5 Mexico has a lot of interesting places to visit. I'm going there on vacation.

______

6 The book is still popular. It was written 50 years ago.

______

VOCABULARY AND LISTENING

Internet Verbs

1 Circle the correct prepositions.

1. Over six million people have subscribed *on* / *to* the Lego channel on YouTube.
2. If I like someone's post, I always comment *on* / *to* it and say something nice.
3. Jenna Marbles vlogs *about* / *of* makeup, her dogs, and her daily life. She has over 18 million followers.
4. Influencers say you have to work very hard to build *on* / *up* a large number of followers.
5. I tried Instagram for a while, but I take terrible photos, so I shut *up* / *down* my account.
6. The app sends you messages about new games, but you can switch *on* / *off* this option if you don't want to see them.

2 Complete the email with the correct form of the verbs in the box.

build up	comment on	delete	follow	post
shut down	~~subscribe~~	switch on	vlog about	

Dear subscriber,

Thank you for [1] *subscribing* to our YouTube channel. You can also [2] ________ us on Twitter and Instagram. Over two years, we have [3] ________ over one million followers thanks to people like you.

On this channel, we will be [4] ________ our favorite video games. If you would like to [5] ________ the videos, we'd love to hear from you, and we'd love you to [6] ________ ideas for new vlogs. If you follow us on Twitter, you can [7] ________ the option to receive new messages from us on your screen. Remember, rude posts will be [8] ________. If you continue to make rude comments, your account will be reported, and it might be [9] ________.

An Interview

3 Guess which numbers in the box match the sentences.

300	50 million	5 billion
over 1 billion	~~2005~~	

1. This is the year YouTube started. *2005*
2. This is the number of YouTube users. ________
3. This is the number of people making videos. ________
4. This is the number of hours of video posted to YouTube every minute. ________
5. This is the number of videos watched every day. ________

8.01 **4** Listen to an interview about the YouTube video channel. Check your answers to Exercise 3.

8.01 **5** Listen again. Are the sentences *T* (true) or *F* (false)? Correct the false sentences

1. Three young men started YouTube after an argument at a dinner party.
   F. They decided they wanted to share videos from a dinner party but found it difficult.
2. Janelle believes that young people watch YouTube more than TV.
   ____
3. Product review videos are not that popular.
   ____
4. People watch YouTube to find out how to do things or how good things are.
   ____
5. One of the most popular YouTubers makes documentaries.
   ____

GRAMMAR IN ACTION

Indefinite, Reflexive, and Reciprocal Pronouns

1 ☆ **Circle the correct indefinite pronouns.**

1 (Someone) / *Anyone* posted this video about my neighborhood.

2 I don't know *nobody* / *anybody* who vlogs about video games.

3 I swear I didn't delete *anything* / *something* from your computer.

4 What's that noise? Is *anybody* / *nobody* there?

5 He's joined Instagram, but *anyone* / *no one* follows him yet.

6 I switched on the computer, but *anything* / *nothing* happened.

2 ☆☆ **Complete the text with the words in the box.**

anything	~~nobody~~	nothing (x2)	someone (x2)	something (x2)

Be careful with what you post on social media because [1] nobody likes rude comments. My grandma used to say, "If you have [2] ______ nice to say, don't say [3] ______." If you disagree with [4] ______, tell them and explain why. There's nothing wrong with disagreeing about [5] ______, but you can really hurt [6] ______ if you're unkind. If you can't discuss [7] ______ politely, then say [8] ______.

3 ☆ **Circle the correct pronouns.**

1 She might have hurt *himself* / (*herself*) when she fell.

2 You shouldn't get annoyed with *yourself* / *ourselves* for something like this.

3 How do I look? I'm going to take a photo of *myself* / *yourself*.

4 Leticia and I met *ourselves* / *each other* at a party two years ago.

5 We really enjoyed *ourselves* / *themselves* on our vacation.

6 It was a difficult project, so they decided to help *themselves* / *one another*.

4 ☆☆ **Underline and correct one mistake in each sentence.**

1 This sport is totally safe. Anything dangerous can happen to you. Nothing

2 Anna taught himself how to vlog about video games. ______

3 Phil and I are really good friends. We talk to ourselves about everything. ______

4 There isn't nothing you can do about ads on TV except switch them off. ______

5 It's nothing serious – I just cut me with a knife. ______

6 I don't know no one at this party. Is there anyone you know here? ______

5 ☆☆ **Complete the text with the correct indefinite or reflexive pronouns or *each other*.**

My sister went to live in Canada last month to work at a big marketing company. We send messages to [1] each other almost every day, and she tells me [2] ______ about her life there. She says she's enjoying [3] ______, but at first it was difficult because she didn't know [4] ______ in Toronto, and she had to do everything [5] ______ without any help. She found an apartment downtown, but there was [6] ______ in it – not even a bed! She lives with another girl now, but they hardly ever see [7] ______ because the other girl works at night. But at least she has [8] ______ to talk to sometimes. We all miss her!

WRITING

An Online Product Review

1 Read the review of an app. What does the writer particularly like about it?

2 Complete the *Useful Language* phrases in the review with the words in the box.

allows	~~designed~~	features	included	missing

Review: PhotoStar App

1 PhotoStar is a new app for smartphones. If you love taking photos with your phone but you think they're pretty boring, you should try this app.

2 PhotoStar is [1] *designed* to be used on photos on your smartphone or tablet. It [2] ________ you to add funny features to your photos like emoticons, animations, and elements like glasses, beards, and funny ears. One of its best [3] ________ is that you can add voice messages using the voice of someone famous. So you can send a funny photo to your friend that has a message with your favorite celebrity's voice. I tried out all the different features and sent some photos to my friends. All of them wanted to know the name of the app. The one thing that's [4] ________ is a better text function so that you can also write funny messages or slogans on your photos. One is [5] ________ with the app, but it isn't very interesting.

3 PhotoStar is free and it has no annoying ads. It offers more features in the paid version, which is very cheap. I've recommended it to all my friends.

STAR RATING ★★★★

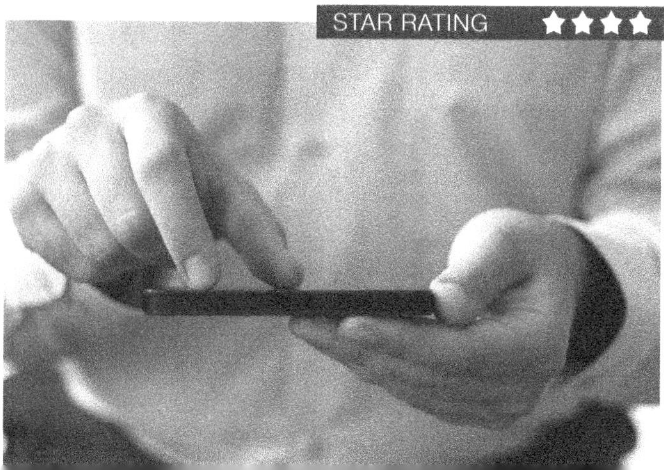

3 Read the review again. In which paragraph (1–3) can you find the following?

a a negative point 2
b a summary of the app ____
c a description of the app ____
d specific features of the app ____
e a recommendation ____

PLAN

4 Choose an app to review and take notes. Think of the positive features. What do you think is missing?

Name of app: ____

A short description: ____

Positive features: ____

What's missing: ____

WRITE

5 Write your review. Remember to include three paragraphs, vocabulary from the unit, and phrases from the *Useful Language* box (see Student's Book, p101).

CHECK

6 Do you ...
- give a star rating?
- say what you like and don't like about the app?
- say whether or not you would buy it?

8 REVIEW

VOCABULARY

1 Complete the sentences with the words in the box.

ad	ad blocker	advertise	brand	buyer	influenced	logo	marketing	product	review	seller	slogan

1 If you are not satisfied with the ________, please return it within 15 days.
2 I can't remember the ________ name, but I know it was yellow.
3 Our company's ________ is "We work harder for you."
4 You can see the company ________ on the back of the phone.
5 Everyone loved the ________ that was shown on TV last December.
6 The products that they ________ on this website are all video games.
7 He works for a ________ company with offices all around the world.
8 A lot of children are ________ by ads on TV.
9 We found a ________ for our old car.
10 A ________ will often want to charge a higher price for the product.
11 I use an ________ so I don't see any ads on websites.
12 Bea always writes a ________ of the products she buys online.

2 Match the beginnings of the sentences 1–8 with the ends a–h.

1 On Twitter, I like following ☐
2 Dave has just posted ☐
3 If you don't want people to comment on your video, ☐
4 As an influencer, Lydia has built up ☐
5 I don't know why I subscribed ☐
6 Lately, Luke has been vlogging ☐
7 If you don't delete ☐
8 They wouldn't have shut down ☐

a you can switch that option off.
b your account if you hadn't posted those terrible things.
c about that new video game – it looks amazing.
d some photos of the party – he looks so funny.
e accounts that post information about soccer.
f that photo, I'm never going to speak to you again!
g to this channel – I don't even like rap music.
h a lot of followers since last year.

GRAMMAR IN ACTION

3 Complete the text with the correct relative pronouns.

The simplest technique [1] ________ marketing companies use to sell their products is repeating the product's name again and again. This technique, [2] ________ is most common on the radio, often doesn't explain the product. On TV, perfume companies, [3] ________ products are all very similar, use a slightly different technique, [4] ________ is to have a stunning image of a beautiful man or woman [5] ________ says the name of the brand at the end. On the Internet, [6] ________ there is often no sound, this technique is hardly ever used.

4 **Complete the sentences with a reflexive pronoun or *each other.***

1 Did you hurt ______ when you dropped all those books?

2 I heard Larry talking to ______ while he was in the bathroom.

3 Diana didn't ask for help from anyone. She did everything ______.

4 Do you and Peter see ______ every day in class?

5 When you're insecure, you have doubts about ______ and your abilities.

5 **Complete the text with the indefinite pronouns in the box.**

anyone	anything	everything	nothing	someone (x2)

My friend said to me the other day that she had seen [1] ______ in an ad who looked like me. I've never been in an ad, and I don't know [2] ______ who has. I watched the ad myself, and the person looked [3] ______ like me at all. [4] ______ about her was different – her hair, her face … there wasn't [5] ______ about her that I could see that was similar to me. Maybe my friend was thinking of [6] ______ else.

CUMULATIVE GRAMMAR

6 **Complete the text with the missing words. Circle the correct options.**

A man named Thomas J. Barratt [1] ______ to be the father of modern advertising. In 1865, Barratt started working in the Pears soap company [2] ______ he created a system of advertising with works of art by [3] ______ famous British painters to advertise the soap. One of the most famous paintings [4] ______ was of a young boy, clearly from a rich family, with a bar of Pears soap in his hand – the soap [5] ______ to the original painting. Barratt knew that [6] ______ Pears soap in people's minds with quality would create a better image. He believed that the product [7] ______ have a good slogan. The company used the slogan, "Good morning. Have you used Pears soap?" for well over 60 years. He also thought that if the company put Pears soap ads everywhere – in magazines, and on posters – [8] ______ would see the ads. However, Barratt also knew that things went out of style quickly, and advertising [9] ______ change, too. Modern advertising has kept many of Barratt's ideas, and it [10] ______ his techniques ever since.

1	a considers	b considered	c has considered	d is considered
2	a which	b where	c when	d that
3	a totally	b a lot	c very	d a little
4	a used	b was using	c have used	d had used
5	a added	b had been added	c had added	d was adding
6	a connect	b connected	c connecting	d connects
7	a has to	b ought to	c must have	d can
8	a anybody	b no one	c someone	d everyone
9	a had to	b must	c could	d have to
10	a is using	b was using	c has been using	d use

9 What's new?

VOCABULARY
Reporting Verbs

1 ☆ **Find 11 more reporting verbs in the word search.**

C	(S	U	G	G	E	S	T)	H	A
A	B	X	G	Y	U	W	T	K	D
P	N	P	R	O	M	I	S	E	M
O	C	N	R	A	D	E	N	Y	I
L	M	C	O	N	F	I	R	M	T
O	R	M	E	U	D	I	L	D	F
G	B	Z	Y	G	N	H	V	I	M
I	N	S	I	S	T	C	B	W	A
Z	R	E	F	U	S	E	E	J	C
E	D	I	S	C	O	V	E	R	C
E	Y	C	O	M	P	L	A	I	N
Z	N	T	D	C	L	A	I	M	A

2 ☆☆ **Match reporting verbs from Exercise 1 with the direct speech sentences.**

1 "No, the government is not going to close any more hospitals." deny

2 "Yes, it's true what you've heard. Our star player is leaving the team." ______

3 "I've told you a hundred times. I don't know who Kevin is." ______

4 "Why don't you look it up on Wikipedia?"

______

5 "No, I'm not doing it. I'm not going shopping with you." ______

6 "I hate watching ads before videos. They're so annoying." ______

3 ☆☆ **Complete the story with the reporting verbs in the box. (See the *Learn to Learn* tip in the Student's Book, p107.)**

admit announced ~~apologize~~ claimed discovered promised

Giles had to [1] apologize to all his followers for telling a big lie! On his vlog, Giles [2] ______ that he had been asked to play in a video game competition. He [3] ______ that the designers of the video game wanted him to play. At the end of his vlog, he [4] ______ to tell everyone all about it the following week. So, we waited for his vlog. Nothing happened. He didn't appear. When the competition came, we all watched, but he wasn't there either. That's when we [5] ______ that he was lying. Giles had to [6] ______ it had all been a lie. He has lost a lot of followers ... including me.

4 ☆☆☆ **Write a sentence using the reporting verb and your own ideas about a time when ... .**

1 a teacher announced something

______

2 someone refused to do something

______

3 a friend apologized

______

4 someone promised that they would do something for you.

______

5 you complained about something

______

Explore It!

Guess the correct answer.

The first 24-hour news channel was CNN, which started in ... .

a 1980 b 1995 c 2000

Find another interesting fact about a news channel or website. Write a question and send it to a classmate in an email, or ask them in the next class.

READING

A Newspaper Story

1 **Read the newspaper story. Choose the best summary.**

a Police solve the mystery of "Piano Man." ☐
b "Piano Man" tells his story. ☐
c "Piano Man": too many questions remain. ☐

2 **Match the underlined words in the newspaper story with the definitions.**

1 a problem, events, or a person that is dealt with by the police *case*
2 strange or not understood ______
3 a person who plays the piano ______
4 walking slowly in no particular direction ______
5 of no use or value ______
6 very well, in a very pleasant way ______

3 **Read the story again. Answer the questions.**

1 What was strange about the man when he was found?
He didn't say anything.
2 Why did the hospital think he played the piano?
______
3 Why did police think he came from Norway?
______
4 Why weren't they able to solve the case?
______
5 How did the man get home?
______
6 What is a "Hollywood ending"?
______

4 **What do you think about this story? What was the man doing?**

______

The Strange Case of "Piano Man"

In 2005, a very strange story hit the news. Newspapers and TV stations reported that a young man had been found wandering the streets in a town in Kent, England. He was wearing a suit and tie, but he refused to speak.

He was taken to a hospital, and the doctors insisted that he was in good health but that he didn't speak. Then he drew a picture of a piano, so people suggested that he might be a pianist. A piano was taken to the hospital, and some newspapers claimed that he played the piano beautifully and that he seemed to be happy.

The nurses asked him where he was from, but he still didn't say anything until one day he pointed to Oslo on a map. The police announced that it was possible that he might come from Norway. They discovered that a ship had traveled from Norway to England when the man was found. Did he jump from the ship and swim to the English coast? The police asked a Norwegian speaker to talk to him, but she told them that he hadn't spoken to her either. One newspaper claimed that he wasn't able to talk at all.

TV and radio stations and newspapers asked everyone to help them to find out who the mysterious "Piano Man" was. Police admitted they had received a lot of calls, but all the information that people gave was useless.

Unfortunately, there's no Hollywood ending to this story. The man was actually Andreas Grassl, a 20-year-old from Germany, who returned there with his parents. Police discovered that he could actually talk. But what was he doing? Why was he in Kent? How did he get there? Why didn't he say anything? Why were all these stories told about him? It all remains a mystery.

GRAMMAR IN ACTION

Reported Speech: Verb Patterns

1 ☆ **Circle the correct option.**

1 My sister told me not to *worry* / *worrying*.
2 She apologized *for* / *to* hiding the keys.
3 Hector refused to *telling* / *tell* me the answer.
4 Sandra insisted *for* / *on* going to the party.
5 I promised *to meet* / *meet* Karla later.
6 My parents told me *staying* / *to stay* home.

2 ☆☆ **Rewrite the sentences using the correct form of the reporting verbs in the box.**

~~admit~~	announce	deny	explain	refuse	tell

1 "All right, it was me. I dropped my drink and it fell on your bag."
Helen *admitted that she had dropped the drink.*
2 "I'm sorry I'm late. My bike got a flat tire on the way to school."
My brother ____
3 "Look, it wasn't me. I would never send you a message like that."
David ____
4 "I'm not going to talk to Andrés ever again!"
Melanie ____
5 "Listen, everyone. Tomorrow there's going to be an exam."
The teacher ____
6 "Go home and lie down. You'll be fine in a few hours."
The doctor ____

3 ☆ **Are the sentences offers (*O*) or suggestions (*S*)?**

1 I'll slice the cake in half if you like. *O*
2 Why don't you check online to see if there are any good movies out? ____
3 I can lend you a nice shirt if you need one. ____
4 I'll hold your bag while you try on the sweater. ____
5 Let's meet after class to discuss your progress. ____
6 I'll ask my dad if he can give us a ride. ____

4 ☆☆ **Rewrite the sentences from Exercise 3. Use the reporting verbs *offered* or *suggested*.**

1 Alison *offered to slice the cake in half.*
2 Tim ____
3 Raquel ____
4 She ____
5 The teacher ____
6 Ada ____

5 ☆☆☆ **Write sentences that are true for you about . . . .**

1 something you tell your parents not to do
____
2 something you promised a friend you would do
____
3 a time when you denied doing something
____
4 a suggestion you made to a friend
____
5 something that you always refuse to do
____

VOCABULARY AND LISTENING

Adverbs of Time and Manner

1 ☆ **Complete the sentences with the adverbs in the box.**

after a while	eventually	fluently	gradually
nowadays	occasionally	~~patiently~~	
regularly	secretly	surprisingly	

1 I waited *patiently* at the movie theater for an hour, but Tim never showed up.

2 Emily only ______ posts photos on social media because she doesn't take many photos.

3 They claimed that they had ______ downloaded people's personal data without anyone knowing.

4 No one has ever heard of him in my country, but ______, he has over one million followers in Japan.

5 At first, I couldn't see anything, but ______, my eyes ______ got used to the dark, and ______, I saw the house in the distance.

6 Our French teacher speaks six languages ______, and he ______ travels to Japan because he's also learning Japanese!

7 I used to send a lot of emails but ______ I usually message people from my phone.

2 ☆☆ **Complete the story with adverbs from Exercise 1. Sometimes more than one answer is possible.**

Paul stood beside the tree and waited [1] *patiently* for the animal rescue people to arrive. He looked up [2] ______ to check that the bird hadn't moved. It was a beautiful creature. A large eagle, Paul thought. [3] ______ the bird tried to take off, moving its wings, but not [4] ______, it couldn't get anywhere because one of its wings was broken. Paul [5] ______ wished he could speak bird language [6] ______, to tell it that everything would be fine. [7] ______, a white van arrived. A man and woman got out. They approached the bird [8] ______ so as not to scare it. The woman threw a blanket over it, and they [9] ______ managed to get it into a cage. When they had gone, Paul walked home looking at the photos on his phone.

A Radio Interview

9.01 **3** ☆ **Listen to an interview about viral videos. Which of these reasons does the man not give for why we share a video?**

It's useful. ☐

It causes positive or negative feelings. ☐

It makes us laugh. ☐

It's important to us. ☐

It has a story. ☐

9.01 **4** ☆☆ **Listen again. Complete the notes with key words and information.**

1 Jonah Cook is a *marketing manager*.

2 There are ______ things you need to do to communicate well.

3 We like to watch a good story until ______ to find out what happens.

4 "How-to" videos are ______ because they help us do something.

5 There are a lot of videos with ______ that show you how to build up followers.

6 We share "how-to" videos because it makes us look ______.

5 ☆☆☆ **Send your answers to Exercise 4 to a friend in an email and compare them. (See the *Learn to Learn* tip in the Student's Book, p110.)**

GRAMMAR IN ACTION

Reported Questions

1 ☆ **Complete the reported questions with one word in each blank.**

1 My teacher asked me where I *was* going.
2 She asked me ______ I was chatting with.
3 The coach asked me what my favorite sport ______.
4 Nicolas asked me ______ I wanted something to eat, but I told him I wasn't hungry.
5 Molly wanted to know if I ______ gone to the party last Friday.
6 Juan asked me if he ______ come to my house to watch the game later.

2 ☆☆☆ **Rewrite the reported questions from Exercise 1 in direct speech.**

1 "*Where are you going*?" my teacher asked me.
2 "______?" she asked.
3 "______?" the coach asked.
4 "______?" Nicolas asked. I told him I wasn't hungry.
5 "______?" Molly asked.
6 "______?" Ean asked me.

3 ☆☆ **Put the words in the correct order to make reported questions.**

1 was / where / asked / the station / We / a police officer
We asked a police officer where the station was.
2 asked / My / been / I'd / where / dad / me
______
3 help / Paul / I / his / bike / me / if / asked / could / fix / him
______
4 tomorrow / to school / ask / me / if / She / didn't / I / was / going
______
5 asked / Marco / me / I'd / Brooke / seen / when
______

Indirect Questions

4 ☆☆ **Complete the interview with a famous rock star. Rewrite the underlined questions as indirect questions.**

A Thanks for talking to me, Jimmy B. First, [1] <u>what was your favorite subject in school?</u>
Can *you tell me what your favorite subject in school was*?
B Sure. It was math.
A [2] <u>Why did you start playing the guitar?</u>
Would you mind ______?
B My dad had a guitar, so I just decided to pick it up one day.
A [3] <u>Are you happy with your latest album?</u>
Could ______?
B Yes, I'm very happy with it. It's my best album so far.
A [4] <u>When is your next tour?</u>
Do ______?
B It will start next spring.

5 ☆☆☆ **Think about questions you have asked this week. Write them as indirect questions.**

Would you mind telling me when our report is due?
______

WRITING

A News Story

1 ☆ **Read the news story. How do the children communicate in the village of Ubang?**

____

2 ☆ **Match the sentences 1–5 with the paragraphs A–C.**

1 an expert's explanation of the Ubang languages [B]
2 an explanation given by the Ubang chief [ ]
3 a fear about the future [ ] and [ ]
4 a general belief about communication between men and women [ ]
5 examples of different words that Ubang men and women have for things [ ]

3 ☆☆ **Complete the *Useful Language* phrases in the news story with the words in the box.**

asked	explained that	nowadays	said	~~surprisingly~~

What Did You Say?

A People, especially older people, often complain that men and women don't understand each other. But there is a Nigerian village where men and women actually do speak different languages because, [1] surprisingly , they use different vocabularies for many things. Ubang people are proud of their language and culture but are afraid that the language will not continue.

B In the village of Ubang, women use the words *okwakwe* for "dog" and *ogbala* for "cup," and men say *abu* and *nko*. And there are many other examples of words that sound different and use completely different letters. When [2] ______ if men and women find it difficult to understand each other, the Ubang village chief [3] ______ everyone understands each other perfectly and that they are very proud of the difference. In fact, there are a lot of words that men and women have in common. Ms. Chi Chi Undie, who has studied the community, says that the men and women of the tribe live very separate lives. "All their children are brought up speaking the women's language fluently," she [4] ______ . When the boys get older, they learn to speak like the men in order to be closer to them.

C [5] ______ , most children are learning English, and the older members of the community ask what is going to happen to their unique language situation. … The village chief is determined that it will survive because, he says, "if the languages die, the Ubang people will exist no more."

PLAN

4 **Write a news story. First, research a current news story on a few websites to get different versions. Take notes on these things in your notebook.**

- A general introduction
- The basic facts of the story (who? what? where?)
- An interesting fact or extra information
- Quotes from the people involved

WRITE

5 **Write your story. Remember to include three paragraphs, language from this unit, and phrases from the *Useful Language* box (see Student's Book, p113).**

CHECK

6 **Do you …**

- include an interesting headline?
- include some extra details in the third paragraph?
- include some direct speech?

9 REVIEW

VOCABULARY

1 Complete the sentences. The first letter is given.

1 Sarah s__________ that we buy a present for James.
2 I said he was lying, and he a__________ I was right.
3 Julia c__________ she met Lionel Messi, but I don't believe her.
4 Remember that you p__________ to help me move my bed later.
5 The students are c__________ that the classroom is too cold.
6 Francesca d__________ that she had fallen asleep in class, but everyone could see her.
7 The president a__________ that he was going to visit our school.
8 Ricardo still hasn't a__________ for breaking my watch.
9 The teacher o__________ to let Sophie take the exam again.
10 Thomas has always i__________ that nobody told him about the trip to France.
11 I can't believe that you are r__________ to talk to Victoria because she lost your sweater.
12 The school principal c__________ that the art teacher had had an accident.

2 Circle the correct adverbs to complete the sentences.

1 Isaac *patiently* / *secretly* hid the box, and nobody knows where it is.
2 I only *gradually* / *occasionally* clean my computer. I should do it more often.
3 They waited *patiently* / *eventually* in line for hours, but there were no tickets left.
4 My dad has a friend who speaks eight languages *nowadays* / *fluently*!
5 I saved ten dollars every week, and *regularly* / *gradually*, I saved enough money for a new phone.
6 *After a while* / *Nowadays*, hardly anyone sends letters to people.
7 The doctor says that my dad should exercise more *regularly* / *occasionally*.
8 The movie was interesting at the beginning, but *secretly* / *after a while*, I got bored and fell asleep.
9 I thought the food would be pretty ordinary, but it was *surprisingly* / *patiently* delicious.
10 Mark sent a message to say he was late, and *eventually* / *gradually*, he arrived at 11:30.

GRAMMAR IN ACTION

3 Match the beginnings of the sentences 1–7 with the endings a–g.

1 We asked the teacher if	☐	a I was doing later.
2 The police told everyone	☐	b that I had to remember the card I had in my hand.
3 Lucas asked me what	☐	c to clear the area because there was a big fire.
4 My parents suggested	☐	d to help me fix my bike.
5 Beatrice offered	☐	e where this street goes?
6 The magician explained	☐	f we had to write in pen or pencil.
7 Could you tell me	☐	g going to the beach for the weekend.

4 Complete the second sentence so that it reports the first. Use no more than three words.

1 "Can you look it up on the Internet?" Ivan asked me.

Ivan asked me ______________ look it up on the Internet.

2 "What did Josh say in the message?" Sara asked her.

Sara asked her what ______________ in the message.

3 "Would you mind inviting me next time?" I asked Ann.

I asked Ann ______________ next time.

4 "Where are you waiting for me?" asked Bella.

Bella asked me ______________ waiting for her.

5 "How did you know the answer?" Leo asked us.

Leo asked us ______________ the answer.

6 "Do you need directions to the station?" asked the police officer.

The police officer asked us ______________ directions to the station.

CUMULATIVE GRAMMAR

5 Complete the text with the missing words. Circle the correct options.

SCIENCE NEWS: Goats Prefer Happy Faces

Everyone loves a happy animal, [1] ______ ? Scientists in England [2] ______ that goats are attracted more by happy faces than by angry ones. It suggests that goats, like other animals [3] ______ humans keep at home or on farms, [4] ______ read human faces and understand human feelings. Previous studies had [5] ______ shown similar results in tests [6] ______ were done with horses and dogs.

In the tests, the reactions of the goats were studied by [7] ______ them in a closed area. Then different faces [8] ______ to people who gave them pasta to eat, [9] ______ is their favorite snack. The goats went to the happy faces more often and spent [10] ______ more time studying the faces with their noses. They also found that if they changed the faces from men to women, it [11] ______ any difference to the goats. Scientists believe the results [12] ______ us understand animals better in the future.

	a	b	c	d
1	doesn't it	does he	don't I	don't they
2	just have discovered	have discovered just	have just discovered	have just discover
3	what	that	if	to
4	can	should	ought to	can't
5	still	never	yet	already
6	who	that	where	whose
7	put	to put	putting	puts
8	attached	are attached	were attaching	were attached
9	which	what	that	who
10	really	a lot	fairly	totally
11	makes	would make	didn't make	hadn't made
12	were helped	help	helped	will help

EXAM TIPS: Listening Skills

Listening: Multiple-Choice Pictures

You will listen to short extracts and choose from different options. This tests your ability to listen for specific information and answer questions about what you hear.

Exam Guide: Multiple Choice

- If the question is about a conversation between a boy and a girl, underline which of the two people you need to answer the question about. For example: *What food will the boy eat?*
- Decide if the question is asking about the past, present, or future. The verb tense and time expressions in the question will help you. For example: *What is the weather like now?* is a completely different question from *What will the weather be like tomorrow?*
- Listen carefully to see if the meaning is positive or negative. For example: *Can you buy some fruit – but not bananas?* tells us that the speaker does not want bananas.
- Usually the answer will come in the middle or at the end of the listening and not at the beginning. This means that you should always wait until the end of each listening before you choose your answer.

REMEMBER!

Don't choose a picture as an answer just because you hear information about it in the listening. Usually you will hear information related to all three pictures!

Listening Practice: Multiple-Choice Pictures

Tip!

Listen for key words and synonyms to help you identify the answer.

1 Choose the correct meaning for the expressions.

1 Are you kidding me?
   A I don't believe you. B That's interesting!
2 You're getting on my nerves.
   A You're funny! B You're irritating me!
3 You'll never know unless you try.
   A You should try. B Are you going to try?
4 You're coming to my party, aren't you?
   A Are you sure you're coming to my party?
   B Can you confirm that you're coming to my party?
5 You must feel really proud of your exam results!
   A I'm sure you feel really happy about your exam results.
   B You ought to feel very happy about your exam results.
6 I get a lot out of playing chess.
   A Playing chess is hard for me. B I really enjoy playing chess.

2 E.01 **You will hear six short extracts. Are the sentences *T* (true) or *F* (false)?**

1 The boy's sister irritates the girl. ____
2 The speaker says everyone should study abroad. ____
3 The boy's coffee is very hot. ____
4 There is a present in the box. ____
5 Some fruit tastes better than it smells. ____
6 The girl thinks going to college is a bad idea. ____

Tip!

Sometimes information later in the listening will contradict or correct the information before. For example:

A *Amy loves skateboarding.*

B *Well, that was before her accident. She hasn't done it since then.*

This is another reason why you need to wait until the end before choosing your answer.

3 E.02 **Listen to the conversation between Ben and his mom. Answer *Yes* or *No*.**

1 Are the dishes washed? ____
2 Does Ben need to do his homework tonight? ____
3 Is Ben going to speak to his friends tonight? ____

4 E.02 **Listen again. What is Ben going to do first? Choose the correct option A, B, or C.**

A

B

C

EXAM TIPS: Reading Skills

Reading: Multiple Matching

Matching People with Activities and Things

You will read descriptions of people and match them with the best options. Remember that there are more options than people, so read carefully! The extra options usually fit only partially, not completely.

Exam Guide: Multiple Matching

- Begin by reading the five descriptions of the people. Underline the key information in each description.
- Next, read all eight texts carefully and underline the key information in each one.
- Then compare the underlined information in the description of the first person with the underlined information in the texts. Which text is the best match for this person?
- Don't choose a text just because it repeats some words from the description of one person. You need to focus on the meaning of the descriptions and the texts and not on individual words.

REMEMBER!

Be very careful when choosing – the text needs to be a perfect match for everything the person wants.

Reading Practice: Multiple Matching

Identifying Meaning

1 Choose the option (A, B, or C) that shows the meaning of the first sentence.

1 Jack wants to do without chocolate for a week.

A Jacks wants to eat less chocolate for seven days.

B Jack thinks he can do without chocolate for seven days.

C Jack would like not to eat chocolate for seven days.

2 Chloe is looking forward to learning to drive.

A Chloe plans to learn to drive.

B Chloe is happy that she will start learning to drive soon.

C In the future, Chloe will learn to drive.

3 Liam has moved to Veracruz.

A Liam is living in Veracruz now.

B Liam has traveled to Veracruz.

C Liam is spending some time in Veracruz.

Synonyms

2 Match the underlined words with the synonyms in the box. There are four extra words.

be born	can	cook in oil	cook in an oven	cut into pieces
heat	know	lived as a child	think	will possibly

1 I'm going to bake a cake. ______
2 Jon grew up in Chicago. ______
3 How long does it take to fry the onions? ______
4 Rachel might go to college. ______
5 I guess they must be brother and sister. ______
6 You need to chop the peppers. ______

Tip! Don't look for words that match exactly. Read the text carefully and underline synonyms of the key information words.

Eliminating Options

3 Read what Laura wants. Then decide which options A–D you can eliminate.

Laura wants to buy a new phone. It must be the latest model, feel very light and smooth, and have a very large display.

A We repair all the latest models of phones …
B Our store has a good selection of phones, including classic old models …
C We have the latest models. They're very light, and have big displays. We're definitely the best place to get a new watch.
D This store specializes in all sorts of digital devices. Its products are expensive, but they look great!

Tip! When you think you have a correct answer, check the incorrect options again to be sure that they don't match.

Finding Differences

4 Read about Sam and Nathan. Find three differences between them.

Sam wants to try out some new recipes. He cooks every day. During the week, he doesn't have much time to cook, but he has time on the weekend to make more complicated dishes. He doesn't eat fried food or food with a very strong flavor.

Nathan likes very spicy food. He wants to buy a book of recipes. He is especially interested in making quick meals in the frying pan.

______
______
______

EXAM TIPS: Listening Skills

Listening: Fill in the Blanks

You'll have to listen and complete notes or sentences. The notes or sentences summarize what you hear. You have to write a word, number, or very short noun phrase in each blank.

Exam guide: Fill in the Blanks

- Pay attention to the instructions. They remind you what you have to do, but more importantly, they tell you what the topic is.
- After the instructions, there is a pause. Use this to read the notes or sentences.
- While you read, try to think about what type of information is missing. It might be a day, a number, a date, or a price, for example.
- The sentences or notes summarize what the speaker says, so you are not going to hear what is written on the page. Pay attention to the key words.
- As you listen, fill in the blanks – remember the answers are one word, a number, or a very short phrase.
- During the second listening, check your answers.

REMEMBER!

Check that your answers make sense in the context if you are given a second opportunity to listen.

Tip!

The sentences and notes will give you clues about what type of information is missing. Read everything carefully.

LISTENING PRACTICE: Fill in the Blanks

1 **Read the notes. What type of information is missing?**

Rent a Bus
Number of seats on our bus: 1 ________
Bus leaves: 10:30 a.m.
Meet at youth club: 2 ________
Price of exhibition entrance: $7
Special group price (over 20 people): 3 $________

E.03 **2** **You will hear some information about a visit to a photography exhibition. Listen and write the correct answer in the blanks (1–3) in Exercise 1. Then listen again and write down the other numbers that you hear.**

____

Tip!

What you read in the questions is not what the person says – it is a summary or paraphrase. Think about the meaning and listen for key words.

3 E.04 **Listen and complete the sentences.**

A Angela's mom told her that her ____________ had won the contest many years ago.

B To find out more about the contest, visit the website – www____________org.

C Angela entered the contest with her ____________.

D The class was given a grant of $ ____________ to build their robot.

4 You will hear an announcement about events coming up at a youth club. Before you listen, read the notes in Exercise 5. What type of information is missing from the blanks?

a type of clothing	a day	the name of a food	a number	a subject	a time

5 E.05 **Listen and complete the notes with one or two words or a number, date, or time.**

Youth Club Events: November

Weekly cooking classes:

Every [1] ____________ at 5 p.m.

Mary

1) bake a chocolate cake; 2) roast [2] ____________

Visit 1:

Date: Friday, the 16th at [3] ____________ p.m.

Helen Fields – fashion designer

Workshop: match colors; choose jeans; decorate a plain white [4] ____________ (must bring)

Visit 2:

Date: Saturday, the 24th at 7 p.m.

Dr. Michael Redding – professor of [5] ____________

Talk: history of logos

Logo contest:

1st prize [6]$ ____________ in cash

Past and Present, Simple and Continuous

- We use the **simple present** to talk about facts, habits, and routines.
  My sister likes pizza.
  I don't read every day.
- We use the **simple past** to talk about completed events and actions in the past.
  I translated the text into Spanish for him.
  I visited Madrid three years ago.
- We use the **present continuous** to talk about actions that are happening now or around now.
  That girl over there is waving at me.
- We use the **past continuous** to talk about actions in progress around a time in the past. We also use ***when*** and ***while*** to mean "during that time," or to connect two events happening at the same time.
  Isabella was wearing a dress last night.
  While I was looking for the dog, he was looking for the ball.

Present Perfect and Simple Past

- We use the **present perfect** when something started or happened in the past and continues to be true until now. We can say how long something has been true but not when it started.
  I've been to Barcelona. (When isn't specified, but it continues to be true.)
  They've been sightseeing. (We don't know when.)
  She's wanted to talk to you since she arrived. (She continues to want to.)
- We use the **simple past** when the moment in which something happened has ended. When it happened isn't always mentioned, usually because it is clear.
  I went to Barcelona in June.
  They went sightseeing yesterday.
  She wanted to talk to you.

GRAMMAR PRACTICE

Past and Present, Simple and Continuous

1 Circle the correct options.

1 I *cut* / *was cutting* my finger yesterday.
2 *Do you go* / *Are you going* to the supermarket now?
3 What *happens* / *is happening* when you push this button?
4 Mary *listened* / *was listening* to music when I *saw* / *was seeing* her.
5 You *don't need* / *aren't needing* to pack a lot of clothes.
6 *Did you buy* / *Were you buying* some bread for a sandwich?

2 Complete the conversation with the correct form of the verbs in parentheses.

MOM Harry, you're going to be late. What [1] *are you doing* (you / do)?
HARRY I [2] ______ (try) to find my keys!
MOM Where [3] ______ (you / normally / leave) them?
HARRY I always [4] ______ (put) them on my desk. But they're not there now.
MOM When [5] ______ (you / have) them last?
HARRY I [6] ______ (have) them in my hand when I [7] ______ (arrive) here yesterday. I [8] ______ (talk) to Jonah on the phone.
MOM Oh, yes, I [9] ______ (remember). You [10] ______ (go) into the living room.
HARRY I [11] ______ (look) there, but I [12] ______ (not find) them.
MOM [13] ______ (you / wear) your coat?
HARRY Yes, I was. Maybe I [14] ______ (leave) them in my coat pocket. Here they are!

Present Perfect and Simple Past

3 Complete the sentences with the present perfect or simple past form of the verbs in the box.

not laugh	not play	paint	~~see~~	sing	tell

1 *Have* you *seen* Scarlett? She's looking for you.
2 Pete ______ very well at the concert yesterday.
3 I ______ you 100 times! Don't call me Timmy!
4 Don't touch the door. They ______ just ______ it.
5 Why ______ you ______ at that joke? It was really funny.
6 Lucas ______ soccer for a month. He's injured.

4 Put the words in the correct order to make sentences.

1 sent / Has / photo / you / Erin / the / ?
Has Erin sent you the photo?
2 tennis / I / liked / you / didn't / know / playing / .
______
3 long / your / taken / a / You / time / to / essay / have / finish / .
______
4 questions / the / didn't / exam / all / answer / on / the / We / .
______
5 you / us / did / Why / come / with / to / decide / ?
______
6 heard / from / We / news / Julia / any / haven't / .
______

Present Perfect Simple

- We use the **present perfect** to talk about actions, experiences, and facts in the past when the exact time is not mentioned or important.
  I've found my favorite T-shirt.
  She has been to the mall.

Present Perfect Continuous

	Affirmative	Negative
He / She / It	has been practicing for years.	hasn't been eating very well.
I / We / You / They	have been practicing for years.	haven't been eating very well.

Questions		
Has	he / she / it	been sleeping a lot?
Have	I / we / you / they	

Short Answers		
Yes,	he / she / it	has.
	I / we / you / they	have.
No,	he / she / it	hasn't.
	I / we / you / they	haven't.

- We use the **present perfect continuous** to talk about an action or a series of actions that started in the past, is still in progress, and we expect to continue.
  I've been studying hard all week.
  She's been exercising since last summer.
- We often use the **present perfect continuous** to say how long we have been doing something.
  I've been taking piano lessons for nine years.
- We use the **present perfect continuous** to focus on the ongoing action rather than the result.
  We've been preparing for the party all day!
- We don't use the **present perfect continuous** with stative verbs (e.g., *like*, *have*, and *know*).
  Emily has liked him since she met him.
  (NOT ~~*Emily has been liking him since she met him.*~~)
  We have had our cat since she was a kitten.
  (NOT ~~*We've been having our cat since she was a kitten.*~~)
- We form the **present perfect continuous** with **subject** + ***has/have*** (***not***) + ***been*** + ***-ing***.
  I've been playing basketball since I was seven.
  She's sick, so she hasn't been coming to school this week.
- We form **present perfect continuous** questions with ***has/have*** + **subject** + ***been*** + ***-ing***.
  Has she been living here for a long time?

Present Perfect Simple and Present Perfect Continuous

- We use the **present perfect simple** to emphasize that the action or event is recently finished. We use the **present perfect continuous** for actions or events that are still going on up to now.
  I've studied for my English test tomorrow.
  (completed action)
  I've been studying for my English test tomorrow.
  (ongoing)

Modifiers

- We use **modifiers** with adjectives to make the meaning stronger and show emphasis. Common modifiers include *a bit*, *a little*, *a lot*, *totally*, *really*, *absolutely*, *extremely*, *pretty*, *fairly*, and *far*.
  He was really upset.
  I felt extremely sorry for him.
  Her parents are pretty strict.
  She can't do anything.
  They work extremely hard.
  They need to relax.
  Her room is really messy.
  There's stuff everywhere!

GRAMMAR PRACTICE

Present Perfect Simple

1 Complete the sentences with the present perfect simple form of the verbs in parentheses.

1 I *haven't worn* (not wear) this dress since last spring!

2 Paul ______ (wait) all his life for this moment.

3 ______ Jane ______ (tell) you what happened yesterday?

4 We ______ (not play) this computer game for months.

5 Our school ______ (organize) a fashion show.

Present Perfect Continuous

2 Complete the sentences with the present perfect continuous form of the verbs in the box.

clean ~~listen~~ rain run wear

1 I *'ve been listening* to this great radio station on my phone.

2 Your face is red. ______ you ______?

3 It ______ all morning, so we can't go out.

4 Her feet hurt because she ______ those high-heeled boots all day.

5 Vanessa ______ her room all morning – it was a mess!

Present Perfect Simple and Present Perfect Continuous

3 Circle the correct options.

1 How many times have you (*seen*) / *been seeing* this movie?

2 I've *folded* / *been folding* all my clothes, and they're in my suitcase now.

3 Have you *sent* / *been sending* the photos to me yet?

4 Dad's tired because he has *painted* / *been painting* all day.

5 Daniel hasn't *read* / *been reading* Laura's message yet, so don't tell him what she said.

6 I've *ordered* / *been ordering* pizza – it'll be here in a few minutes.

4 Complete the conversation with the present perfect simple or continuous form of the verbs in parentheses.

TIM Hi, Mia. I [1] *haven't seen* (not see) you all day. What [2] ______ (you / do)?

MIA Oh, hi, Tim. I [3] ______ (study) for an exam. It's history. I [4] ______ (always / find) it hard to study history.

TIM Me, too. I [5] ______ (even / not start) yet. I [6] ______ (try) to write that essay for English class. I [7] ______ (not finish) it yet, though.

MIA I have. Do you want to see it? I [8] ______ (write) about my last vacation. I'm really happy with it.

TIM That's funny. I [9] ______ (do) the same thing. Maybe the teacher's going to think we [10] ______ (copy) each other!

Modifiers

5 Circle the correct options.

1 I'm not buying these jeans. They're *absolutely* / (*much too*) big for me.

2 The movie was *really* / *totally* good and *a bit* / *extremely* funny.

3 Lydia's dress was *totally* / *a lot* amazing, and her brother looked *pretty* / *a little* handsome.

4 These jeans are *a bit* / *pretty* shorter than those jeans.

6 Match the beginnings with the endings.

1 The exam was really — e

2 I'm really

3 Diego thought the story was fairly

4 Edwin's party was a lot more

5 Liam takes totally amazing

6 The food was pretty

a fun than Carl's party last month.

b good, but I didn't like the music.

c sorry, but I can't talk now.

d amusing, but nobody else liked it.

e difficult, but I think I passed.

f photos, but he never shares them.

GRAMMAR REFERENCE

Used To, Would, and Simple Past

- ***Used to*** emphasizes that past states, habits, and actions are now finished.
  It used to be a castle, but now it's a museum.
  She used to play piano. Nowadays, she just sings.
- ***Used to*** does not have a present form. For present habits and states, we use the simple present.
  My cousin visits us every summer.
  (NOT ~~*My cousin use to visit us every summer.*~~)
- We use ***used to*** and ***would*** to talk about habits and actions in the past that are different today.
  They used to run on Tuesdays, but now they run on Fridays.
  When I was young, my parents would take me for a walk every day.
- We also use ***used to***, but not ***would***, to talk about states and feelings in the past that are different today.
  My grandfather used to have black hair, but now it's white.
  (NOT ~~*My grandfather would have black hair …*~~)
  She used to love volleyball, but she doesn't play anymore.
  (NOT ~~*She would love volleyball …*~~)
- We do not use ***used to*** or ***would*** to talk about things that only happened once or to say how many times something happened.
  Last year, I went to Mexico.
  (NOT ~~*Last year, I used to go to Mexico.*~~)
  Yesterday, I called my dad three times.
  (NOT ~~*Yesterday, I would call my dad three times.*~~)
- We put question words at the beginning of the question.
  What things did you use to do when you were younger?
- We don't often use ***would*** in questions and negative sentences.
- ***Used to*** is like any regular verb. The past tense ends in ***d***, but in questions and negative forms, the verb does not end in ***d***.
  I used to like playing, but I didn't use to like practicing.
  Did you use to have a bike when you were younger?

Past Perfect with *Never, Ever, Already, By (Then), By the Time*

- We use the **past perfect** with other past tenses to talk about actions or states that happened before the main past action or state.
  We hadn't seen the news, so we didn't know about the storms.
  I couldn't call you on Friday because I had left my phone at home.
- We use **adverbs** and **adverbial phrases** such as *already, never, ever, by the time,* and *by then* with the past perfect.
- ***Already***, ***never***, and ***ever*** come before the past participle, but ***yet*** comes at the end of the sentence.
  We had never been to New York until last year.
  They've gone to school, but they haven't had breakfast yet.
- We use ***already*** to emphasize that something had happened.
  I had already finished my test before class was over.
- If something had happened ***by the time*** something else happened, it happened before it.
  They had already heard the news by the time I told them.
- If something had happened ***by then***, it happened before then.
  I finally arrived at the party, but by then all the food had gone.

GRAMMAR PRACTICE

Used To, *Would*, and Simple Past

1 Complete the sentences with *used to* and the verbs in parentheses.

1 I didn't use to like (not like) wearing dresses when I was younger.
2 Edwin ______ (eat) a lot of candy until his dentist told him to stop.
3 Adela ______ (not look) forward to PE classes because she wasn't very fit.
4 Our soccer team ______ (win) every game, but now they're terrible!
5 My dad ______ (not have) a cell phone when he was 15.
6 My teachers ______ (not give) us much homework.

2 Make questions with *used to* or the simple past. Sometimes both are possible.

1 When / Helen / buy / this car / ?
When did Helen buy this car?
2 there / always / be / a movie theater here / ?
______
3 your dad / have / a bike / when he was a teenager / ?
______
4 you / hear / what happened yesterday / ?
______
5 What types of music / you / listen to / when you were younger / ?
______

3 Choose the correct sentences. Sometimes both are correct.

1 (a) When she younger, my aunt used to live in Miami.
b When she was younger, my aunt would live in Miami.
2 a When I was five, I wouldn't eat vegetables.
b When I was five, I didn't use to eat vegetables.
3 a There used to be a lot more stores on this street.
b There would be a lot more stores on this street.
4 a My dad used to have a long beard.
b My dad would have a long beard.

Past Perfect with *Never*, *Ever*, *Already*, *By (Then)*, *By the Time*

4 Circle the correct options.

1 I was excited because I'd (*never*) / *already* been to a wedding before.
2 Had the teacher *already* / *never* started the class when Paul arrived?
3 By *then* / *the time* you called, it was too late to do anything.
4 When the movie started, they'd *never* / *already* eaten all the pizza.
5 I started running, but *by then* / *by the time*, the man had disappeared.
6 When we took my grandmother to Los Angeles, she had *never* / *ever* flown before.

5 Complete the text with the words in the box.

already	by	had	had already	~~never~~	then

I was very nervous. I'd [1] never played the guitar in front of people before. I walked onto the stage. [2] ______ the time I'd picked up the guitar, my hands were shaking. They [3] ______ turned the lights off, so I couldn't really see much. I put the strap around my neck, but by [4] ______, the rest of the band had [5] ______ started playing the first song! I put my hands on the guitar to play ... and there was no sound. Someone [6] ______ pulled the plug!

6 Use the prompts to write simple past and past perfect sentences.

1 They / not sleep / all night because / there / be / a big storm
They hadn't slept all night because there was a big storm.
2 By the time we / get / there, our team / score
______
3 I / try / to cancel my order yesterday, but by then, / they / already send / it
______
4 Until last week, Camilla / never / speak / in English
______
5 When you / arrive, / Dennis / already / find / his keys
______

GRAMMAR REFERENCE

Future Forms

- We use ***be going to*** to talk about future plans and intentions and predictions that we feel sure about.
  After I graduate, I'm going to travel the world.
  My sister is going to stay with my grandparents this summer.
  I'm going to feel sick if I eat all of that!
- We use ***will*** to talk about what is going to happen in the future, especially things that you are certain about or things that are planned.
  I'll see him tomorrow.
  I won't cook later – I'll be out.
- We use ***may*** (***not***) or ***might*** (***not***) instead of ***will*** (***not***) to show that we feel less sure about a future action or event but think it is probable.
  I might not go to college.
  I may get a job with my dad.
  When he gets here, he may want to speak to you.
  Don't call after ten o'clock – we may be watching a movie.

Present Continuous for Future

- We use the **present continuous** to talk about future arrangements when the time is fixed.
  They're getting married this summer.
  What are you doing this weekend? – I'm going shopping with my parents.
  She isn't coming to the party. She's spending the day with her cousins.

Simple Present for Future

- We use the **simple present** to talk about events that are scheduled or timetabled.
  The lesson starts at 9:30 tomorrow instead of 10:30.
  They don't go back to school until next Monday.

Future Continuous

Affirmative/Negative		
I / You / He / She / It / We / You / They	will	be flying this time next week.
I / You / He / She / It / We / You / They	won't	

Questions		
Will	I / you / he / she / it / we / you / they	be flying this time next week?

Short Answers		
Yes,	I / you / he / she / it / we / you / they	will.
No,	I / you / he / she / it / we / you / they	won't.

- We form the **future continuous** with ***will/may/might*** + **be** + ***-ing***.
- We use the **future continuous** to talk about actions we believe will be in progress at a future time.
  In five years, he'll be living in Veracruz and working as a teacher.
  By 2025, everyone will be wearing smartwatches.
- We can also use the **future continuous** to talk about future plans.
  I'll be leaving at 2 p.m. I'm picking my little brother up from school, so I can't be late.
- We put question words at the beginning of a question.
  What will you be doing in 20 years?
  When will computers be cooking dinner for us?

Future Perfect

Affirmative/Negative		
I / You / He / She / It / We / You / They	will have finished	the project by 2050.
I / You / He / She / It / We / You / They	won't have finished	

Questions			
Will	I / you / he / she / it / we / you / they	have finished	the project by 2050?

Short Answers		
Yes,	I / you / he / she / it / we / you / they	will.
No,	I / you / he / she / it / we / you / they	won't.

- We form the **future perfect** with ***will*** + ***have*** + **past participle.**
- We use the **future perfect** for actions that will be completed before a certain time in the future.

GRAMMAR PRACTICE

Future Forms

1 (Circle) the correct options.

1 Mike's not sure yet, but he *'s going to* / (*might*) get a new bike.
2 Do you think it *'s going to* / *might* be a sunny day tomorrow?
3 Some scientists say the world's temperature *will* / *going to* rise by four degrees in the next ten years.
4 Enjoy your vacation. I'm sure you *'ll* / *might* have a great time.
5 Tracy is certain she *is going to* / *might* study biology in college. It's her favorite subject.
6 I'm not feeling very well, so I *may not* / *won't* go to the game. I'll text you later.

2 Complete the sentences with the correct future form of the verbs in parentheses.

1 This restaurant *doesn't open* (not open) until 5 p.m. this evening.
2 Do you think you ______ (pass) all your classes?
3 What time ______ (Tim / meet) us tomorrow?
4 I've decided I ______ (not buy) a new printer.
5 Larry hasn't decided yet, but he ______ (not have) dinner with us.
6 I ______ (order) pizza at the restaurant tonight.

3 Complete the conversations with the correct form of the verbs in the box.

buy	need	~~overcook~~	start

1 A Can I help you with dinner?
B Yes. You fry the chicken because I *'ll* probably *overcook* it!
2 A Where are you going?
B Into town. I ______ a new coat.
3 A What time do you want to meet?
B The concert ______ at 8 p.m., so let's say 7:30.
4 A Is there enough food for everyone?
B I don't know. I think we ______ more bread.

Future Continuous and Future Perfect

4 Complete the sentences with the future continuous form of the verbs in parentheses.

1 What *will you be doing* (you / do) this time tomorrow?
2 My jeans are dirty, so I ______ (not wear) them tomorrow.
3 The music teacher says she ______ (not teach) us how to play this song.
4 While you're working hard, I ______ (enjoy) myself on vacation.
5 You can't meet him later; you ______ (write) your English essay.
6 Tomorrow's a national holiday, so we ______ (prepare) a special meal!

5 Complete the text with the future perfect form of the verbs in the box.

drink	eat	laugh	see	~~sleep~~	spend

What do humans do in one year? By this time next year, you [1] *will have slept* for 2,372 hours and you [2] ______ over 1,000 hours on the Internet. You [3] ______ probably ______ some funny things, which means you [4] ______ for a total of 36.5 hours. If you're American, you [5] ______ around 46 slices of pizza, and you [6] ______ probably ______ well over 800 liters of water.

6 Correct the mistake in each sentence.

1 This time tomorrow, I'll ~~have~~ lying on the beach in Italy. *be*
2 In 20 years, we'll be built robots to do the cooking for us. ______
3 By the time tomorrow, I'll have finished all my exams. ______
4 I be not doing anything later, so call me. ______
5 Will have you started dinner when I get home? ______
6 What will be you wearing to Itzel's party? ______

GRAMMAR REFERENCE

Modals of Deduction and Possibility

- We often use ***can***, ***can't***, ***could***, ***may***, ***might***, and ***must*** + **infinitive without *to*** to say how possible or probable we think an action or event is.
  It can't be him! He never wears a hat to a party!
  She's late. She might be stuck in traffic.
  You must be tired after your long trip.
- We use ***can*** to make general statements about possibilities.
  They say that drinking too much coffee can be bad for you.
  Try drinking more water; it can help you feel more awake!
- We use ***can't*** to say that we think something is impossible or cannot be true.
  That can't be Samantha. She's in China!
  They can't be at home. I saw them leaving an hour ago.
- We use ***could***, ***may***, and ***might*** to say we think something is possible.
  You could have an infection; that's why you're feeling bad.
  A *Who's that man?*
  B *I don't know. He may be her husband.*
  It might be cold outside, so I'll take a coat.
- We use ***must*** when we think something is highly probable.
  She's not answering her phone. She must be busy.

Obligation, Prohibition, Necessity, and Advice

- We use ***must*** and ***have to*** to say that it is necessary to do something.
  Visitors must complete the form and then give it to the receptionist.
  We have to fill in this form and then send it to the office.
- We often use ***must*** when the obligation comes from the speaker – it's something the speaker considers important.
  You must do your homework before you go to Greg's house.
  I must get my grandfather a present for his birthday. I forgot last year!
- ***Must*** is followed by an infinitive without *to*.
- We use ***have to*** to say what it is necessary to do.
  You have to answer all the questions on the exam.
  He has to wear a uniform in school.
- We often use ***have to*** when we talk about laws or rules.
  You have to get good exam results to get into this college.
  He's angry because he has to take his hat off in school.
- ***Have to*** is follow by an infinitive without *to*.
- We use ***don't have to*** to say that it is not necessary to do something but that you can do it if you want.
  You don't have to help me with my experiment.
  She doesn't have to get up early tomorrow.
- Question words go at the beginning of the question.
  How much homework do you have to do every day?
  When do we have to make a decision?
- We use ***can't*** and ***must not*** to say something is prohibited by law or rules.
  I can't take my phone to school – it's the rule.
  You must not use your calculator during the exam.
- We use ***need to*** to express necessity in the present. We use ***don't need to*** to show a lack of necessity.
  I need to get home before my parents get angry.
  They don't need to leave now. It's still early.
- We use ***should('nt)*** and ***ought to*** to give advice. ***Should('nt)*** and ***ought to*** both mean "I (don't) think it's a good idea for someone to do this."
  You should take the bus. It will be faster.
  They shouldn't eat that. They're going to get sick.
  We ought to pay attention. This might be on the exam.

Past Obligation

- We use ***had to*** to say that it was necessary to do something in the past.
  I had to leave school early because I wasn't feeling well.
  They didn't have to come, but they did.
  Did you have to do chores when you were younger?
  Before we took the exam, we had to study a lot.

GRAMMAR PRACTICE

Modals of Deduction and Possibility

1 Circle the correct options.

1 I'm not sure, but I think this gold *may not* / *can't* be real.
2 Reading in bed at night *can* / *must* help you fall asleep faster.
3 I don't know what's in the box. It *could* / *can* be a present.
4 Harry failed two exams. He *couldn't* / *can't* be very happy.
5 Take a drink of water. You *might* / *must* be very thirsty after the game.
6 The doctor's not very sure. She says it *might* / *must* be serious.

2 Use the prompts to write the second sentence.

1 I haven't eaten all day. You / be very hungry
You must be very hungry.
2 It's eleven o'clock at night. Freya / be in bed
______
3 I feel sick. You / need to sit down
______
4 That boy looks like Freddie, but Freddie's in Mexico. That / be Freddie
______
5 Max got up late. He / not arrive on time for his first class
______
6 That cheese is three weeks old! It / be very smelly
______

Obligation, Prohibition, Necessity, and Advice

3 Are the sentences about obligation (*O*), prohibition (*P*), necessity (*N*), or advice (*A*)?

1 You must not use your phone in class. P
2 I probably don't need to wear a coat today. ______
3 I think Lauren should study engineering. ______
4 You ought to try turning the computer off. ______
5 You must write at least 100 words. ______
6 What do I have to do to be successful? ______

4 Complete the email with the phrases in the box.

don't have to worry	~~don't need to bring~~
have to take	must not forget
need to pack	ought to buy

Hi Evelyn,

I'm so glad you're coming to visit us. It's really warm here, so you [1] don't need to bring a coat. However, you [2] ______ your swimsuit because we're going to the beach. We'll [3] ______ the train, so I [4] ______ our tickets tomorrow. You [5] ______ about bringing a towel because we have a lot, but you [6] ______ your sunscreen!

See you on Friday!

5 Complete the second sentence so that it means the same as the first. Use no more than three words.

1 Don't shout. I can hear everything you're saying.
You don't need to shout because I can hear everything you say.
2 It's not a very good idea to call him now.
You probably ______ him now.
3 I had an appointment with the doctor yesterday.
I ______ and see the doctor yesterday.
4 There's no need to worry about making lunch.
You ______ to worry about making lunch.
5 No running in the hallways.
Students ______ in the hallways.
6 That car must be very expensive.
That car ______ cheap.

Past Obligation

6 Complete the sentences about past obligations with the correct form of *have to* and the verb in parentheses.

1 Julieta ______ (go) to school early on Thursday.
2 Did students ______ (gather) in the auditorium?
3 She ______ (not write) another paper.

GRAMMAR REFERENCE

UNIT 5

The Passive

Simple Present		
Spanish	is	spoken in many countries.
Tigers	aren't	found in Africa.

Simple Past		
Writing	was	invented in Asia.
Planes	weren't	used until the 1900s.

Will		
The prize	will be	awarded next week.
The food	won't be	served until 10 p.m.

Questions			
Will	your project	be	finished by next week?

- We use the **passive** when we don't know or are not interested in who or what does an action.
- To form the **passive**, we use the appropriate form of ***to be*** + **past participle**.
  Millions of emails are written every day.
  Brian wasn't invited to the party.
  The microwave will be repaired tomorrow.
- We use the **simple present passive** to talk about facts in the present.
  English is spoken in most hotels and tourist offices.
- We use the **simple past passive** to talk about facts in the past.
  The first video game console was made in 1972.
- We use ***will*** with the **passive** to talk about facts and actions we believe will happen in the future.
  Results will be emailed to students next week.
- We use ***by*** with the **passive** to show who or what was responsible for an action.
  The book was written by a marketing expert.
- To form questions in the present and past, we use the appropriate form of ***to be*** + **subject** + **past participle**. We put *Wh-* question words before ***be***.
  Was the light bulb really invented by Edison?
  Where is the most coffee drunk in the world?
- To form questions with ***will***, we use ***will*** + **subject** + ***be*** + **past participle**.
  When will the next drama club meeting be held?

Question Tags

Main Clause	***To Be / To Do / To Have* / Modal + Subject Pronoun**
They aren't ready,	are they?
They are ready,	aren't they?
We don't need a pencil,	do we?
We need a pen,	don't we?
He was sick,	wasn't he?
He wasn't sick,	was he?
She can't run a marathon,	can she?
She can run a marathon,	can't she?
You won't be late,	will you?
You'll be late,	won't you?
You haven't seen it,	have you?
You've seen it,	haven't you?

- We use **question tags** at the end of statements to invite a response from the listener.
  A *You're an athlete, aren't you?*
  B *Yes, I am.*
- To create **question tags**, we use ***to be***, ***to do***, ***to have***, or a **modal verb**, plus a **subject**. The subject is normally a pronoun.
- Positive sentences have negative question tags and negative sentences have positive tags.
- When we use the auxiliary verbs ***to be***, ***to do***, ***to have***, a **modal verb**, or the main verb ***to be*** in the main clause, this verb is used in the tag.

GRAMMAR PRACTICE

The Passive

1 Complete the sentences with the passive form of the verbs in parentheses.

1 Our groceries *will be delivered* (deliver) to our house tomorrow morning.

2 These problems ________ (solve) a long time ago.

3 ________ phone batteries ________ (produce) in this factory?

4 A lot of time ________ (waste) if we don't do something now.

5 It was delicious. The meat ________ (chop) into small pieces.

6 My computer ________ (not connect) to Wi-Fi.

2 Use the prompts to write questions in the passive. Use the tense in parentheses.

1 When / the books / deliver / ? (past)

When were the books delivered?

2 Why / flies / attract / to the smell of food / ? (present)

____

3 How / these images / create / ? (past)

____

4 Where / we / pick up / after the museum visit / ? (*will*)

____

5 How / the meat / cook / ? (past)

____

6 When / a time machine / develop / ? (*will*)

____

3 Rewrite the sentences in the passive.

1 This lake supplies water to our town.

Water *is supplied to our town from this lake.*

2 They will send your grades to you in a week.

Your grades ________

3 We measured the ingredients very carefully.

The ingredients ________

4 They grill the fish over a fire.

The fish ________

4 Complete the text with the passive form of the verbs in parentheses.

The city of Dubai is incredible. Before oil [1] *was discovered* (discover) in 1966, it was a small town, but it [2] ________ (develop) into a modern city where millions of tourists [3] ________ (attract) to its shopping malls. In 1999, the seven-star Burj Al Arab [4] ________ (complete), and the 828-meter tall Burj Khalifa [5] ________ (open) in 2010. A new city with air conditioning [6] ________ (plan) for the future. Hotels and apartments [7] ________ (connect) with seven kilometers of stores.

Question Tags

5 Complete the questions with the correct verbs.

1 James *isn't* coming to lunch tomorrow, is he?

2 They ________ have to take the train, do they?

3 You ________ deliver the message later, won't you?

4 Robbie ________ going to call us today, wasn't he?

5 They ________ flying to Spain, are they?

6 She ________ be able to play, will she?

7 You ________ yoga every day, don't you?

8 Felicia ________ in class yesterday, was she?

6 Complete the questions with the correct questions tags.

1 You don't know the answer, *do you*?

2 Dad picked up his car from the garage, ________?

3 Everyone knows the answer, ________?

4 They can't see the screen, ________?

5 Elena doesn't want to help us, ________?

6 You won't tell anyone what I told you, ________?

7 Grace listens to classical music a lot, ________?

8 You can't be in two places at once, ________?

First Conditional

- We use **first conditional** sentences to talk about possible situations in the present or future and say what we think the result will be.
- We often use ***if*** + **simple present** to describe the possible action or event.
  We'll find tickets if we go online at 7 a.m.
- We can use ***unless*** + **simple present** instead of ***if not***.
  Unless we hurry up, we'll miss the bus.
- We use ***will/won't*** + **infinitive** when we are sure of the result and ***may*** or ***might*** + **infinitive** when we are less sure.
  If we don't leave now, we won't catch the 8:30 train.
  If my uncle doesn't feel better, he may not travel.
- When we use ***if*** to start the sentence, we use a comma between the two parts.
  If I have enough money, I'll go to the concert.
- We normally use ***will*** to make first conditional questions. It is unusual to use ***may*** or ***might***.
  Will you practice with me this evening if you have time?

Second Conditional

- We use **second conditional** sentences to talk about imaginary situations and the possible consequences.
- We use ***if*** + **simple past** to describe the imaginary situation and ***would***, ***could***, or ***might*** for the consequence.
  If I didn't have a cat, I'd get a rabbit.
- We use ***would*** (***not***) when we are sure of the consequence.
  He would do better in school if he didn't spend all his time playing basketball.
- We use ***could*** (***not***) to express a possibility or ability as a consequence.
  If it was Friday night, we could go to the movies.
- We use ***might*** (***not***) to show we are less sure about the consequence.
  If I had more free time, I might take up the guitar.
- We can use ***was*** or ***were*** in the ***if-*** part of the sentence with *I*, *he/she*, and *it*.
  If it wasn't/weren't so spicy, I could finish it.
  I wouldn't say anything if I were/was you.

Third Conditional

Possible Situation in the Past	**Imaginary Consequence**
(*if* + past perfect)	(*would have* + infinitive)
If I had seen your message,	I would have called you.
If I hadn't seen your message,	I wouldn't have called you.
Imaginary Consequence	**Possible Situation in the Past**
(*would have* + infinitive)	(*if* + past perfect)
I would have called you	if I had seen your message.
I wouldn't have called you	if I hadn't seen your message.
Questions	
If he had been the chef,	what would he have prepared?
If you had let me help you,	wouldn't you have done better?

- We use the **third conditional** to talk about possible or imaginary situations in the past and the imaginary past consequences.
  If you hadn't read the story, the ending of the movie would have been a surprise.
  They would have found the exam easy if they'd worked harder.
- We use ***if*** + **past perfect** to describe a possible or imaginary past situation.
  If I hadn't missed the shot, we would have won the game.
  The book would have been better if the hero hadn't guessed that Jason was the bad guy.
- We use ***would*** (***not***) + ***have*** + **past participle** when we are sure of the imaginary past consequence.
  We would have seen his new car if he'd been at home.
  If she'd won the game, she wouldn't have been sad.
- We often use the **third conditional** to talk about things we regret doing.
  If I hadn't posted that photo, my parents wouldn't have found out.
  My sunglasses wouldn't have broken if I hadn't left them on the sofa.

GRAMMAR PRACTICE

First Conditional

1 Match the beginnings of the sentences with the ends.

1 If I get lost on the way,
2 If you season the chicken first,
3 Sean won't come to lunch
4 We might solve the problem faster
5 Unless you listen to the teacher,
6 They'll go sailing

a you won't understand.
b unless we go for pizza.
c it might taste better.
d unless it rains.
e I'll call you.
f if we sit down and talk.

2 Complete the sentences with the correct form of the verbs in parentheses.

1 If you *listen* (listen) very carefully, you *'ll hear* (hear) a bird singing.
2 You ________ (not understand) Molly unless you ________ (get) to know her better.
3 Ruby ________ (not have) fun unless she ________ (join) in the game.
4 If Jason ________ (waste) any more time, he ________ (be) late for school.
5 We ________ (not be) able to watch the video unless we ________ (connect) to Wi-Fi.

Second Conditional

3 Circle the correct options.

1 If you *had* / *have* a new dog, what *you would* / *would you* name it?
2 If Brian *would go* / *went* to bed earlier, he *wasn't* / *wouldn't* always be late for school.
3 If I *could* / *can* have any job, I *'d work* / *worked* in a chocolate factory.
4 What *would you* / *did you* do if you *would find* / *found* a phone on the street?
5 If my mom *doesn't* / *didn't* work so hard, I think she *'d* / *'ll* be a lot happier.

4 Use the prompts to write second conditional questions.

1 If there / be / no electricity for a week, what / you / do / ?
If there was no electricity for a week, what would you do?
2 If animals / can communicate / with humans, what / they / say / ?
____
3 you / go / to Mars / if / you / have / the chance / ?
____
4 What / you / do / all day if you / live / on a desert island / ?
____

Third Conditional

5 Complete the sentences with the correct form of the verbs in parentheses.

1 If you *had taken* (take) more interest in the subject, you *wouldn't have failed* (not fail) the exam.
2 I ________ (not get) lost if you ________ (not tell) me to turn left.
3 Henry ________ (finish) the marathon if we ________ (encourage) him a bit more.
4 We ________ (not miss) our stop if we ________ (not fall) asleep on the bus.
5 What ________ (happen) if Rocio ________ (press) that button?

6 Complete the third conditional sentences in the conversation with the correct form of the verbs in the box.

buy	give	go	~~invite~~	look	not have	not hurt

SARA If Alice [1] *had invited* you to her party, [2] ________ you ________?
DANY Of course. And I [3] ________ her a nice present for her birthday.
SARA Really? What [4] ________ you ________ for her?
DANY I probably [5] ________ for something small, like some earrings.
SARA So, why didn't she invite you?
DANY It's a long story. But if I [6] ________ her feelings when she needed me to be her friend, we [7] ________ that big argument a few weeks ago.

Gerunds and Infinitives

Gerunds

- We can use a **gerund** as a noun and to make noun phrases.
  Running is great exercise.
  My favorite free-time activity is kitesurfing.
  Being the youngest child can be difficult sometimes.
  They think having a school dance is a terrible idea.
- We also use **gerunds** after prepositions.
  My aunt isn't very good at cooking, but she tries very hard.
  They spend a lot of money on buying clothes.
  We're thinking of giving up singing lessons.
  I'm looking forward to seeing you this summer.
- We use **gerunds** after certain verbs and expressions. Some common verbs and expressions that are followed by a gerund are *avoid, finish, enjoy, practice, miss, be good/bad at, can't stand,* and *don't mind.*
  They enjoy working on the same team.
  I don't mind helping you clean your room.
- With most verbs, we add ***-ing*** to the **infinitive** (without *to*).
  eat – eating *watch – watching* *buy – buying*
- For verbs ending in **-e**, we remove the **-e** and add ***-ing***.
  have – having *write – writing* *save – saving*
- For verbs ending in a **vowel** and a **consonant**, we usually double the consonant and add ***-ing***.
  get – getting *run – running* *shop – shopping*
- In American English, when words end in a **vowel** + ***l***, the ***l*** is not doubled.
  travel – traveling *cancel – canceling*

Infinitives

- We usually use the **infinitive with *to*** after adjectives.
  He was lucky to get tickets for the show.
  I'm very pleased to meet you!
  My teacher's very easy to talk to.
- We also use the **infinitive with *to*** after certain verbs. Some common verbs that are followed by an **infinitive with *to*** are *decide, want, refuse, hope, would like.*
  Kaitlyn decided to help me with my homework.
  We would like to buy two tickets, please.
  They refused to come with us.
- Some verbs need an object before the **infinitive with *to***.
  My mom taught me to ride a bike.
  I didn't invite Elizabeth to come with us.
- Some verbs can have an object before **the infinitive with *to***.
  They asked us to turn the music down.
  She'd like everyone to arrive by 8 a.m.
- We can use a **gerund** or **infinitive** after *remember, forget,* and *stop*, but it changes the meaning.
  Remember to do your assignment. (= Don't forget to do it.)
  Do you remember feeling so happy after we won? (= Do you have a memory of that moment?)
  Don't forget your book bag. (= Bring your book bag.)
  We'll never forget winning the championship. (= We'll always have a memory of that moment.)
  We stopped to eat something on our trip. (= We paused for a moment.)
  They stopped eating junk food last year. (= They quit eating junk food.)

Subject and Object Questions

- When we use **subject questions**, we are trying to find out information about the subject of the question. We don't use an auxiliary verb (*do, does, did*), the word order is inverted, and the *Wh-* word becomes the subject of the sentence.
  Who ate the last piece of cake?
  What happened?
- When we use **object questions**, we are trying to find out information about the object of the question and we use an auxiliary verb (*do, does, did*).
  Who does Tania like? (= We want to know who Tania likes.)
  What did Brad want? (= We want to know what Brad wanted.)
- To compare **subject and object questions** that are similar:
  Topic: *Mike likes eating vegetables.*
  Who likes eating vegetables? (subject question) (*Who = Mike*)
  What does Mike like eating? (object question) (*What = likes eating vegetables*)

GRAMMAR PRACTICE

UNIT 7

Gerunds and Infinitives

1 Complete the sentences with the gerund or infinitive form of the verbs in parentheses.

1 It's easy *to get* (get) lost in this city.
2 Kyle refuses ______ (help) me with the project.
3 ______ (be) a police officer can be a dangerous job.
4 My mom has decided ______ (sell) her car.
5 My grandmother enjoys ______ (listen) to the radio.
6 Are you afraid of ______ (fly)?

2 Complete the sentences with the gerund or infinitive form of the verbs in the box.

drive	go	play	~~show~~	solve	take	use

1 I'll be happy *to show* you around my school.
2 We're looking forward to ______ skiing this winter.
3 Have you finished ______ my computer?
4 Would you like ______ video games later?
5 ______ public transportation in big cities is often quicker than ______.
6 This problem might be complicated ______.

3 Complete the email with the correct form of the verbs in parentheses.

Hi Hollie,

I hope you're well. Do you remember [1] *inviting* (invite) me [2] ______ (come) and stay with you a few months ago? Well, I'm really pleased [3] ______ (tell) you that I'm going to be in the U.S. next month. My parents have decided [4] ______ (send) me to Boston for a month because they would like me [5] ______ (practice) my English. I don't mind [6] ______ (travel) to Boston at all. In fact, I'm really looking forward to [7] ______ (see) you again.

I really hope [8] ______ (hear) from you soon.

Love, Amber

4 Circle the correct options.

1 I don't remember *to tell* / *telling* you what Sarah told me.
2 Have you forgotten *to do* / *doing* your homework again?
3 Samuel can't stop *to listen* / *listening* to that song. He loves it.
4 We worked on the project all day, and we only stopped *to eat* / *eating* lunch.
5 I've never forgotten *to win* / *winning* that art contest.
6 Sophie didn't remember *to set* / *setting* her alarm clock, so she was late.

Subject and Object Questions

5 Write subject questions for these answers.

1 William decided not to go to the party.
Who decided not to go to the party?
2 Class 5A is going to the National Museum tomorrow.
______
3 Nobody sent me a message on my birthday.
______
4 A rock fell on my dad's car.
______

6 Circle the correct options.

1 Who *invented* / *did invent* the telephone?
2 What *studies your sister* / *does your sister study*?
3 Who *is going* / *he going* to tell George?
4 What *did happen* / *happened* when she found out?
5 Who *can ask* / *can we ask* to come and help us tomorrow?
6 Which team *beat* / *did you beat* last year?

Defining Relative Clauses

- We use **defining relative clauses** to give essential information about a person, place, or thing.
  My aunt has a friend who makes great cookies.
  This is the movie that I told you about.
- We use **relative pronouns** at the beginning of relative clauses. We do <u>not</u> repeat the subject pronoun when the subject of the pronoun and following clause are the same.
  I know a lot of people who live in Veracruz.
  (NOT ~~*I know a lot of people who they live in Veracruz.*~~)
- We use ***who*** or ***that*** to talk about people.
  The woman who/that lives next door is very friendly.
  I like the new person who/that works in the café.
- We use ***that*** to talk about things.
  I don't enjoy books that have sad endings.
  He wants to buy some boots that he can wear with his new hat.
- We use ***where*** to talk about places.
  That's the office where my uncle works.
  Let's go to the restaurant where I had my birthday dinner.
- We use ***whose*** to talk about possessions.
  Do you remember the boy whose phone was lost?

Non-Defining Relative Clauses

- We use **non-defining relative clauses** to give extra information about a person or thing. We don't need it to understand who or what is being referred to. It is not necessary information. Non-defining relative clauses are introduced by a relative pronoun, and we use commas around them.
  Ms. Parker, who studied in Italy, is my teacher.
  They just visited Madrid, where Javier is from.
  Last night, we had dinner at John's Pizza Parlor, which we'd never tried before.
  My dad, whose name is Wayne, is 45 years old.
- We don't use ***that*** to introduce a non-defining relative clause. We use **which**, not *that*, for things.
  Sam, who scored three goals in the first game, was amazing.
  (NOT ~~*Sam, that scored three goals in the first game, was amazing.*~~)
  We're having lasagna, which is my favorite dish, for dinner.
  (NOT ~~*We're having lasagna, that is my favorite dish, for dinner.*~~)

Indefinite Pronouns

anybody	everybody	nobody	somebody
anyone	everyone	no one	someone
anything	everything	nothing	something
anywhere	everywhere	nowhere	somewhere

- We use **indefinite pronouns** to refer to people, places, and things in a general way. To create **indefinite pronouns**, we combine *any*, *every*, *no*, and *some* with *body*, *one*, *thing*, or *where*. We write them as one single word, except for *no one*.
  Is anybody here? = Is anyone here?
  Everybody is late today. = Everyone is late today.
  Nobody was there last night. = No one was there last night.
  Can somebody help me? = Can someone help me?
  Is something wrong? = Is anything wrong?

Reflexive Pronouns

I	→	myself	it	→	itself
you	→	yourself	we	→	ourselves
he	→	himself	you	→	yourselves
she	→	herself	they	→	themselves

- We use **reflexive pronouns** when the subject and the object of a verb are the same.
  I sing to myself when I'm alone.
  (NOT ~~*I sing to me when I'm alone.*~~)
  She bought herself a new shirt.
  (NOT ~~*She bought she a new shirt.*~~)
- We can also use **reflexive pronouns** to emphasize that someone did something alone, without help.
  He didn't buy the cookies – he made them himself.
  He's good at baking.

Reciprocal Pronouns

- We use ***each other*** or ***one another*** when each of the two (or more) subjects do the verb to the other subject(s).
  Dave and Ellen sent each other presents. (Dave sent Ellen a present, and Ellen sent Dave a present.)
  The triplets really love each other. They're always together.
  We message one another all the time.

GRAMMAR PRACTICE

Defining Relative Clauses

1 Match the beginnings of the sentences with the ends.

1 Is that the movie that — b
2 Rugby is a sport that
3 This is the park that
4 We have a neighbor who
5 This company has a slogan that
6 That's the student whose

a has a big lake in the middle of it.
b stars Daniel Radcliffe?
c says, "Power to shoes."
d plays the drums.
e chair broke in French class.
f is played between teams of 15 players.

2 Complete the sentences with the correct relative pronoun.

1 I really like that new ad *that* has a song by Mark Ronson.
2 That's the movie theater ______ Mark dropped a whole bucket of popcorn.
3 She's the teacher ______ laptop was stolen from the classroom.
4 It's a radio station ______ plays mostly rock and pop.
5 This is the hotel ______ we stayed on our last vacation.

Non-Defining Relative Clauses

3 Correct the mistake in each sentence.

1 That ad, ~~what~~ was on TV last night, was really funny. *which*
2 This fish, which we bought it in the supermarket, was very expensive. ______
3 Maya, who's dad comes from Australia, works in marketing. ______
4 Theo's review of the movie, that Lucas sent me, was hilarious. ______
5 Dublin, which Mike has lived since he was five, is the capital of Ireland. ______
6 My friend, which I was following on social media, has blocked me. ______

Indefinite Pronouns

4 Complete the sentences with the correct indefinite pronoun.

1 I don't know *anything* about advertising.
2 My sister deleted ______ on my computer by accident.
3 There are ads for that brand ______!
4 ______ at the party was really nice. I had a great time.
5 The teacher wanted ______ to answer the question, but ______ knew the answer.
6 Paula says she can't find her glasses ______.

Reflexive and Reciprocal Pronouns

5 Complete the conversation with the pronouns in the box.

anything	anywhere	each other	~~everyone~~
himself	nobody	someone	themselves

MIA So how was Phil's party?

NOAH Oh, it was a lot of fun. [1] *Everyone* really enjoyed [2] ______. And the food was delicious.

MIA Phil's a good cook. Did he make it all [3] ______?

NOAH Yes, … well he says [4] ______ helped him, but I think his sister made the cake.

MIA So, did [5] ______ interesting happen?

NOAH Not really … Sam and Katie had had an argument and weren't speaking to [6] ______. Oh, and Carmen lost her coat, and she couldn't find it [7] ______. It turned out that [8] ______ had taken it home by mistake!

Reported Speech: Verb Patterns

Independent Clauses

Direct Speech	Reported Speech
Simple Present "I **want** some new shoes."	**Simple Past** He said (that) he **wanted** some new shoes.
Simple Past "I **had** a great time."	**Past Perfect** She said (that) she **had had** a great time.
Present Perfect "We**'ve** just **seen** a show about a fire."	**Past Perfect** She said (that) they **had** just **seen** a show about a fire.
Present Continuous "We**'re growing** our own vegetables."	**Past Continuous** He said (that) they **were growing** their own vegetables.
will "They **will** need to bring a laptop."	***would*** She said (that) they **would** need to bring a laptop.
can "You **can** do it."	***could*** He said (that) I **could** do it.
must "We **must** buy some bread."	***had to*** She said (that) we **had to** buy some bread.
have to "I **have to** wear a uniform."	***had to*** She said (that) she **had to** wear a uniform.

- We can report speech using an **independent clause** and ***that***. *That* is optional.
- When we report somebody's words, we often have to change the verb forms – see the table above for how the verb forms change.
- We often need to change pronouns in reported speech.
  *"**You** have to leave before 11 p.m." – He said (that) **we** had to leave before 11 p.m.*

Gerunds and Infinitives

- We can also report statements using gerunds (**subject** + **past tense verb** + **gerund**), prepositions with gerunds (**subject** + **past tense verb** + **preposition** + **gerund**), or infinitives (**subject** + **past tense verb** + **infinitive**).
- **... + gerund**
  *"Let's take the bus instead of walking." – She **suggested taking** the bus instead of walking.*
- **... + preposition + gerund**
  *Joe said, "I insist we cut the lawn." – Joe **insisted on cutting** the lawn.*
- **... + infinitive**
  *"I can carry the bag for you." – She **offered to carry** the bag for me.*

Reported Questions

- When we report questions, we usually make the same changes to the verb forms, pronouns, and time references as when we report statements.
- When we report questions with a *Wh-* word, we don't add an auxiliary verb and the word order is the same as in affirmative sentences.
  He asked me what I'd done over the weekend.
  (NOT ~~*He asked me what had I done over the weekend.*~~)
  Connor asked when the school trip was.
  (NOT ~~*Connor asked when was the school trip.*~~)
- When we report *Yes/No* questions, we use ***if***.
  "Did you tell the truth?" – They asked him if he'd told the truth.
- We don't use a question mark when we report questions.
  "Where did you go after school?" – My parents asked me where I'd been after school.

Indirect Questions

- **Indirect questions** are a type of reported question. We use indirect questions when we want to sound more polite or formal.
  How did you finish your homework so fast? – Would you mind telling me how you finished your homework so fast?
- When we ask indirect *Yes/No* questions, we use ***if*** or ***whether***.
  Did they see the movie? – Do you know whether they saw the movie?
- We do not use the auxiliary verb *to do* in indirect questions.
  When does this class start? – Could you tell me when this class starts?
  (NOT ~~*Could you tell me when does this class start*~~?)

GRAMMAR PRACTICE

UNIT 9

Reported Speech: Verb Patterns

1 Write the statements in reported speech.

1 "I don't want to go out for lunch."
   Alison said (that) she didn't want to go out for lunch.
2 "We won't waste any more time."
   They told us ______
3 "I can help you make lunch."
   Joshua said ______
4 "I haven't bought your birthday present yet."
   Andy said to Amy ______
5 "Heidi's moving to Australia next week."
   You told me ______

2 Complete the reported statements with two or three words.

1 "Write an essay about technology."
   The teacher told *me to write* an essay about technology.
2 "Don't touch my new car!"
   My dad told ______ touch his new car!
3 "Tell them to keep the noise down."
   Martha told me ______ to keep the noise down.
4 "Don't say anything to Charlie about the concert."
   She ______ to say anything to Charlie about the concert.

3 Complete the reported statements with the correct form of the verbs in the box.

~~correct~~	drive	help	not tell	turn

1 Helen asked us *to correct* her essay before she gave it to the teacher.
2 My friend's dad offered ______ us to school.
3 They suggested ______ Thomas what had happened.
4 When did Ethan offer ______ you with your math homework?
5 Who suggested ______ the computer on and off?

Reported Questions

4 Rewrite the questions in reported speech.

1 "Are you going to make dinner?" Jake asked Jazmin.
   Jake asked Jazmin if she was going to make dinner.
2 "What will make you change your mind?" Maria asked me.
   ______
3 "Have you ever been to Vienna?" I asked my friend.
   ______
4 "When is the next exam?" Leah asked the teacher.
   ______
5 "Do you change your mind often?" Josue asked her.
   ______

5 Correct the mistake in each sentence.

1 They asked us ~~could we~~ help them. *if we could*
2 The teacher asked me why hadn't I done my homework. ______
3 The doctor asked me where it does hurt.
   ______
4 Paula wanted to know if could she borrow my phone. ______
5 My dad asked me what did happen.
   ______

Indirect Questions

6 Complete the second question so that it means the same as the first. Use no more than three words.

1 Can I try a piece of cake?
   Would you mind *if I tried* a piece of cake?
2 When is the next bus?
   Could you ______ the next bus is?
3 Do you go out all the time?
   Can you tell me ______ out all the time?
4 Where's my hat?
   Do you ______ my hat is?
5 Is there a soccer game tonight?
   Would you mind telling me ______ a soccer game tonight?

LANGUAGE BANK

STARTER

Vocabulary

Travel

accommodation backpacking resort
sightseeing tourist attractions trip

Music and Theater

audience lines part
rehearsal scene show

Ways of Communicating

describe greet post shake hands
shout smile translate wave whisper

Grammar in Action

Past and Present, Simple and Continuous
Present Perfect and Simple Past

Writing

Useful Language

Starting and Ending an Informal Email

Hello … / Hi …
How are you? / Thanks for your email. / How are things?
I'm writing to … / I just wanted to say …
See you soon. / Bye for now. / Write back soon.
Take care, … / Love, …

UNIT 1

Vocabulary

Describing Clothes and Shoes

baggy checkered cotton denim
flowery high-heeled leather long-sleeved
plain polka-dot striped tight

Verbs Related to Clothes and Shoes

fit fold go out of style
go with hang up look good on match
unzip wear out zip up

Grammar in Action

Present Perfect Simple and Present Perfect Continuous
Modifiers

Speaking

Everyday English

check out
fashion victim
in
out there

Useful Language

I don't know if …
I'm not a huge fan of …
I think maybe …
That's … uh … different!
They're not exactly my style.

Writing

Useful Language

Great post!
I had no idea that …
It got me thinking about …
Since reading your post, I've …
Thanks for sharing!
We decided to …

LANGUAGE BANK

UNIT 2

Vocabulary

Phrasal Verbs: Changes

do without end up go back go through
look forward to move out move to
settle down sign up try out
turn down turn out

Parts of Objects

button cord cover display handle
key lens lid plug strap

Grammar in Action

Used To, *Would*, and Simple Past
Past Perfect with *Never*, *Ever*, *Already*, *By* (*Then*), *By the Time*

Speaking

Everyday English

all over again
I'm not surprised.
old-school
That's it.

Useful Language

Is it some kind of … ?
I've messed it up.
Like this, you mean?
What you do is, you …
You'll have to …

Writing

Useful Language

first
in addition
in conclusion
second
therefore
this means that

UNIT 3

Vocabulary

Cooking Verbs

bake boil chop fry grate
grill overcook peel roast
season slice spread

Quantities

a bag of a chunk of a cup of a handful of
a piece of a pinch of a slice of
a splash of a spoonful of a sprinkle of

Grammar in Action

Future Forms
Future Continuous and Future Perfect

Speaking

Everyday English

a piece of cake
forever
Is that it?
tasty

Useful Language

Don't forget to … (+ verb)
Once that's done, …
Start by … (+ *-ing*)
While that's … (+ *-ing*)
You'll need …

Writing

Useful Language

… is here to stay
… isn't going anywhere
Watch this space
… will be around forever
… will be the norm

LANGUAGE BANK

UNIT 4

Vocabulary

The Five Senses

feel   feel like   look   look like
smell   smell like   sound
sound like   taste   taste like   touch

Describing Texture, Sound, Taste, Etc.

colorful   faint   rough   sharp   shiny
smelly   smooth   sour   spicy   transparent

Grammar in Action

Modals of Deduction and Possibility
Obligation, Prohibition, Necessity, and Advice
Past Obligation

Speaking

Everyday English

Bingo!
I give up!
I guess so.
nice and warm/hot, etc.
Sure, why not?

Useful Language

Guess again.
Guess what it is / they are.
I guess they must be …
Perhaps it's something (+ *adjective*)
They're definitely some kind of …

Writing

Useful Language

According to …
and grew up in …
At the age of …
including …
… is known as …
… was born on …

UNIT 5

Vocabulary

Processes

attract   collect   communicate   connect
create   deliver   develop   measure
produce   solve   supply   waste

Extreme Adjectives

awful   boiling   deafening   enormous
fascinating   freezing   gorgeous
marvelous   stunning   terrifying

Grammar in Action

The Passive
Question Tags

Speaking

Everyday English

… and everything
I'd say it was …
Oh, man
Um, not exactly.
Wanna …?

Useful Language

Are you kidding me?
I can't believe you actually …
I find that hard to believe.
Seriously?
You can't be serious.

Writing

Useful Language

… deserves to win because …
I'm absolutely certain that …
The highlight of a visit to … is …
the … that impressed me the most was …
Without a doubt, …

LANGUAGE BANK

UNIT 6

Vocabulary

Verb Collocations with *To Get*, *To Take*, and *To Have*

get a lot out of   get bored   get lost
get on my nerves   get to know
have doubts   have fun   have the chance
take advantage of   take an interest in
take pleasure in   take risks

Inspiration and Challenge

Nouns	**Verbs**
bravery	achieve
challenge	encourage
determination	inspire
obstacle	overcome
opportunity	support

Grammar in action

First and Second Conditional
Third Conditional

Speaking

Everyday English

Come on!
Good for you!
not really
seriously
You've got to be kidding!

Useful Language

Encouraging

Don't worry, you'll be fine.
You can do it!
You'll feel really proud afterward.
You'll never know unless you try.

Responding

That's easy for you to say.
What if … ?

Writing

Useful Language

For example, … / For instance, … / such as …
Furthermore, … / On the one hand, …
I personally believe (that) …
On the other hand, …
In conclusion, …

UNIT 7

Vocabulary

Feelings

amused   annoyed   down   eager   glad
grateful   hopeful   hurt   insecure
peaceful   ridiculous   satisfied   thrilled

Expressions with *Heart* and *Mind*

bear in mind   be close to my heart
break someone's heart   change my mind
cross my mind   have something on my mind
learn by heart   make up my mind
put my heart into something   slip my mind

Grammar in Action

Gerunds and Infinitives
Subject and Object Questions

Speaking

Everyday English

kind of harsh
Don't mention it.
I swear
stressed out
That's kind of you …

Useful Language

I can imagine.
Is there anything I can do to help?
It'll be alright, you'll see.
That's not very nice.
What's the matter?

Writing

Useful Language

It might be better (not) to …
It would definitely help to …
I would recommend … (+ *-ing*)
Whatever you do, don't …
Why don't you suggest … (+ *-ing*)?

LANGUAGE BANK

UNIT 8

Vocabulary

Advertising

ad   ad blocker   advertise   brand
buyer   influence   logo   marketing company
product   review   seller   slogan

Internet Verbs

build up   comment on   delete   follow
post   shut down   subscribe to
switch off   switch on   vlog

Grammar in Action

Defining Relative Clauses
Non-Defining Relative Clauses
Indefinite, Reflexive, and Reciprocal Pronouns

Speaking

Everyday English

handy
I don't have a clue.
no-brainer
What's up?

Useful Language

I can't recommend it/them enough!
I don't know where to start!
Is it easy to use?
It's the best thing …
(It) would be ideal for …
You really ought to …

Writing

Useful Language

… is included.
It allows you to …
It is designed to be used …
One of its best features is …
The one thing that's missing is …

UNIT 9

Vocabulary

Reporting Verbs

admit   announce   apologize   claim
complain   confirm   deny   discover
insist   promise   refuse   suggest

Adverbs of Time and Manner

after a while   eventually   fluently
gradually   nowadays   occasionally
patiently   regularly   secretly   surprisingly

Grammar in Action

Reported Speech: Verb Patterns
Reported Questions
Indirect Questions

Speaking

Everyday English

Hey!
Let me guess.
show-off
kind of
to make matters worse

Useful Language

Basically, what happened was …
It was so (+ *adjective*)
So, anyway, …
The next thing I knew …
You'll never guess what happened …

Writing

Useful Language

A man/woman from …
He/She announced/explained/admitted that …
"…," he/she said
Surprisingly/Nowadays, etc., …
When asked … he/she answered/explained/said …